LIBRARY OF NEW TESTAMENT STUDIES

626

Formerly the Journal for the Study of the New Testament Supplement Series

Editor
Chris Keith

Editorial Board
Dale C. Allison, John M. G. Barclay, Lynn H. Cohick, R. Alan Culpepper,
Craig A. Evans, Robert Fowler, Simon J. Gathercole, Juan Hernandez Jr.,
John S. Kloppenborg, Michael Labahn, Love L. Sechrest, Robert Wall,
Catrin H. Williams, Britanny Wilson

Jesus as Teacher in the Gospel of Mark

The Function of a Motif

Evan Hershman

LONDON • NEW YORK • OXFORD • NEW DELHI • SYDNEY

T&T CLARK
Bloomsbury Publishing Plc
50 Bedford Square, London, WC1B 3DP, UK
1385 Broadway, New York, NY 10018, USA
29 Earlsfort Terrace, Dublin 2, Ireland

BLOOMSBURY, T&T CLARK and the T&T Clark logo are trademarks of
Bloomsbury Publishing Plc

First published in Great Britain 2020
This paperback edition published in 2021

Copyright © Evan Hershman, 2020

Evan Hershman has asserted his right under the Copyright, Designs and Patents Act, 1988, to be identified as Author of this work.

For legal purposes the Acknowledgments on p. viii constitute an extension of this copyright page.

All rights reserved. No part of this publication may be reproduced or transmitted in any form or by any means, electronic or mechanical, including photocopying, recording, or any information storage or retrieval system, without prior permission in writing from the publishers.

Bloomsbury Publishing Plc does not have any control over, or responsibility for, any third-party websites referred to or in this book. All internet addresses given in this book were correct at the time of going to press. The author and publisher regret any inconvenience caused if addresses have changed or sites have ceased to exist, but can accept no responsibility for any such changes.

A catalogue record for this book is available from the British Library.

A catalog record for this book is available from the Library of Congress.

ISBN: HB: 978-0-5676-9244-3
PB: 978-0-5677-0519-8
ePDF: 978-0-5676-9245-0
ePUB: 978-0-5676-9247-4

Series: Library of New Testament Studies, ISSN 2513-8790, volume 626

Typeset by Newgen KnowledgeWorks Pvt. Ltd., Chennai, India

To find out more about our authors and books visit www.bloomsbury.com and sign up for our newsletters.

To my parents, with love

Contents

Acknowledgments	viii
Introduction	1
1 Greek and Greco-Roman Texts on Teachers and Teaching	23
2 Teaching and Authority in the First Half of Mark	73
3 Teaching and Authority in the Second Half of Mark	131
Conclusion	165
Bibliography	175
Index of Ancient Sources	183
Index of Modern Authors	189

Acknowledgments

This study began its life as my doctoral dissertation, completed at the Graduate Theological Union and defended in the spring of 2018. During the completion of the dissertation and the present revised form in which it is now presented, I was supported and assisted by many people.

Thanks are due first of all to my adviser, supervisor, and committee chair, Professor Jean-François Racine. Without his unflagging support, and the many conversations we had concerning my research and its completion, this study would never have seen the light of day, either as a dissertation or as a published work. Professor Eugene Park and Professor Anthony Long of the University of California, Berkeley, served as well on my committee. I thank Professor Long for welcoming me to his classes on ancient Greek philosophy, which first interested me in placing the Gospel of Mark in conversation with writings from the wider Greco-Roman world.

I also wish to thank my friend, Dr. Philip Erwin. Our many conversations on the New Testament and early Christianity provided a sounding board for the ideas developed here. Phil's encouragement kept me working on this book even when I was convinced it would never be finished.

Last, my parents provided space and time for me to work through the long process of revising the dissertation and submitting it for publication as a monograph. This book is dedicated to them with all my love and thanks.

Introduction

The Gospel of Mark refers to Jesus as "teacher" (διδάσκαλος), or as engaged in the act of teaching, proportionally more than either of the other synoptic Gospels.[1] It is therefore a reasonable assumption that Mark is particularly interested in Jesus's teaching. But although Mark frequently refers to Jesus's teaching, the Gospel contains relatively little of the actual content of Jesus's teaching compared to Matthew and Luke. That is, although Mark describes Jesus as teacher, we are not often told exactly *what* it is he taught. It is the aim of this study to examine Mark's image of Jesus as teacher in order to understand this paradox. This introduction will discuss the state of scholarly discussion on the subject of the Markan Jesus as teacher, make preliminary methodological remarks, and then briefly describe what is to come in the following chapters.

The State of the Discussion

Mark's portrayal of Jesus as teacher has gone mostly unexamined in the scholarly literature. To the present writer's knowledge, only one full monograph has been devoted to the subject, which will be discussed below. Beyond that, the subject comes up only incidentally in commentaries and in works devoted to other topics related to Mark. Even scholars who do make a deliberate effort to discuss the Markan portrayal of Jesus's teaching seem mostly uninterested in what this portrayal means in the context of the Markan narrative.

---

[1] Mark uses the noun διδάσκαλος and the verb διδάσκειν a combined total of twenty-nine times, compared to Matthew's twenty-five uses and Luke's thirty. Thus, when accounting for the fact that Mark is significantly shorter than either of the other two, Mark's proportional usage is much higher.

As a salient example, consider Adela Yarbro Collins's magisterial commentary on the Gospel.[2] Collins includes a lengthy section on "Jesus as Teacher" and says of this section, "Mark's portrayal of Jesus as teacher will be examined in relation to the social role of teacher (in the narrow sense) in the cultural context of the first century C.E."[3]

What this means in practice, however, is that the section on "Jesus as Teacher" consists largely of a catalog of parallels drawn from Jewish and Greco-Roman texts, with a few comments to the effect that Jesus's teaching in Mark concerns the "eschatological plan of God."[4] Collins does not discuss the role that Jesus's teachings play in either the Markan narrative or the rhetorical aims of the Gospel. She discusses the cultural parallels and makes remarks about the putative content of Jesus's teaching but does not discuss the *function* of the image of the teacher in Mark. Further, she often supplies the parallels without explaining why they matter for understanding Mark. As a result, the portrayal of Jesus's teaching in Mark is tacitly considered to be in a one-to-one relationship with historical data about teachers and their teaching in the Greco-Roman world. This is a highly questionable assumption. One of the conclusions of the following study is that Mark draws upon the well-known cultural commonplace of the itinerant teacher but does so for distinct narrative and rhetorical purposes that are not simply equivalent to the various historical and literary parallels.

Most commentaries do not go as far as Collins in including an actual lengthy discussion of Jesus's teaching. This may be partly due to the limitations of the genre: Most commentaries are much shorter than Collins's and thus do not have the luxury of synthesizing their conclusions about every aspect of the Gospel. Yet even longer commentaries do not single out the subject of Jesus's teaching as worthy of special remark. For instance, Joel Marcus's two-volume commentary includes a lengthy introduction.[5] But as for the various types of content singled out for special note, we find sections on eschatological or apocalyptic elements, a discussion of Mark's relationship to Pauline theology,

---

[2] Adela Yarbro Collins, *Mark*, Hermeneia (Minneapolis, MN: Fortress Press, 2007).
[3] Ibid., 73.
[4] Ibid., 76.
[5] Joel Marcus, *Mark 1-8: A New Translation with Commentary*, AB 27 (2000; repr. New Haven, CT: Yale University Press, 2005), 17–79.

and a critique of various proposals about "corrective Christology" in the Gospel but no mention of Jesus as teacher, despite the frequency of this theme in Mark.[6]

This inattention persists in the commentary proper. To give just one example, in his discussion of Mk 1:21-28 (which this study takes as a critical passage for the understanding of the Markan Jesus's teaching), Marcus is content to offer a historical parallel drawn from our limited knowledge about teaching in first-century synagogues.[7] Even though the passage both begins and ends with remarks that Jesus's teaching drew him attention from onlookers, Marcus does not explain *what*, exactly, Jesus is teaching here or why Mark should mention it. He is more interested in the exorcism in this passage, with his remarks about Jesus's teaching limited to describing its "eschatological newness" and its connection to the Gospel's theme of apocalyptic confrontation between Jesus and the demons.[8]

Other commentaries also overlook the theme of Jesus as teacher. Darrell Bock devotes the entire introduction of his commentary to a defense of Mark's historical reliability.[9] If we use 1:21-28 as a test case again, his interpretation is almost entirely mistaken. He correctly notes the importance of the theme of Jesus's "authority" (ἐξουσία) (1:22, 27), which will be of particular importance in our own study. But he then goes on to interpret Jesus's teaching entirely by means of historical "background" material and by implicit harmonization with Matthew and Luke—for example, he argues that Jesus must be appealing to scripture in his teaching, despite the fact that no citation from scripture occurs in the scene.[10] Still less does he explain *why* Mark depicts Jesus teaching in this way—although given that Bock seems to regard the Gospel as almost entirely historically accurate, he no doubt thinks that Mark is just reporting "what really happened."

Examples could be multiplied across the standard commentaries. The trend is that although commentators frequently produce a wealth of philological and historical material as parallels to Mark's portrayal of Jesus as teacher, they

---

[6] Ibid., 70–9.
[7] Ibid., 191–2.
[8] Ibid., 192–3.
[9] Darrell Bock, *Mark*, New Cambridge Bible Commentary (Cambridge: Cambridge University Press, 2015).
[10] Ibid., 126.

entirely overlook the question of why Mark portrays Jesus's teaching in such an oblique manner—that is, why Mark so often refers to Jesus's teaching yet does not often describe what that teaching is. Scholars also tend to assimilate the picture of Jesus as teacher to the Gospel's apocalyptic or eschatological themes. To be clear, the problem is *not* that Mark is not heavily invested in depicting the course of Jesus's life and death in apocalyptic terms. This is undeniable, for it has been known since the epochal works of Weiss and Schweitzer that the synoptic Gospels portray Jesus by means of motifs familiar from Jewish apocalyptic literature. The problem, rather, is that this conclusion has yet to be integrated with the data we observed above, which suggests that it is also a major concern of Mark to depict Jesus as a teacher. One of the burdens of a study of the Markan Jesus as teacher must therefore be to tie up this scholarly loose end by showing how the teaching motif in Mark relates to the Gospel's apocalyptic orientation.

In the commentary genre, there is one notable exception to the trend of ignoring the motif of Jesus as teacher in Mark. M. Eugene Boring, in his commentary, takes the theme of Jesus as teacher quite seriously and particularly notes how the theme of Jesus's authority serves as a means of linking the teaching motif with other aspects of the Gospel.[11] His work will be referred to frequently in the following study.

Overall, commentaries offer little aid in understanding Mark's portrayal of Jesus's teaching. Outside occasional perceptive remarks about individual passages, such as noting the importance of Jesus's authority in critical scenes like 1:21-28, the subject goes undiscussed, and few if any commentaries bother to integrate their conclusions about individual teaching-related passages into an overall interpretation of the teaching motif in the Gospel. Obviously, as indicated above, the limitations of the genre likely contribute to this oversight, for not even the lengthiest commentaries can reasonably be expected to offer in-depth treatments of every single issue that might be raised concerning the text. This is the province of more specialized studies.

---

[11] M. Eugene Boring, *Mark: A Commentary*, NTL (Louisville, KY: Westminster John Knox, 2006). See esp. his discussions of Mk 1:21-28 and 4:1ff., two passages that are extremely important for understanding the Markan portrayal of Jesus's teaching.

Vernon Robbins

We turn, then, to examples from outside the realm of commentaries. As alluded to above, only one monograph, to the present writer's knowledge, has been written about the subject of Jesus as teacher in Mark: Vernon Robbins's *Jesus the Teacher*.[12] Given the singular place that Robbins's work therefore occupies in the discussion of the subject, it is worthwhile to discuss it in detail.

Robbins's project originates with his conviction that Markan scholarship has neglected to study the Gospel in comparison with Greco-Roman literature, as opposed to just biblical and Jewish texts.[13] This neglect has led to a conclusion that Robbins considers erroneous: that, since the form of the Gospels, of which Mark is the first, seems unparalleled within Jewish literature, the Gospels are unique among ancient literature.[14] By contrast, Robbins proposes that the literary antecedents of Mark can be made clear via a comparison with non-Jewish literature, although certain forms from Jewish literature are found in Mark as well.[15]

Robbins proposes to study various types of rhetorical *forms* commonly found in Greco-Roman literature and to elucidate how they are used in Mark and to what effect. He uses the term "forms" not in the sense commonly found in New Testament form criticism but rather in a sense derived from the work of Kenneth Burke: "A work has form in so far as one part of it leads a reader to anticipate another part, to be gratified by the sequence."[16] Therefore, Robbins isolates four kinds of "form" in Mark: (1) minor form, (2) progressive form, (3) conventional form, and (4) repetitive form.[17] *Minor* form is close to what the form critics have meant by "form": a miracle story, a controversy, a scholastic dialogue, and so on. *Progressive* form refers to the unfolding of the

---

[12] Vernon. K. Robbins, *Jesus the Teacher: A Socio-Rhetorical Interpretation of Mark* (1984; repr. Minneapolis, MN: Fortress Press, 2009).
[13] Ibid., 1–3, 12.
[14] This conviction that the Gospels are "unique" seems to have mostly disappeared since the time of Robbins's writing in 1984, largely under the influence of the renewed trend toward interpreting the Gospels as Greco-Roman *bioi* or "lives," which received its most influential statement in Richard A. Burridge, *What Are the Gospels?: A Comparison with Graeco-Roman Biography*, SNTSMS 70 (1992; paperback ed. Cambridge: Cambridge University Press, 1995).
[15] Robbins, *Jesus the Teacher*, 4–5.
[16] Ibid., 7, quoting Kenneth Burke, *Counter-Statement* (Berkeley: University of California Press, 1931), 124.
[17] Ibid., 7–10.

narrative, either by means of "logical" progression," where the events of the narrative cause the reader to expect something to occur, and this expectation is then fulfilled, or by means of "qualitative" progression," where unexpected shifts and turns in plot and characterization introduced and integrated smoothly into the overall narrative.[18] *Conventional form* refers to categorical expectations that a reader or audience brings with them to the narrative based on cultural conventions and traditions—genre would be an example of such a convention. And finally, *repetitive* form refers to the repetition of themes, ideas, or motifs in a text—"the consistent maintaining of a principle in new guises … [a] restatement of the same thing in different ways."[19] The forms, in other words, do not necessarily refer to portions of text: They refer more to a kind of expectation evoked in the reader, whether through textual repetition or cultural and literary convention.

It is an examination of these various forms, which leads Robbins to conclude that Mark contains a distinctive hybrid of two kinds of repetitive form.[20] From Jewish prophetic literature, Mark incorporates the repetitive pattern of prophetic speech found in books like Isaiah and Jeremiah as well as in the narratives about Elijah and Elisha. In this repetitive form, the prophet repeatedly announces "the word of the Lord" and is vindicated when that word comes to pass. However, Robbins argues that the Gospel of Mark puts a different twist on this prophetic form, because Jesus in Mark is never said to describe his message as "the word of the Lord."[21] Rather, Jesus preaches "the gospel of God," which is ambiguous enough to be identified both with a message announced by Jesus and a message *about* Jesus:

> In other words, the action and speech of God are remote enough that the action and speech of Jesus become the essential content of the gospel. Indeed, the centrality of Jesus' speech and action in Mark leads the author to make virtually no distinction between "Jesus" and "the gospel."[22]

What this change from the biblical pattern suggests to Robbins is that Mark is heavily influenced by another repetitive pattern: the pattern of

---

[18] Ibid., 9–10.
[19] Burke, *Counter-Statement*, 125, quoted in Robbins, *Jesus the Teacher*, 10.
[20] Robbins, *Jesus the Teacher*, ch. 3.
[21] Ibid., 59: "There are no repetitive forms in Mark insisting that the word of the Lord comes to Jesus."
[22] Ibid., 58.

"disciple-gathering teachers in Greco-Roman literature."[23] This is because Mark shares with such literature "a socio-rhetorical pattern that emphasizes the teacher's self-embodiment of the system of thought and action he teaches."[24] In other words, whereas in biblical prophetic literature the prophet's words are authorized by the fact that they are simply the reporting of the "word of the Lord," in Greco-Roman literature about disciple-gathering teachers (including Mark, according to Robbins), the teacher's teaching is shown to be correct by the teacher's own faithfulness to his teaching and the consistency of his words and deeds. Robbins adduces the *Memorabilia* of Xenophon as the earliest extant example of a work depicting a "disciple-gathering teacher" in Greek literature. In such works, Robbins finds a repetitive form whereby a teacher-protagonist exemplifies his way of life to disciples, who then join him in adhering to the program of thought and action which the teacher embodies. Robbins quotes Xenophon to describe this repetitive form: "All teachers themselves show their disciples how they themselves do what they teach, and lead them on by speech" (*Mem.* 1.2.17).[25]

Therefore, the basic pattern that underlies much of Mark's narrative results from the combination of Jewish traditions about the prophet whose words are authorized by God and the Greco-Roman notion of the disciple-gathering teacher who is demonstrated as trustworthy by his adherence to his own program and his success in passing that program on to disciples. On the basis of such a pattern, Robbins develops a thorough outline of Mark's Gospel based around a repeated pattern of new roles and titles being attributed to Jesus, who then transmits each new aspect of his program to his disciples.[26]

However, the influence of the Greco-Roman tradition of the disciple-gathering teacher is not apparent only at the level of repetitive form—that is, at the level of the individual pericope or episode. Rather, Robbins also detects a longer conventional form held in common between Greco-Roman teaching narratives and the Gospel. In this conventional form, a disciple-gathering teacher is shown at the height of his adult life and career as he gathers disciples, passes on his system or program to them, and dies or otherwise departs from

---

[23] Ibid., 60.
[24] Ibid.
[25] Cited and translated by Robbins, *Jesus the Teacher*, 64.
[26] Robbins, *Jesus the Teacher*, ch. 2.

his followers and entrusts them with the duty of carrying on his program. This conventional form is detailed over three chapters, in which Robbins examines various Greco-Roman literature as well as the Gospel of Mark, contending that these texts share in common the conventional form of the disciple-gathering teacher.[27]

But Robbins also notes a distinctive element of Mark that complicates its status as a narrative about a disciple-gathering teacher. In Greco-Roman narratives of disciple-gathering teachers, it is typical for the teacher to be portrayed as successfully passing on his program to faithful students.[28] In Mark, by contrast, it is well-known that the disciples ultimately fail to accept Jesus's message. The Twelve flee from Jesus in the garden, Peter denies him three times, and the women who go to the tomb flee in fear. Therefore, the expectation set up by the conventional form of the disciple-gathering teacher—that the students will learn from and profit by the teaching of their master—is thwarted in the case of Mark's Gospel: "Mark's gospel differs from both Xenophon's *Memorabilia* and Philostratus' *Apollonius* in the portrayal of a lack of fulfillment of true discipleship by anyone in the narrative."[29] This, for Robbins, is what is most distinctive about Mark. He suggests that the effect for the historical audience encountering the Gospel would have been to consider themselves as the real hearers of Jesus's teaching, challenged to succeed in carrying out Jesus's program where the disciples in the narrative failed:

> Since no one in the Mark's gospel fully adopts the system of thought and action taught and enacted by Jesus, the reader is the object of a special summons to perpetuate the system of thought and action "to all nations for the sake of Jesus and the gospel." ... Possessed by noticeable uncertainty, the reader is asked to respond with greater resolution and sustained commitment than anyone featured in the narrative actually did.[30]

Robbins's thesis is intricate and compelling. Since he is one of the few scholars to have thoroughly engaged the subject of the portrayal of Jesus as teacher in Mark's Gospel, his work deserves careful consideration.

---

[27] Ibid., chs. 4–6.
[28] Ibid., 204–9.
[29] Ibid., 208.
[30] Ibid., 209.

The present study is in full agreement with Robbins's contention that Mark draws heavily upon traditions and forms inherited from Greco-Roman literature about disciple-gathering teachers. His exegetical conclusions are also generally sound. There is no space to engage all of them in detail, but several of his proposals are noteworthy. His identification of a regular pattern whereby Mark introduces new attributes of Jesus as the Gospel progresses is particularly interesting. Further, Robbins also correctly identifies the tension between the motif of Jesus the disciple-gathering teacher and the fact that the disciples fail to learn from and pass on the teacher's ideas. The oddity of the Markan portrayal of the disciples has of course been a subject of considerable scholarly discussion, but Robbins is the first to note how strange the Markan portrayal of the disciples is not just in comparison with later Christian hagiography about "the Twelve" but also with other Greco-Roman literature that draws on the conventional form of the disciple-gathering teacher. Finally, Robbins advances beyond earlier studies in an attempt to examine the theme of Jesus as teacher throughout the whole of Mark's Gospel rather than just examining individual passages.

That said, *Jesus the Teacher* contains a significant lacuna. Robbins focuses on *form* to the exclusion of *content* in his study of Jesus's teaching. He correctly identifies that Mark shares many forms in common with Greco-Roman literature about disciple-gathering teachers—both large forms, such as the overall pattern of the teacher–disciple relationship, and smaller forms, such as the teacher's summoning of students to follow him. But he spends far less time discussing the *content* of Jesus's teaching and how it compares to the content of the teachings propounded by the protagonists of other literature about disciple-gathering teachers. He speaks frequently of the Markan Jesus's "program of thought and action" but does not clearly spell out what this "program" is. He identifies the form of Jesus's teaching in Mark—the well-known narrative of the disciple-gathering teacher—but does not explain what the teacher teaches. He supplies a number of possible candidates—the "kingdom of God," the teachings about suffering and death found in the passion predictions—but does not sufficiently elaborate.

The present study foregrounds the issue of the content of Jesus's teaching. One of the most important conclusions to be drawn here is that Mark differs significantly from other Greco-Roman texts about teachers and teaching in terms of the content of its protagonist's teaching. Jesus's teaching differs from that of teachers from related literature by the critical fact that *Jesus's teaching is about himself.* It is Christological in focus and intent. Robbins's focus on the similarities in *form* between Mark and other Greco-Roman literature leads him to overlook this important distinction.

This issue aside, Robbins's study remains invaluable. He has correctly identified the centrality in the Gospel of the theme of Jesus's teaching, as many other scholars do not. He also provides a wealth of comparative insight into his placing Mark alongside Greco-Roman texts from Xenophon, Plato, Philostratus, and others. The present study includes a chapter (Chapter 1) on Greco-Roman texts concerning teachers and teaching, not to dispute Robbins's own analysis of such texts but to add to it by focusing on content, rather than form.

Other Works: Burton Mack and Robert Fowler

Robbins's work is the only full-length monograph specifically devoted to examining the subject of the Markan Jesus as teacher. Nevertheless, there are two other scholars who, while not focusing specifically on Jesus's teachings, have nevertheless made contributions to the discussion of the subject in the course of projects focused elsewhere. Burton Mack's groundbreaking and controversial work on Mark includes a provocative interpretation of the Markan teaching motif, while Robert Fowler's examination of the Gospel from the perspective of reader-response criticism correctly identifies the theme of Jesus's *authority* as critical for the Gospel's portrayal of Jesus. Both Mack and Fowler also offer helpful methodological points that are congruent with the present study. Let us examine the work of each of these authors in turn.

Mack's contribution to the discussion of Jesus's teachings is found in his 1988 work, *A Myth of Innocence*.[31] His proposals on the subject have generally been overlooked, for two reasons. First, his controversial proposals concerning other topics, especially the historical Jesus, have dominated discussion of the

---

[31] Burton L. Mack, *A Myth of Innocence: Mark and Christian Origins* (Philadelphia, PA: Fortress Press, 1988).

book.³² And second, his interpretation of Mark is embedded in a thoroughgoing reinterpretation of Christian origins, which has come in for a great deal of criticism.³³ But Mack's view of the Markan Jesus's teaching is an innovative one, which deserves careful consideration.

Mack's analysis of the teaching motif in Mark is contained in his chapters on the Markan parables (ch. 6) and pronouncement stories (ch. 7). Mack argues that the evangelist reconfigured and rewrote earlier traditions relating the teachings of Jesus so that they would no longer enlighten or teach, as would be usual in Greco-Roman literature about teachers and teaching, but rather so that they would justify a dualistic, apocalyptic mentality in the wake of the destruction of the Jerusalem temple in 70 CE. Interpreting the rejection of "the gospel" as "persecution," Mark sought to show that Jesus had predicted just such circumstances from the beginning and further that Jesus had already pronounced judgment on the community's "persecutors" during his own ministry, while assuring the "elect" of their eventual vindication. The "parables discourse" of Mk 4, for example, does not make plain what Jesus's teaching about the kingdom of God is but rather shows that no one except the elect ever had hope of understanding it or of escaping God's judgment on the present age. Jesus in Mark does not teach but pronounces doom on Mark's adversaries.

> Mark did not wish to portray Jesus addressing his generation publicly with instruction about the kingdom of God as if his world could have accepted it and changed. What Jesus says in Mark's Gospel is not instruction to those within the story at all. What Jesus says in the story functioned as pronouncement, a sign of his imperious authority, a behavior that triggered and sealed a predetermined fate of ultimate consequence both for the Christian community and for the opponents of Jesus. What Jesus said then is instructive only for the reader in Mark's own time.³⁴

---

[32] Specifically, his much-criticized thesis that the earliest layers of the Jesus tradition depict Jesus as akin to a Cynic sage. Mack himself acknowledges that the chapter on the historical Jesus distracted attention away from the book's main thesis in an essay responding to various reviewers: Burton Mack, "A Myth of Innocence at Sea," *Cont* 1, no. 2 (Winter–Spring 1991), 45.

[33] For one response to Mack's project, see especially Larry Hurtado, "The Gospel of Mark: Evolutionary or Revolutionary Document?" *JSNT* 13, no. 40 (September 1990), 15–32. A more positive set of evaluations is found in a multiauthored retrospective of *A Myth of Innocence* in *JAAR* 83.3 (September 2015).

[34] Mack, *Myth of Innocence*, 171.

The pronouncement stories are similar in function. Whereas the pre-Markan pronouncement stories are similar to the witty *chreiai* of Cynic sages, Mark has, according to Mack, retooled the pronouncements so that instead of offering genuine insight, the Markan Jesus merely asserts his own absolute authority, using logic and argument that no one other than the committed Christian "insider" could accept. This violated all the usual tenets of debate according to Greco-Roman rhetorical conventions and confirms for Mack that the Gospel of Mark is meant to rationalize a sectarian mentality.[35]

The reader need not endorse all aspects of Mack's thesis. In particular, his interpretation is often tinged with a note of moral disapproval of Mark's portrayal of Jesus. He tends to negatively judge the Markan Jesus's teachings by their degree of deviation from the earlier Jesus traditions purportedly found in Q and the *Gospel of Thomas*. But regardless, Mack's interpretation of the Markan Jesus as teacher and his methodological innovations deserve much greater scholarly attention than they have heretofore received.

The first strength of Mack's approach is that he studies carefully how the motif of Jesus's teaching functions in the overall narrative. His exegesis does not remain at the level of individual passages but pays attention to how Mark's picture of Jesus as teacher fits with other aspects of the Gospel, especially Mark's apocalyptic perspective.

Second, when he draws on parallels from Greco-Roman literature, he does not simply point out parallels in surface details such as form or terminology; rather, it is the *function* of the image of the teacher, which is under review. Mack notices that Mark does not portray Jesus as a teacher for the same reason that, say, Xenophon or Philostratus portrayed their own protagonists in such a fashion. Mark's Jesus plays a role in his narrative, which cannot automatically be assimilated to the roles played by teachers and teaching in other texts.

Finally, Mack correctly recognizes that the portrayal of Jesus's teachings in the Gospel is *Mark's* own construction. He is clear that Mark is not just reporting historical "facts" about Jesus or compiling earlier traditions. Rather, Mark's editorial intervention and authorial invention are responsible for the overall impression of Jesus's teaching that one receives when reading the Gospel. This might seem like a trite observation, considering that New

---

[35] Ibid., 203–7.

Testament scholarship now widely rejects the older form-critical thesis that judged the evangelists to be mere editors or collectors of traditions.[36] But considering how little interest scholars have shown in how the teachings of Jesus mesh with Mark's overall narrative, it seems as though the influence of the form-critical thesis still holds sway as far as the subject of Jesus's teachings is concerned. Mack's attempt to understand the teaching motif as primarily a Markan creation is a major step forward. Whatever the historical provenance of the teaching material in Mark, its present form is thoroughly a product of Mark's authorial voice. This methodological move has greatly influenced the analysis to follow.

Unfortunately, Mack's work is weakened by the combination of his interpretation of Mark and his historical skepticism. For he maintains not only that the presentation of Jesus's teachings in the Gospel is, in its present form, the creation of the evangelist. He goes further and tries to demonstrate that this presentation is thoroughly fabricated and unhistorical. As a result, his arguments about Mark frequently mix with his claims about earlier Jesus tradition in Q and the *Gospel of Thomas*. The present work dissents from Mack's approach insofar as the text of Mark will be interpreted without complicating matters by raising issues of historicity.

Aside from Mack's methodological insights, he also correctly identifies the importance of the theme of Jesus's *authority* in relation to his teaching in Mark. Mack's interpretation of the pronouncement stories is on the right track in identifying the way in which Mark makes Jesus's authority the central focus of his debates with opponents. We will adduce considerable evidence in support of this conclusion in the study to follow.

The work of Robert Fowler also takes note of the theme of Jesus's authority. Fowler's project is to read Mark through reader-response theory: He wants to pay attention to the *experience of reading* Mark's Gospel. For "the text imposes powerful constraints upon the reading experience, constraints that to this point have been acknowledged only sporadically and unsystematically."[37]

---

[36] The older form-critical view was clearly stated by Martin Dibelius, *From Tradition to Gospel*, trans. Bertram Lee Woolf (New York: Charles Scribner's, 1965), 3: "The literary understanding of the synoptics begins with the recognition that they are collections of material. The composers are only to the smallest extent authors."

[37] Robert M. Fowler, *Let the Reader Understand: Reader-Response Criticism and the Gospel of Mark* (Minneapolis, MN: Fortress Press, 1991), 15.

These "constraints," in Fowler's estimation, are comprised of the ways in which various elements of the text invite the reader to read and understand the text in a certain way. Fowler wants to "explore the 'rhetoric of fiction' in Mark's Gospel: the ways the Gospel writers 'tries, unconsciously or consciously, to impose his fictional world upon the reader' and 'the author's means of controlling his reader.'"[38]

Fowler's analysis draws upon the categories devised by Seymour Chatman, which identify the "implied author," "implied narrator," "implied narratee," and "implied reader" in the narrative.[39] He suggests that the rhetoric of narrative, including Mark's Gospel, works to "persuade the reader that [the narrator] is reliable."[40] In some narratives, the narrator is unreliable—that is, a significant gap exists between the viewpoint of the implied author and the implied narrator. But in Mark this gap does not exist. The implied author, the implied narrator, and the protagonist (Jesus) share the same viewpoint.[41] Thus, any credibility which Jesus receives in the narrative will also accrue to both implied narrator and implied author.

> In Mark we never have to deal with a narrator's unreliability. To the contrary, we have reliability and authority in spades; that *exousia* (authority) and *dynamis* (power) are recurring themes at the story level of the narrative is no accident. The implied author puts forth a reliable, authoritative narrator, who puts forth a reliable, authoritative protagonist named Jesus. If the rhetoric of the narrative is successful, then the *exousia* and *dynamis* attributed to Jesus by the narrator will implicitly garner *exousia* and *dynamis* for the narrator himself, and in turn for the implied author.[42]

Among the means Fowler identifies by which the Gospel of Mark creates an aura of authority for its narrator is its construal of the relationship between the protagonist Jesus and the narrator. The narrator, first of all, is basically omniscient, knowing everything that Jesus does and why. Second, when Jesus speaks, he does so with the narrator's voice. Both the narrator and Jesus share

---

[38] Ibid., 61, citing Wayne C. Booth, *The Rhetoric of Fiction*, 2nd ed. (Chicago, IL: University of Chicago Press, 1983), xiii.
[39] Seymour Chatman, *Story and Discourse: Narrative Structure in Fiction and Film* (Ithaca, NY: Cornell University Press), 1978. See esp. the diagram that Fowler presents on his p. 31.
[40] Fowler, *Let the Reader Understand*, 61.
[41] Ibid., 77–8.
[42] Ibid., 61.

special inside knowledge (e.g., knowledge of the scribes' thoughts in Mk 2:6-8).[43] The narrative also makes frequent use of repetition, where either the narrator or Jesus predicts something and then the other brings it to pass—as when the narrator shares information and Jesus demonstrates knowledge of the same information (Fowler cites 8:1-2) or when Jesus predicts something and then the narrator reports that it happens, as in the call of the disciples.[44]

So, like Mack, Fowler demonstrates that the idea of "authority" is a critical one in Mark's Gospel. The present study will also draw this conclusion. Fowler's approach is somewhat different than ours, however; he discusses the authority of the *narrator* from the perspective of reader-response criticism, whereas the present work does not use this kind of terminology and focuses mostly on the figure of Jesus within the narrative. Nevertheless, the point is basically the same: "Authority" plays a key role in Mark.

Fowler's work achieves far more than this one insight, however. His most noteworthy achievement is his rigorous and consistent application of Chatman's distinction between "story" and "discourse" to the Gospel. For Chatman, the "story" refers to the events described in the narrative, while the "discourse" refers to *how* these events described: "The what of a narrative I call its 'story'; the way I call its 'discourse.'"[45]

Fowler not only recognizes this distinction in his analysis of Mark but also employs the distinction to make a bold claim regarding the overall locus of meaning in the Gospel. In his analysis, much of Mark's narrative functions not on the level of story but of discourse. That is to say, many parts of the Gospel make little sense on the level of the story but make perfect sense on the level of the discourse. One prominent example he identifies is the Son of Humanity sayings: Despite all the sayings about the Son of Humanity in the Gospel, only on one possible occasion do the characters in the story react to Jesus's mentioning of the Son of Humanity.[46] The reader of the Gospel, meanwhile, is in the position to interpret these sayings, having access to information and a backward-looking perspective that none of the characters (except Jesus) do.

---

[43] Ibid., 125.
[44] Ibid., 74–5.
[45] Chatman, *Story and Discourse*, 9.
[46] The one instance where a character possibly reacts to Jesus's invocation of the Son of Humanity is in the high priest's words at Jesus's trial (14:62-63), but Fowler doubts that this is the case even here; see Fowler, *Let the Reader Understand*, 118–19.

An even more noticeable example of discourse-oriented narrative is Mk 13: In Fowler's estimation, this entire chapter speaks not to the characters ostensibly listening to Jesus in the scene but to the reader or hearer of the narrative. (This fits nicely with Burton Mack's observation about the teaching of Jesus in Mark in general: Only the audience is truly instructed.)[47] Even smaller elements of Mark, from its opening self-description as "Gospel," to scripture citations, to parenthetical remarks by the narrator, indicate to Fowler that the Gospel's discourse has far more impact on the reader than its story does on the characters.

The point is that Fowler has, by distinguishing between story and discourse, identified the peculiarly inward-looking, even self-referential, nature of Mark's Gospel. Like Mack, he correctly notes how much of what the narrative relates is meant for the audience, not the characters. This in itself is not entirely an unusual observation: It has long been the scholarly custom to explain aspects of the Gospels with reference to the situation in the "communities" to which they were written. But Fowler goes beyond this. He does not simply note *that* the Gospel refers to events and persons outside the story; he identifies *how* this is accomplished: through the speech of Jesus, through parenthetical remarks, and through relating to the reader "inside knowledge of characters' thoughts and motivations; in short, through the discourse."

Fowler's employment of the reader-response theory has also enabled him to describe why it has been the case that scholars have so often decided that Mark is a clumsy or incompetent author. A classic example is the two feeding narratives. It was once a common theory that Mark inadvertently or foolishly included two variants of the same traditional story. Fowler suggests that what has happened is that scholars have stumbled over their own experience of reading: Because they cannot accept the idea that the disciples could be so obtuse as not to recognize what Jesus is doing when he feeds a multitude for the second time, they resort to blaming the author for his stupidity or repetitiveness. In other words, the reading experience itself has given rise to interpretive problems.[48] Fowler proposes that this stumbling on the part of the reader may be deliberately induced by the narrative: The confusion is

---

[47] Fowler, *Let the Reader Understand*, 82–7; for Mack, see n. 34.
[48] Ibid., 11, 171.

purposefully caused so that the reader has occasion to reflect critically on how they ought to understand the characters of the disciples.[49]

During research for this study, the present author arrived independently at similar conclusions to Fowler's. Specifically, this project identified early on the importance of the theme of authority in the Gospel. Also independently arrived at was the observation that Mark is frequently concerned with the discourse, far more than with the story (although this terminological distinction was not precisely in mind when this thesis was formulated). That Fowler arrives at similar conclusions to the present author about major aspects of Mark lends credence to the arguments made here, especially considering that he approaches the text with a different methodology.

The Method and Plan of This Study

The following study examines selected Markan passages concerning Jesus's activity as a teacher. These passages will be examined in order to determine the *function* of Mark's portrayal of Jesus as a teacher: the role the motif plays in the internal development of the Gospel narrative and its probable effect on the Markan audience. This description prompts the question of how best to categorize the methodology employed. To answer this question, it is necessary to outline the basic presuppositions that underlie the present work.

First, we assume here that the author of Mark is a creative author, not merely a reporter of historical "facts" or inherited tradition. Thus, like Burton Mack's study of Mark (discussed above), it is assumed that the final form of the text is first and foremost a literary creation, and that this creation was deliberate. The various aspects of Mark are not to be explained through authorial oversight or clumsy editing.[50]

Second, it is assumed that the narrative was composed for a definite historical occasion and setting, and that something can be said about this historical occasion. This means that the function of Mark's image of Jesus as

---

[49] Ibid., 10–11.
[50] As in, to use one of Fowler's examples (see above n.50), the older explanation for the presence of two feeding miracles in Mark: that the author was either so bound to tradition that they felt bound to include two variants of the same story or that they were simply careless.

teacher will be examined both from an internal perspective and an external one: internally, with respect to its place in Mark's narrative, and externally, with reference to the probable historical occasion of its writing.

This combination of both literary and historical interests distinguishes the present work from certain "narrative-critical" approaches that, strongly influenced by the so-called New Criticism, claim to limit themselves entirely to "the world within the text" and ignore the impact of historical factors.[51] A strict narrative-critical approach has been eschewed here. The reason for this is that the present writer shares with Fowler the conviction that much of Mark's narrative works primarily on the level of (to use Chatman's terms) the discourse, rather than the story: that is, many of the things that the characters do and say are meant primarily to influence the audience of the story and only secondarily with an eye toward the thorough and consistent development of the narrative's plot and characters. This does not mean we revert to the conclusion that the evangelist was unskilled, only that they crafted the Gospel to influence the audience and not simply to spin a good yarn in the manner of a modern novelist. To de-historicize the Gospel by analyzing it as a timeless literary product overlooks just how much of the text has been crafted as a discourse meant for a specific time and place.

This study therefore most closely aligns with the interpretive method that has been called *composition criticism*. This is a term suggested by Ernst Haenchen as a substitute for the term "redaction criticism" and may be considered a variant of the latter.[52] While redaction criticism, as it is usually defined, attempts to understand the interests of a New Testament author based on the changes made to existing source material, composition criticism expands the field of interest to include not only the small changes made to sources but also to the overall arrangement, placement, and creation of material in general. This wider focus is particularly appropriate for the study of Mark, since Mark's sources are nonextant, and the question of identifying Markan redaction is a particularly vexed one.[53] Because this study focuses on the influence of a

---

[51] On the influence of the New Criticism upon biblical "narrative criticism," see James L. Resseguie, *Narrative Criticism of the New Testament: An Introduction* (Grand Rapids, MI: Baker Academic, 2005), 21–5.

[52] Ernst Haenchen, *Der Weg Jesu: Eine Erklärung des Markus-Evangeliums und der kanonischen Parallelen*, 2nd ed. (Berlin: Walter de Gruyter, 1968), 24.

[53] See, e.g., the discussion in C. Clifton Black, *The Disciples According to Mark: Markan Redaction in Current Debate*, 2nd ed., JSNTSup 27 (Grand Rapids, MI: William B. Eerdmans, 2012).

specific motif—that of Jesus's teaching—on the overall message and impact of Mark, it may therefore be considered closely aligned with composition criticism.

The influence of *rhetorical criticism* may also be felt at certain junctures, insofar as the present study takes the view that the Gospel is meant to persuade an audience. Although we do not, as some rhetorical critics do, apply to Mark the complex terminology of ancient rhetoric, we will nevertheless compare the overall rhetorical impact of Mark with the probable aims of other Greek and Greco-Roman literature about teachers and teaching.

This study proceeds through three chapters and a conclusion. The first chapter is an analysis of three selected non-Christian texts featuring teachers and teaching, drawn from different genres. The three different texts are the *Memorabilia* of Xenophon, the *Discourses* of Epictetus, and Philostratus's *Life of Apollonius of Tyana*. This chapter is included for two reasons: first, to establish a background for our analysis of Mark, and second, to expand upon the comparison of Mark with Greek and Greco-Roman texts found in the work of Vernon Robbins (see above). The common traits and themes shared by literature concerning teachers and teaching will be identified, with an eye toward the extent to which Mark does or does not follow the typical patterns for such literature. The chapter's conclusion will argue that Mark's rhetorical aim is quite different from the aims of the other texts examined. Among the tasks of our analysis of Mark, therefore, is to provide evidence for this view.

Chapters 2 and 3 divide between them the task of interpreting the Gospel of Mark itself. The second chapter deals with relevant passages in the Gospel's first half concerning Jesus's teachings, while the third chapter moves to the second half. Throughout, the case will be made that the motif of Jesus as teacher in Mark's Gospel serves three functions in the narrative. First, it serves to advance the portrayal of Jesus as a figure endowed with a unique form of *authority* (ἐξουσία). Chapter 2 will contain an extended discussion of this concept. The second function of the teaching motif is that it *advances the Gospel's plot*. We will demonstrate that depictions of Jesus's teaching in Mark often serve the distinctly nondidactic purpose of moving the narrative forward by using the occasions when Jesus teaches to introduce new ideas that propel the plot. And third, the image of Jesus as teacher is often used to address the Gospel audience: The character of Jesus frequently breaks the fourth wall, so to speak, to address the audience even when he seems to be talking to characters in the story, like the disciples.

Finally, the conclusion will summarize and synthesize our results and discuss the ways in which the Gospel's portrayal of Jesus as teacher fits with Mark's likely historical context.

A Note on Sources

Before beginning our study of the Greek and Greco-Roman sources that will be our points of comparison, it is necessary to respond to one obvious objection that might be raised: Why compare the Gospel of Mark with Greek and Greco-Roman sources, rather than *Jewish* ones? Aren't Jewish texts the most proximate background to the Gospel?

The answer, as far as the portrayal of Jesus as teacher is concerned, is *no*. While the Gospel of Mark is obviously indebted to biblical sources, considering its many explicit and implicit references to the Jewish scriptures, its portrayal of Jesus's teaching is far more akin to non-biblical texts. The word διδάσκαλος, which Mark uses to refer to Jesus, appears only twice in the LXX: once to refer to a court official in the book of Esther (Esth 6:1) and once as a title for Aristobulus in an epistle embedded in 2 Maccabees (2 Macc 1:10). Neither reference is of consequence for our understanding of Mark's portrayal of Jesus as teacher.

The situation with the verbal form, διδάσκειν, is different. The verb occurs over one hundred times in the LXX. But a careful examination reveals that the context for its usage is quite different from that found in Mark. The verb is primarily used to refer to instruction in the Law. This explains its frequent usage in the book of Deuteronomy, where the Israelites are frequently enjoined to obey the law that Moses has taught them (i.e., 4:1, 14; 5:31; 6:1; 31:19) and to teach this same law to their children (i.e., 4:10, 11:19). Thus, Moses "teaches." But *what* he teaches is quite different from what the Markan Jesus teaches. As we shall see in this study, Jesus in Mark is not consistently portrayed as a teacher of the Mosaic Law; while he opines on legal issues from time to time, the Markan purpose of such scenes is to enhance Jesus's divinely granted authority, not to depict Jesus as passing on a program of legal interpretation.

Outside of Deuteronomy, usage of the verb is similar: The psalms frequently speak of God "teaching" his ways (i.e., Ps 25:4, 71:17, 94:10; 119:68) or of the psalmist "teaching" others in such matters (i.e., 34:11, 51:13). Ezra and various figures associated with him are described as teachers of the Law, just as Moses was (1 Esd 8:23, 9:48; 2 Esd 7:10, 18:8). It is interesting that the biblical figures often associated with the Markan Jesus, the prophets Elijah and Elisha, are never described as teachers or as teaching.

The biblical texts, then, are not the most salient points of comparison for the present study. But what about non-biblical Jewish literature? The most obvious examples would be the works of Philo and Josephus. But the present work has elected not to compare Mark with these particular texts either. The reason for this is that these texts already show signs of influence by the same types of Greco-Roman literature with which we compare Mark in the following chapters. That is, Philo, Josephus, and Mark all portray their "teachers" in ways that resemble texts like the ones we survey in this chapter, rather than on biblical models. While space does not permit an extended discussion of the use Josephus and Philo make of "teachers" in their works, a few brief examples will make the point.

Josephus portrays Moses as a "teacher" of sorts but a teacher after the pattern of famous lawgivers of the Greco-Roman world, such as Solon or Lycurgus (*Ant.* 3.93-94). Abraham, too, is a teacher, but a teacher of specialized kinds of technical knowledge: He is a kind of "wise man" who instructs the Egyptians among who he sojourns in the sciences of astrology and mathematics (*Ant.* 1.168). This portrayal thus portrays Abraham, the patriarch of Israel, as the source of foreign wisdom. Needless to say, Jesus in Mark does not teach such skills. Nor is he portrayed as expounding a new law or code of behavior, as we shall see.

Philo also frequently refers to the great figures of Israel's past as "teachers," but, like Josephus, does so in a manner that shows considerable overlap with non-Jewish Hellenistic texts. For instance, in Philo's exposition of the Decalogue, Moses is portrayed as the ultimate teacher of self-mastery (ἐγκράτεια) and control of the passions, both popular subjects of Greco-Roman philosophical discourse. The patriarch Joseph, too, is such a teacher, expounding "virtue" to those imprisoned with him in Philo's retelling of the tale from Genesis of Joseph's imprisonment (*Joseph* 16.86-87). Philo's tendency, then, is to make the great figures of Israel's past into "teachers" of proper living, particularly of self-control and mastery of desire. This is especially indicated by his tendency to view the "teachings" of Moses as restraints on the passions and the biblical stories of Abraham as allegories for the soul's forsaking earthly things in favor of divine illumination. As we shall see, the concern with mastery of desire is also a central motif of Xenophon's *Memorabilia*, which demonstrates Philo's affinity with Greek traditions about teachers and teaching.

These few examples make clear that both Josephus and Philo portray "teaching" figures in ways similar to Greco-Roman writings such as those we will examine in the next chapter. Moses and others renowned for their "teaching" have been cast in the mold of Greek lawgivers and philosophers, and traditional "teachings" like the strictures of Torah are interpreted as lessons in attaining virtue. Therefore, we commit no methodological error by comparing Mark directly with the same kinds of texts upon which Josephus and Philo draw, rather than upon these Jewish authors' own writings.

1

Greek and Greco-Roman Texts on Teachers and Teaching

We begin with a discussion of selected Greek and Greco-Roman texts that discuss teachers and teaching. The selected texts vary widely in their dates of writing, from the period of classical Athens to the time of the Roman Empire. These texts have been selected in order to demonstrate the themes and motifs that persist in this literature before, during, and after the period in which the Gospel of Mark was written. The selected texts are the *Memorabilia* of Xenophon, the *Discourses* of Epictetus as recorded by Arrian, and Philostratus's *Life of Apollonius of Tyana*. We will analyze each text with respect to its form, content, and purpose, paying particular attention to the questions of *what* the teacher depicted in each text is teaching and *how* they are teaching it. After discussing each of these texts in turn, we will then examine how they, individually and collectively, compare with the Gospel of Mark. These observations will serve as a transition to the study of the Gospel itself.

Before proceeding to the analysis of the texts, it is worthwhile to discuss briefly the role played by *education* in general in the social and cultural life of the ancient Mediterranean. An extensive literature exists on the subject of ancient education, and there is no need here to summarize it.[1] In any case, much of this literature is concerned with the technical formalities of literate education, the details of which are relatively unimportant in examining the Gospel of Mark. However, a word must be said about the *general aims* of ancient education.

---

[1] The classic work on the subject is H. I. Marrou, *A History of Education in Antiquity*, trans. George Lamb (1948; Madison: University of Wisconsin, 1982).

Among the most persistent themes throughout ancient discussion of education is a concern with the inculcation of cultural and moral values. Education in our own day tends to be (theoretically) concerned with preparation for various career paths, setting moral or ethical concerns aside.[2] Nothing could be further from the case with ancient education. Greek education, for example, began as a means of promoting the virtues of the elite warrior class that takes center stage in Homer's *Iliad* and *Odyssey*.[3] These virtues included both physical prowess as well as intellectual skill. The Homeric poems themselves became the central texts of Greek (and later Greco-Roman) education, and Homer himself was credited as "having educated all Greece," as Plato would write: The philosopher alludes to persons who thought all of life should be fashioned in accordance with Homeric example (*Resp.* 606e).

It is precisely the extent of Homer's influence that prompted Plato's extended attacks on poetry in the *Republic*. But Plato's conviction that poetry inculcated bad morals by filling the heads of the young with salacious stories about the gods is an indication that he shared the general view that education ought to promote the right kind of values.

The ubiquity of the belief that education should promote proper values is demonstrated by the shock and horror occasioned in some quarters by the teachings of the early Sophists. These wandering teachers would attract students by demonstrating their rhetorical skill at conversing fluently on any subject and promising to teach their students the skill in public speaking necessary for a political career in the Athenian democracy.[4] The Sophists' critics (Plato not least among them) charged that the Sophists did a grave disservice to their students and to the *polis* by placing technical rhetorical skill ahead of the search for truth, which the philosophers prized.[5] The negative contrast of rhetoric with philosophy became a regular trope, enduring into late antiquity: In the fifth century CE, Augustine of Hippo, in highly Platonic

---

[2] Of course, this is not to say that modern education does not inculcate values anyway, even if these values are not openly acknowledged.
[3] Marrou, *Education*, ch. 1; Frederick A. G. Beck, *Greek Education: 450–350 B.C.* (New York: Barnes and Noble, 1964), 55–64; Mark Royal, Iain McDougall, and J. C. Yardley, *Greek and Roman Education: A Sourcebook*, Routledge Sourcebooks for the Ancient World (New York: Routledge, 2009), 2.
[4] Marrou, *Education*, 48–51.
[5] Ibid., 58.

fashion, lambasted the rhetorical education that he had received in his youth for emphasizing empty style and showiness over truth (*Conf.* 1.18).

Despite the philosophical criticism of rhetoric, teachers of rhetoric also had their own stake in questions about the values imparted by education. The standard rhetorical handbooks of the Hellenistic and Roman periods took care to emphasize that the literary examples supplied for student use should be limited to those which contained values worthy of imitation (μιμήσις).[6] The specific examples chosen were used in turn to reinforce those same values: "The actions of men and gods [in literature] were explained and judged in terms of accepted *mores* and so were used to confirm them."[7] Rhetorical theory from Aristotle onward also argued that a speaker ought to establish common ground with an audience on the basis of shared cultural standards.[8]

Nor was it only in "higher" education in rhetoric or philosophy that a concern for moral and ethical training prevailed. Robert Kaster has studied in detail the social role of the grammarian, the "elementary" teacher who first taught students language and literature. He emphasizes that in ancient society, the skills of reading and writing were bound up with the concern of the elite and privileged to define themselves over and against their putative inferiors. Consequently, the command of language imparted by the grammarian was more than a basic skill; it was a mark of elite culture: "its acquisition signaled that one possessed discipline, an appetite for toil, and the other ethical qualities that marked a man fit to share the burden of government."[9] The grammarian was a "guardian of tradition," transmitting both language usage preserved uncorrupted by the purported vulgarities of the common folk and "the persons, events, and beliefs that marked the limits of vice and virtue."[10]

The technical skills imparted by education were so inextricably bound up with moral pronouncements that it is a key fact to keep in mind when discussing ancient literature on teachers and teaching. To be specific, two of the texts to be examined, those of Xenophon and Philostratus, are keen to

---

[6] Burton L. Mack and Vernon K. Robbins, *Patterns of Persuasion in the Gospels* (Sonoma, CA: Polebridge, 1989), 42–3.
[7] Robert A. Kaster, *Guardians of Language: The Grammarian and Society in Late Antiquity* (Berkeley: University of California, 1988), 12 (italics original).
[8] Mack and Robbins, *Patterns*, 38.
[9] Kaster, *Guardians*, 27.
[10] Ibid., 18.

demonstrate that their subjects behaved in conformity with conventional, or at least widely recognized, standards of virtuous behavior and to answer charges that their subjects' teachings had a deleterious effect on their followers or on society. To anticipate a later conclusion, we will argue that one thing that sets Mark apart from other such texts on teachers and teaching is the Gospel's lack of such apologetic concerns.

The Memorabilia *of Xenophon*

The earliest of the four texts to be examined in this chapter is the *Memorabilia* of Xenophon, written in the fourth century BCE.[11] Xenophon (ca. 430–355?), a wealthy Athenian who became famous for his military exploits, knew Socrates when he himself was a young man. He wrote the four books of the *Memorabilia* as a defense of Socrates after the philosopher's condemnation and death in 399 and as a record of conversations that he attests occurred between Socrates and various interlocutors.

Because Xenophon's account of Socrates's life and views contains significant differences from the more influential version of Plato, his "Socratic" works have regularly played a part in debates concerning the "historical Socrates."[12] However, since our focus here is on the *Memorabilia* as a literary work rather than on questions of historical accuracy, there is no need to deal with the vexed "Socratic question." Therefore, we will not discuss the reliability of Xenophon as a reporter of the views of the historical Socrates. It is Socrates the teacher portrayed in the work itself, not the historical teacher Socrates, who can profitably be compared with Jesus the teacher in the Gospel of Mark.

At its broadest level, the *Memorabilia* is structured into two parts. The first is a short section at the beginning of the work in which Xenophon attempts

---

[11] "The dating of Xenophon's Socratic works can only be approximate: we have no precise information about where or how they were published." Jeffrey Henderson, introduction to *Xenophon*, vol. 4, trans. E. C. Marchant and O. J. Todd, revised by Jeffrey Henderson, LCL 168 (Cambridge, MA: Harvard University Press, 2013), xv.

[12] On the historical issues and the extant sources concerning Socrates, see W. K. C. Guthrie, *Socrates* (London: Cambridge University Press, 1971), 5–57, and Sara Ahbel-Rappe and Rachana Kamtekar, *A Companion to Socrates* (Malden, MA: Blackwell, 2006), section 1.

to refute the charges against Socrates, with himself as the implied narrator (1.1-2). It is worthy of summarization here, since several of its themes will be important for the work as a whole.

After recounting the charges made against Socrates—that he introduced new gods while not recognizing the established ones and that he corrupted the Athenian youth—Xenophon deals with each charge in turn. In response to the accusation of impiety, he portrays Socrates as a model of traditional religiosity: Socrates worshiped the traditional gods, offering them sacrifices both publicly and privately (1.1-2), and never took up for discussion the cosmological matters popularly associated with philosophers (1.1.11-15).[13] His appeal to his famous "divine sign" is, Xenophon argues, no more remarkable than everyday practices of divination accepted by common opinion and tradition (1.1.2-5). Finally, Socrates frequently exhorted his companions to seek advice from the gods about everyday matters (1.1.6-9).

Next, at 1.2, Xenophon addresses the charge that Socrates corrupted the Athenian youth. Xenophon responds by listing Socrates's virtues. Foremost among these is Socrates's "continence" or "self-control" (ἐγκράτεια):

> It is also amazing to me that some were convinced that Socrates corrupted the youth. Beyond what I have already said, he was the most self-controlled [ἐγκρατέσατος] of all persons with respect to the desire for sex and food, and he was the strongest of all with respect to cold and heat and all harsh things. And what is more, so educated was he in needing only what was moderate, that, even having very little, he was quite easily satisfied. (1.2.1, author's translation)

"Self-control" is a key aspect of Xenophon's presentation of Socrates and his teaching, and we will return to it later. In the present context, self-control is the chief virtue of Socrates, which he passed on to his companions not so much by direct teaching as by his own example (1.2.3, 8). But shortly after this, Xenophon does say that Socrates also taught continence or self-control by means of his words. Socrates teaches both by example and by speaking:

---

[13] The claim that Socrates was wholly uninterested in questions of nature and cosmology seems contradicted by the *Memorabilia* itself. For instance, Socrates gives a detailed examination of the natural world in 1.4, as he tries to convince Aristodemus of the existence of divine providence toward human beings.

I find that all teachers show their disciples how they themselves practice what they teach, and persuade them by argument. And so it was with Socrates: he showed his companions that he was a gentleman [καλὸν κἀγαθόν] himself, and talked most excellently of goodness and of all things that concern human life. (1.2.17-18, LCL)

The more specific aspect of the charge that Socrates corrupted the youth is then summarized: He taught the youth to despise their elders and the laws of the city (1.2.9). This charge is personified by Critias and Alcibiades, notorious political figures who both associated with Socrates (1.2.12). Xenophon's response is to argue that these two did not care to actually learn what Socrates had to teach but only associated with the philosopher because they hoped to learn how to speak well from him and thereby improve their political standing (1.2.14-15). Further, they neglected to maintain the lifestyle of moderation or self-control, which they had learned from Socrates, and fell into ambition and lawlessness (1.2.24).

In the concluding summary of the opening defense, Xenophon reiterates the claim made throughout the first two chapters: that, far from being impious or corrupting the youth, Socrates was extremely pious by the most conventional assessments of the city and improved the youth greatly by exhorting them to self-control above all else, which he demonstrated in his own conduct.

1.3 onward consists of the "memorabilia" [ἀπομνημονεύματα] proper: "In order to support my opinion that he benefited his associates alike by actions that revealed his own character and by his conversation, I will set down what I recollect of these" (1.3.1, LCL). The conversations at first seem to be a completely random assortment and further seem not to have any strong connection with the opening defense portion of the text. The opinion of much scholarship has been that that the *Memorabilia* is not a unified work and was perhaps a combination of two disparate works: a "defense" and a collection of remembrances.[14]

The work of Vivienne Gray calls into question this earlier scholarly opinion. Her argument is that there existed

---

[14] Vivienne J. Gray, *The Framing of Socrates: The Literary Interpretation of Xenophon's Memorabilia*, Hermes Zeitschrift für Klassische Philologie 79 (Stuttgart: Franz Steiner, 1998), 9–10, discusses scholarly criticism of the *Memorabilia*'s alleged structural problems.

a rhetorical precedent for the bipartite combination of defence and exposition in the combination in various types of lawcourt speech of a refutation of the charges against a defendant and positive exposition of the virtues of his life.[15]

Gray argues further that the *Memorabilia* also employs the technique known as "amplification" in ancient rhetorical theory in order to fully bring out the nuances and complexities of the teachings of Socrates. This amplification leads to the unfolding, as the work proceeds, of more complex understandings of the methods and aims of Socrates's teachings.[16]

Based on the work of Gray, we may take it as well-founded that there is a certain unity in the *Memorabilia*.[17] While there is neither space nor need here to summarize the entirety of the "recollections" in 1.4 and following, the comparison of Xenophon's work with the Gospel of Mark requires that we now turn to the most important aspect of the discussion: the portrayal of Socrates the teacher and his teaching in the *Memorabilia*. In other words, what does the Socrates of Xenophon teach, and how does he teach it? We will take particular notice of the way the themes of the defense connect with the portrayal of Socrates's teaching, thus lending further credibility to Gray's contention that the *Memorabilia* is indeed a unified work whose structure shows evidence of careful forethought.

The subjects of Socrates's teaching throughout much of the work follow naturally from the claims made in the defense: that Socrates was pious, and that he benefited those who followed him, rather than corrupting them as his accusers said. Therefore, in response to the charges, Xenophon relates numerous conversations between Socrates and interlocutors that demonstrate both of these attributes, especially the latter. On the theme of Socrates's piety, we are given a number of conversations concerning the philosopher's views on the gods as well as snippets of his words that reveal the same. In 1.3, the section that begins the "recollections" portion of the text, we are told straightaway that Socrates's piety was completely conventional and in accordance with the established laws:

---

[15] Gray, *Framing*, 7.
[16] Ibid., 16–25.
[17] Ibid., ch. 8. Christopher Bruell, introduction to *Xenophon: Memorabilia*, trans. Amy L. Bonnette (Ithaca, NY: Cornell University Press, 1994), contains a summary of the *Memorabilia* as a whole, including discussion of the themes that unite various subsections.

First, then, for his attitude towards the gods; his deeds and words were clearly consistent with the answer given by the Priestess at Delphi to those who inquire about their duty regarding sacrifice or the cult of ancestors or any other such matters, for the answer of the Priestess is that those who follows the customs of the state would act piously, and that is how Socrates acted himself and counseled others to act, and to take any other course he considered presumption and folly. (1.3.1, LCL)

A while later, we read one of the most extended conversations of Socrates in the text: "what I once heard him say about the divinity in conversation with Aristodemus the dwarf, as he was called" (1.4.2, LCL). Aristodemus "was not known to sacrifice to the gods or pray or use divination and actually made fun of those who did so" (1.4.2, LCL). Socrates seeks to persuade Aristodemus of the reality of divine providence, especially the gods' care for human beings. Via a series of leading questions, Socrates argues that the natural world is so perfectly designed from a teleological perspective, with different creatures so well suited to their needs and ends, that the existence of divine providence is undeniable. Though the line of argument bears some resemblance to classic "arguments from design," the point of Socrates's case is to argue not for the existence of a designer but rather for the gods' unending beneficent care for the world, especially for human beings. Finally, to clinch his case, Socrates appeals to social convention: The most powerful and successful cities are those which are most devoted to the gods (1.4.16). This invocation of conventional mores underscores Xenophon's point, first made in the defense in 1.1-2, that Socrates was perfectly obedient to the laws of the city, contrary to the charges made against him. The conversation ends with Socrates proclaiming the gods' omnipresence and benevolent providence: "Then you will know that such is the greatness and such the nature of the deity that it sees everything and hears everything alike, and is present everywhere and takes care of everything" (1.4.18, LCL).

This conversation is the most extended presentation in the *Memorabilia* of the idea, expressed in the defense (1.1-2), that Socrates was pious in thoroughly conventional ways that would be approved of by "respectable" Athenians. The only distinctive aspects of Socrates's piety were his invocation of his "divine sign" (1.1.2-4) and his belief that divine knowledge was absolute—Xenophon claims that most other people believed that the gods were beneficent but not all-knowing (1.1.19).

The notion that Socrates behaved in accordance with Athenian law and convention is a recurrent theme in the *Memorabilia*. Socrates behaves in socially appropriate ways for a respectable Athenian gentleman and encourages his followers to do the same. Xenophon's attempts to portray Socrates in this way are sometimes at odds with what is reported in the defense: For example, in 1.2.9-11, Xenophon admits that Socrates criticized the selection of officials by lot in the Athenian democracy.

Beyond the emphasis on Socrates's piety, many of the conversations suggest Socrates's concern for the institutions and norms of the city-state. Socrates chides his own son for not paying proper respect to his mother (2.2). He encourages Chairephon to reconcile with his brother Chairecrates (2.3). There are a number of conversations on the subject of friendship, how one should find, keep, and make use of the best kinds of people as one's friends (2.4-6). He even expounds business advice to Aristarchus and Eutherus, advising the former on how to put his relatives to work in trying economic times and counseling the latter on how to provide for himself in old age (2.7-8). And in the third book of the *Memorabilia*, we find the lengthiest topical grouping of discussions in the text: an extended series of conversations on political leadership and generalship (3.1-7).

Only toward the end of the text do the topics under review suddenly shift. Beginning at about 3.8, we begin to find topics that are more similar to what the reader of Plato might associate with Socrates: the nature of concepts such as courage, wisdom, and virtue. 3.8 concerns the nature of the "good": In conversation with Aristippus, Socrates asserts that "good" and "noble" are terms that apply to any given thing differently, for a good horse is not the same as a good basket, and they are both in turn different from a good cure for fever, and so on. 3.9 discusses whether courage is natural or taught and extends to Socrates's views on the nature of wisdom itself. 4.2 and 4.4 both discuss justice and injustice.

Even in these more abstract discussions, we once again find the recurrent theme of Socrates's adherence to convention: In 4.4, he argues that justice is the same as adherence to the laws (understood broadly as both the written statutes of the cities and the unwritten customs held in common by all cities).

And throughout these conversations, Xenophon as implied narrator is keen to point out how Socrates continually benefited his companions and made them better (e.g., 3.8.1, 4.1, 4.2).

How is one to account for this range of topics addressed by Socrates in the *Memorabilia*? Despite an initial impression of a lack of order or purpose, there is, as we have seen, some logic in the way the conversations are arranged. Conversations are grouped together by their broad subject, such as friendship or leadership. Also, the broad order of the conversations beginning at 1.3 follows the order in which the charges were addressed in 1.1-2. In the defense, the notion of Socrates's impiety was rebutted first, followed by the charge that Socrates corrupted the youth. In parallel, 1.3 opens with a narrative exposition of Socrates's virtues, which follows the same order: Socrates' piety is discussed (1.3.1-4), then his self-discipline in matters of food, drink, and sex—the opposite of the vices attributed to Critias and Alcibiades, the supposed prime examples of Socrates's pernicious influence (1.3.5-15).

Vivienne Gray has further argued that the *Memorabilia* shares many characteristics in common with Greek wisdom literature.[18] Such literature tended to cover a wide variety of topics, and the wide range of subjects touched upon in Socrates's conversations are "partly a result of the rhetorical desire to prove Socrates as completely wise as possible and partly a compromise with wisdom literature, which regularly covered such a range."[19]

Finally, the fact that the dialectical discussions of justice, wisdom, and so on appear at the end of the text appears well-matched to Xenophon's view of the relationship between self-control (one of his favorite themes) and virtue. This brings us to a discussion of the most important way in which Xenophon unifies the topics of Socrates's teaching: the overarching themes of Socrates's teaching program. Beyond structural organization and groupings of the conversations by topic, the teaching of Socrates in the *Memorabilia* is unified by the attention paid to three quintessential themes: "self-control," "usefulness," and the importance of practice and training for virtue. These three themes are repeatedly invoked throughout all four books of the *Memorabilia*.

---

[18] Gray, *Framing*, ch. 9.
[19] Ibid., 10.

Ἐγκράτεια, "self-control," is an extremely common and important theme in the work. Its centrality has been noted by Louis-André Dorion. Citing 1.2, which we touched on earlier, Dorion identifies three key terms: "*enkrateia* (self-mastery with regard to bodily pleasures), *karteria* (endurance of physical pain), and *autarkeia* (self-sufficiency)." He points out the frequent appearance of these three ideas in the *Memorabilia* and says that "this triad forms the core of Socratic ethics in Xenophon's writings."[20] And preeminent among these three is ἐγκράτεια.

Dorion highlights the importance of the theme of ἐγκράτεια for Xenophon's Socrates by comparing him with the Socrates found in the dialogues of Plato.[21] As he observes, the emphasis on ἐγκράτεια in the *Memorabilia* demonstrates that the ethical system of Xenophon's Socrates incorporates a concept almost entirely foreign to that of his Platonic counterpart: the notion of ἀκρασία or "weakness of will." Plato attributes to Socrates the view that knowledge alone is sufficient for virtue; that is, that a person who is in possession of knowledge of what is good will not attempt to act in opposition to that good. This doctrine is given forthright expression in *Protagoras* 358d:

> Then surely, I went on, no one willingly goes after evil or what he thinks to be evil; it is not in human nature, apparently, to do so—to wish to go after what one thinks to be evil in preference to the good; and when compelled to choose one of two evils, nobody will choose the greater when he may the lesser. (LCL)

But turning from Plato to Xenophon, one finds this notion expressly contradicted. While it is true that Xenophon seems on occasion to express views similar to Plato, for the most part the Socrates of the *Memorabilia* accepts as fundamental the idea that a lack of ἐγκράτεια prevents one from becoming virtuous.[22] Dorion singles out 1.5.4, which reads,

---

[20] Louis-André Dorion, "Xenophon's Socrates," trans. Stephen Menn, in *A Companion to Socrates*, 97.
[21] Dorion, "*Akrasia* et *enktraeia* dans les Mémorables," in his *L'autre Socrates: Études sur les écrits socratiques de Xénophon* (Paris: Les Belles Lettres, 2013), 93–122.
[22] Gregory Vlastos, *Socrates: Ironist and Moral Philosopher* (Ithaca, NY: Cornell University, 1991), 99–101, cites *Mem.* 3.9.5 as an example of a passage where Xenophon's Socrates seems to teach a partial version of the Platonic notion of the "impossibility of incontinence" (p. 100). However, much hinges on how one chooses to translate the verb προελέσθαι in this passage. According to Liddell-Scott-Jones, it can mean either "to prefer" or "to choose before others." If one follows Vlastos and translates it as "prefer," then it is not clear that the passage actually teaches the impossibility of weakness of will: Just because one with knowledge will always "prefer" the good does not mean they will actually choose it. By contrast, if we follow Marchant, Todd, and Henderson (LCL) in

> Should every man not hold self-control to be the foundation of all virtue, and first lay this foundation firmly in his soul? For who without his can learn any good or practice it creditably? (LCL)[23]

The importance of the theme of ἐγκράτεια in the *Memorabilia* is demonstrated by the emphasis given to it in the defense and in several of the summary statements with which Xenophon introduces various conversations between Socrates and his interlocutors. We have already noted 1.2.1, where ἐγκράτεια is listed first and foremost among Socrates's virtues. 1.2.2-8 emphasizes that this self-control was key among the things that Socrates took pains to pass on to his companions, by his own example. The theme of Socrates's self-discipline and control of his desires recurs toward the beginning of the conversations proper in 1.3.5-8. A short speech of Socrates on the subject is presented at 1.5.1, and the section concludes as follows: "Such were his words; but his own self-control was shown yet more clearly by his deeds than by his words" (1.5.6, LCL). And outside the summary statements from the narrator, ἐγκράτεια appears in the defense section when Critias and Alcibiades are presented as being deceitful in their association with Socrates, since they had no desire to imitate Socrates's own moderation of pleasures. The two of them are portrayed as exact opposites of Socrates, ruthless and uncontrolled in seeking gratification of their desires. Finally, toward the end of the work, there is a lengthy discussion between Socrates and Euthydemus (4.5.1-12) on the subject of self-control, which makes it the basis of not only virtue but also advanced philosophical discussion in the form of dialectic (4.5.11):

> Only the self-controlled [τοῖς ἐγκρατέσι] can consider the things that matter most, and sorting them out after their kind, by word and deed alike, choose the good and reject the evil. (LCL)

Ἐγκράτεια is therefore crucial in the *Memorabilia*. Self-control is a key aspect both of Socrates's own character and of the program that he teaches to his own students. It serves to unite many of the disparate conversations and tie

---

translating the verb as "choose," then the passage does seem to suggest that weakness of will is impossible.

[23] Dorion, "*Akrasia* et *enktraeia*," 94.

together the defense with the conversations. It is a central element in Socrates's teaching.

A second, no less prevalent motif that helps unify the work is that of Socrates's "usefulness" or "helpfulness" (ὠφελία, ὠφέλιμος) to his companions. Gray notes the centrality for Xenophon, of this aspect of Socrates's character, and cites over sixty instances of the term in various forms across all four books of the *Memorabilia*. The programmatic statement of Socrates's "usefulness" occurs in the narratorial remark that opens the "conversations" section of the work:

> In order to support my opinion that he benefited [or "was useful to," ὠφελεῖν] his associates alike by actions that revealed his own character and by his conversation, I will set down what I recollect of these. (1.3.1, LCL)

Following 1.3, some form of the term appears "in almost every episode of the work."[24]

Many different types of people, activities, and things can be "useful" or "useless" according to Xenophon's Socrates. For one, weighty matters such as politics can be arenas for displaying one's usefulness. In a conversation between Socrates and Glaucon (3.6), we learn that Glaucon wishes to take part in public affairs but makes a fool of himself whenever he speaks in public on matters of civic concern. Socrates declares to Glaucon that usefulness is the prime prerequisite of doing well in politics: "Well, Glaucon, since you want to win honor, isn't it obvious that you must benefit your city [ὠφελητέα σοι ἡ πόλις ἐστί]?" (3.6.3, LCL)

Usefulness is also the primary measure of a philosopher's worth. Aside from the various asides about Socrates's usefulness, Socrates is also given the opportunity to defend his own usefulness against the criticism of the sophist Antiphon. In a pair of conversations (1.6.1-14), Antiphon implicitly challenges the usefulness of Socrates's teachings. First (1.6.1-10), Antiphon taunts Socrates that while philosophy ought to make its adherents happier, Socrates only makes his companions miserable, because he teaches them to live a life of material deprivation. Socrates retorts that he himself has learned to be satisfied with little and take enjoyment from the most basic sorts of food

---

[24] Gray, *Framing*, 11.

and drink, which in the final equation makes him much happier than a man who is dependent upon physical pleasures and material comfort.

The following conversation (1.6.7-14) has Antiphon declare that Socrates's teaching must be of no worth, because if Socrates himself valued it, he would charge money to his students rather than give it away for free. Socrates answers the charge by comparing sophists to prostitutes, offering their services to all and sundry for money, while saying that his practice of seeking good friends with whom to share wisdom and virtue is widely recognized as the way of a gentleman (καλὸν κἀγαθόν) (1.6.13).

Even matters more prosaic than politics and philosophy are discussed with reference to usefulness. In 2.7, Socrates strikes upon a conversation with a gloomy Aristarchus, who is at his wits' end because his household is filled with idle female relatives who had fled civil disorder elsewhere, and he cannot find the means to provide for them. Socrates suggests that Aristarchus set his relatives to work making "useful" things like bread and clothes (2.7.5). In this way, the women themselves will become both useful and happier because they are no longer idle. And when Aristarchus, after implementing this scheme, says that the women are now complaining that he himself does nothing while they are hard at work, Socrates responds that they ought to think of Aristarchus as like the sheepdog who keeps the flock from harm—this, analogously, is Aristarchus's own usefulness to his relatives.

Everything from household skills to the arena of politics, then, is considered in the *Memorabilia* from the perspective of usefulness. But not only does the term recur frequently in individual cases, it is in fact a key theme that, like "self-control," ties together the defense section with the conversations. Recall that in 1.3 Xenophon begins the conversations by announcing that his recollections will prove the claim made in the defense that Socrates was useful to his companions. Since usefulness is often contrasted with the witting or unwitting causation of harm to self and others, it is thus the opposite of "corrupting the youth," which is what Socrates's accusers said he did. That Socrates was useful to others is Xenophon's answer to the charge that Socrates harmed others instead. Like self-control, usefulness is something that Socrates both possessed himself and tried to encourage in his companions.

Finally, it is worth noting that the theme of usefulness is closely related to that of self-control. Dorion notes that self-control is the prerequisite in the *Memorabilia* not just for virtue but also for usefulness:

> For Socrates[x] [Xenophon's Socrates], a person's usefulness is grounded in *enkrateia*: this is what allows him to be useful to himself, and then his usefulness then extends, thanks to his exercise of virtue, to his household, his friends, and finally his city and fellow citizens.[25]

This contention, that Xenophon grounds usefulness in self-control, is readily demonstrated from the text. As just one example, consider 4.5.6: Socrates encourages Euthydemus toward the view that "incontinence [ἀκρασία] prevents [people] from attending to useful things [ὠφελοῦσι] and understanding them by drawing them away to things pleasant" (LCL). We have, then, a further indication that the *Memorabilia* is in fact a carefully designed work, rather than just a jumble of assorted conversations. The conversations have been organized around careful themes, and those themes have been linked with one another, as in the case of self-control and usefulness.

The final theme of the *Memorabilia* to be considered cannot be reduced to a single technical term, but it is quite important nevertheless. This theme is the repeated claim, both by the narrator and by Socrates himself, that both knowledge and practice are required for the completion of any task that makes one "noble and good (καλὸν κἀγαθόν)" and thus are indispensable for virtue.

The theme is sounded early on in the text by Xenophon as narrator. Speaking for himself, he responds to the view that if Socrates were a good example to the Athenian youth, then Critias and Alcibiades would never have strayed from the virtues that Socrates taught.

> But many self-styled philosophers may reply: A just man can never become unjust; a prudent man can never become wanton; in fact no one having learned any kind of knowledge can become ignorant of it. I do not hold with this view. I notice that as those who do not train the body cannot perform the functions proper to the body, so those who do not train the soul cannot perform the functions of the soul: for they cannot do what they ought to do nor avoid what they ought not to do. (1.2.19, LCL)

---

[25] Dorion, "Xenophon's Socrates," 99.

This view that one must "train" (ἀσκεῖν) to become reliably virtuous in attaining the good or useful in any arena of life is a regular theme in the *Memorabilia*. It is also another point at which Xenophon stands in direct contradiction of Plato. For Plato's Socrates, since knowledge alone is a sufficient condition for virtuous behavior, not only can there be no such thing as ἀκρασία, but there also cannot be any need for training or practice in virtue, outside the acquisition of the required knowledge. For Xenophon, by contrast, various arts, skills, and behaviors can lapse without practice: Just as one's body can become weak without regular physical exercise, so too can the soul lose virtue without proper reinforcement.

In fact, Socrates regards both knowledge and practice as indispensable in any arena of life. For instance, Socrates frequently converses with individuals wish to attain positions of rank and renown in the city-state: leadership of the polis or generalship. We discussed in a different context Socrates's encounter with Glaucon, who clumsily attempts to participate in politics (3.6). What becomes clear over the course of the conversation is that although Glaucon has the *desire* to participate in politics, he does not have the requisite *knowledge*. He knows nothing, for instance, of how to grow the city's economy or manage its military affairs. When Glaucon's ignorance becomes clear, Socrates advises him to brush up on what he needs to know, if he wants to fulfill his ambitions (3.6.18).

The relationship between practice or training and innate talent is made clear in 3.9, when Socrates is asked whether courage is something taught or natural (διδακτὸν ἢ φυσικόν). Socrates's reply is that although different people may have greater or lesser natural inclinations toward courageous behavior, he thinks "that every man's nature acquires more courage by learning and practice" (3.9.1, LCL). This maxim, that one must practice in order to hone one's natural gifts, is then applied to all skills and practices generally in 3.9.3. And a while later, to drive home the point, Socrates imparts his views on the nature of rulership: Only those who actually have knowledge of how to rule can truly be considered rulers (3.9.10). 4.1.4 nicely sums up the general idea: Talented youths whose gifts are properly directed and focused become good citizens, while those whose gifts are not so channeled become wicked. (This is likely a jab at Critias and Alcibiades.)

From these three concepts that recur throughout the text—self-control, usefulness, and practice or knowledge—we form an outline of Xenophon's philosophy of education. The aim of education is the production of a person who possesses happiness (εὐδαιμονία) by virtue of being useful to friends, family, and society. The foundation of this education toward happiness is self-control or self-mastery (1.5.4). Without it, one cannot be virtuous or useful. Especially, without self-control, one cannot acquire the knowledge necessary to do well at anything or discipline oneself to practice at it (4.1.5). This is why Socrates exhorts his hearers to self-control and tries to correct their excesses of desire. But even if one is self-controlled, one must also properly know the limits of one's own skill and knowledge. This is why Socrates is so intent on dispelling the illusions of knowledge under which Glaucon (3.6) and Euthydemus (4.2) labor.

Having spent a great deal of time discussing *what* Socrates teaches, a question remains to be answered: *How* does he teach it? The most salient feature of the teaching method of Xenophon's Socrates is that he does not rely on ironic use of the *elenchus*, or cross-examination of an interlocutor's beliefs, as does the version of Socrates in Plato.[26] Traces of the *elenchus* can still be found in the *Memorabilia*: the conversation with Aristodemus about divine providence, for example.[27] But there is a key difference from the Platonic presentation of Socratic conversation. Even in conversations where an interlocutor's beliefs are subjected to rigorous examination, Socrates is never portrayed as professing ignorance on a subject or as seeking to discover a conclusion that is not clear at the beginning of the discussion.[28] This is partly because Xenophon usually presents in advance with his editorial introductions to each conversation what the "point" of the dialogue is, but it is also because Socrates, in confronting various interlocutors, already has a strong position on whatever issue is being discussed, a position that he hopes the interlocutor will adopt. For example, in one conversation where Xenophon himself is present as the philosopher's interlocutor, Socrates seeks to persuade Xenophon that Critobulus's reckless pursuit of a beautiful youth is dangerous (1.3.8-13). On another occasion, he

---

[26] The *elenchus* is discussed in more detail below in the section on the *Discourses* of Epictetus.
[27] The relative absence of the ironic *elenchus*, and the traces of it which do remain, is discussed by Gray, *Framing*, 13-16.
[28] As noticed by Dorion, "Xenophon's Socrates," 95.

upbraids his son Lamprocles for not sufficiently respecting his mother (2.2). In 2.6, he instructs Critobulus on the best method of seeking a good friend. The tendency toward positive instruction, rather than just the tearing down of mistaken opinions, is perhaps the most notable difference between Xenophon's Socrates and the early Plato's.

On a related note, we should not neglect the impact made on a reader's impression of Socrates's teaching by the comments that Xenophon himself makes as narrator on the substance and style of Socrates's words. The very fact that Xenophon offers his own defense of Socrates in 1.1-2, and peppers the whole text with editorial asides on the goals and outcomes of Socrates's teaching, encourages the reader to view Socrates as having a definite program of moral improvement that he imparts to his companions. This was possibly Xenophon's means of answering the charge made by Socrates's accusers that he taught his young students to despise established laws and authorities by subjecting those laws and authorities to rigorous negative criticism (1.4.1). But regardless of the reasons for it, the editorial asides of the narrator also play a role in the inculcation of the teachings that are presented for consideration in the *Memorabilia*. Xenophon himself, in his role as implied narrator, is virtually a co-teacher alongside his literary Socrates, offering guidance on how to interpret Socrates's words.

The *Discourses* of Epictetus

Epictetus (c. 50-c. 135 CE), a former slave who studied with the Stoic teacher Musonius Rufus, began teaching in Rome but relocated to the Greek city of Nicopolis after Domitian's banishment of philosophers from Italy in 95 CE. For the rest of his life, he instructed well-to-do young men, partly in the Stoic "classics" such as the writings of Chrysippus, but especially through his own discourses, in which he presented his interpretation of Stoic philosophy.[29] Epictetus is one of the best-known Stoic thinkers, his words having been

---

[29] An excellent discussion of the background and social status of Epictetus's students is found in P. A. Brunt, "From Epictetus to Arrian," in his *Studies in Stoicism*, ed. Miriam Griffin and Alison Samuels, with the assistance of Michael Crawford (Oxford: Oxford University, 2013), 332–42.

copiously preserved by his student Arrian, who studied with Epictetus for some time during the reign of Trajan, Domitian's successor. These posthumous publications include four extant books of *Discourses* (another four are lost) and a small digest, the *Enchiridion* or "handbook."

While some scholars have doubted the historical reliability of these works, and view the "Epictetus" depicted in them as almost entirely the creation of Arrian, the majority opinion is that these works, and the *Discourses* in particular, provide a more or less accurate portrait of Epictetus and his teaching, although Arrian has certainly intervened in their organization and presentation.[30] Most notably, the koine Greek of the *Discourses* is substantially different from the style of the works known to have been composed by Arrian himself.[31] In any event, as with the work of Xenophon, our concern here is not with the historical figure behind the work but with the teacher and his teachings as they appear in the work itself.

Formally, the *Discourses* take the form of speeches of Epictetus and conversations between the philosopher and various interlocutors. Editorial introductions present the subject of each discourse. Sometimes we are informed that a particular discourse was addressed to a specific individual (i.e., 2.4, 2.14, 2.24, 3.7); at other times to a group or "type" of person, such as a rival philosophical school, or people guilty of a certain vice (1.5, 2.15, 2.20, 4.13). Much of the time, however, the editorial introductions concern the topic of each discourse, as either a declarative statement or a question to be answered—for instance, 1.1, "On the things which we control and those we do not" (Περὶ τῶν ἐφ' ἡμῖν καὶ οὐκ ἐφ' ἡμῖν), or 3.10, "how is it necessary to deal with illnesses?" (Πῶς φέρειν δεῖ τὰς νόσους).[32] There is relatively little order or thematic grouping in the way the discourses are arranged, although the beginning of book 1 does deal with some of the most fundamental precepts of Epictetus's teaching, and the discourses directed at specific individuals or types (as opposed to those titled after their topic) become somewhat more common in books 3 and 4. Since four books of the *Discourses* are no longer

---

[30] On the reliability of the *Discourses*, see A. A. Long, *Epictetus: A Stoic and Socratic Guide to Life* (Oxford: Oxford University, 2002), 40–1.
[31] Christopher Gill, introduction to *Discourses, Fragments, Handbook* by Epictetus, trans. Robin Hard (Oxford: Oxford University, 2014), ix.
[32] My translations.

extant, it is difficult to make strong judgments about the literary structure of the work as a whole.

Although the discourses predominately present the speech of Epictetus himself, there are also narrative elements in several of the discourses. In these cases, Arrian typically describes a certain individual entering Epictetus's classroom or challenging him on a certain topic, at which point Epictetus will engage the interlocutor in conversation.[33] The extent to which these conversations constitute true dialogue or dialectic varies—sometimes, genuine conversation gives way to a full-blown speech by Epictetus, with the interlocutor fading out of the scene, such as in 3.1, where a conversation with a vain student of rhetoric eventually results in the student himself no longer speaking, while Epictetus gives a speech and poses rhetorical questions in lieu of actual ones from a real interlocutor. This style, where a speaker imagines questions from a potential interlocutor and then answers them as part of a hortatory address, is often called *diatribe* and is well-known to students of the New Testament particularly from the letters of Paul.[34] Indeed, even when no real interlocutor is present, Epictetus will often supply an imaginary one to point out the most common objections to the position he is advancing so that he can refute them.

However, there are also some discourses where the interlocutor becomes a full participant in the conversation. A good example is 1.11, "Of family affection" (LCL). In this discourse, Epictetus asks an "official" (τινος ... τῶν ἐν τέλει) question about his family life. The man replies that his family has brought him misery: In particular, he was recently brought to much misery when his young daughter was ill and near death. "I could not bear even to stay by her sick bed but I up [*sic*] and ran away, until someone brought me word

---

[33] In some instances, the entrance of a particular person serves no purpose other than to set the scene of the occasion for a specific discourse; Epictetus does not engage with the entrant as an interlocutor but simply presents a discourse based on the issues raised by the very presence of the newcomer (e.g., 2.14).

[34] See, e.g., Stanley K. Stowers, *A Rereading of Romans: Justice, Jews, and Gentiles* (New Haven, CT: Yale University), 1994, esp. 11–15. However, Long (*Epictetus*, 49, 90) has reservations about using "diatribe" as a description of Epictetus's teachings in the *Discourses*, primarily because of their highly Socratic aims (on which see below) and the distance between Epictetus the teacher and the traditional practitioners of diatribe, the rhetoricians. That said, "Epictetus' discourses have *some* affinity with the so-called diatribe tradition," as Long says (49). Here, the intention is no more than to point out the affinity to the diatribe tradition based on the formal conceit of using an imaginary interlocutor (as opposed to a real one) to advance the point being made.

that she was well again" (1.11.4, LCL). Although the official is convinced that he was acting "naturally" (φυσικῶς) in doing this, Epictetus challenges him to defend this belief, since Epictetus holds that what is done in accordance with nature is right. The man attempts to defend his actions, but Epictetus eventually convinces him that what he did was not in accordance with nature but rather was the result of wrong judgment (1.11.27ff.). Throughout, the interlocutor is an active participant in the conversation. The style is quite similar to that of the early Socratic dialogues of Plato. This Socratic style is an important feature of the *Discourses*, which we will discuss further below.

These, then, are the basic characteristics of the *Discourses*. We can now ask the same questions we asked concerning the portrayal of Socrates in Xenophon: What does the Epictetus of the *Discourses* teach, and how does he teach it? Although older scholarship considered Epictetus's teachings to be mere repetition of older Stoic ethical ideas, more recent work has overturned this judgment. In both respects—the content and manner of the teaching—Epictetus draws on the Stoic tradition but also introduces his own ideas.[35]

The basis of his ethical teaching is presented in the very first section of the *Discourses*, which discusses "things which are under our control and not under our control" (1.1, LCL). In the Stoic view, the universe is entirely determined by a single principle, called reason or God, which causes everything to happen in deterministic fashion. Because of this, the vast majority of things that occur cannot be controlled or affected by human beings: "Not under our control are the body, the parts of the body, possessions, parents, brothers, children, country—in a word, all that with which we associate" (1.22.10, LCL). I cannot, for instance, ultimately control whether I will be struck with a debilitating illness or whether my crops will fail due to inclement weather. I can take precautions such as trying to care for my body or plan for emergencies, but in the end, I cannot shape these things according to my will; therefore, they are not "up to me."[36] These things are "externals" and play no role in Epictetus's account of the good. For unlike Aristotle, who held that

---

[35] Long, *Epictetus*, 2–3.
[36] As noted by William O. Stephens, *Stoic Ethics: Epictetus and Happiness as Freedom* (London: Continuum, 2007), 8, these things are "not under my control" not because I can have no effect on them whatsoever (as my examples about staying healthy and preparing for unexpected disaster indicate) but rather that they are not "free, unhindered, and unimpeded," as is the case with things that are actually "under my control."

some measure of material prosperity was necessary for the truly happy life, the Stoics, including Epictetus, argue "that a certain kind of internal state of the soul is not only a sufficient condition of *eudaimonia*, but is moreover its only condition."[37]

If, because the universe is deterministic, so much is not under our control, what *is* under our control? Only, says Epictetus, our ability to make proper use of our own "impressions" (φαντασίαι):

> As was fitting, therefore, the gods have put under our control only the most excellent faculty of all and that which dominates the rest, namely, the power to make correct use of external impressions, but all the others they have not put under our control. (1.22.10, LCL)

Or, as he puts it elsewhere, "The function of the good and excellent man is to deal with his impressions in accordance with nature" (3.3.1, LCL). One deals with one's impressions properly by controlling "desire" (ὄρεξις) and "aversion" (ἔκκλισις). In a deterministic universe, we cannot ultimately control what sense impressions we receive or the events we experience, only the judgments we make about them, and it is our judgments about things, rather than the things themselves, which cause us to view them as good or bad:

> Epictetus constantly insists that what disturbs people is not an event as such—death or illness, for instance—but rather their judgement about this event, or the way they describe it and its bearing on themselves. By intruding evaluative judgments onto events, people make essentially neutral or indifferent circumstances bad or good.[38]

The source of human unhappiness, then, is that we judge things to be good or bad, which are not in fact so. Epictetus and the Stoics hold to the Platonic tradition that no one willingly does wrong; rather, people assent to what they believe to be good and never willingly do what they believe is bad (i.e., 1.18.1-4; 2.26.1-3). One of Epictetus's most vivid expositions of this notion is his interpretation of Medea's intention to kill her children in Euripides's play (1.28). Epictetus imagines an interlocutor objecting to his doctrine that no one willingly does bad by quoting Medea's declaration that she knows what

---

[37] Stephens, 1. For Aristotle's view, see *Eth. nic.* 1099a31-b7.
[38] Long, *Epictetus*, 28.

she intends to do is bad, but that out of anger she will do it anyway (Euripides *Med.* 1078-9). Epictetus counters that Medea only acts in this way because she judges that it is better to kill her children out of revenge than not to do so. If she thought what she was doing was bad, she would not do it (1.28.7).[39] What Medea does is, in fact, bad, but because she does not know that, but rather thinks it is good, she is to be pitied rather than reviled (1.28.9). It is because we lack the ability to properly understand what is actually good and bad that we come to grief: We do not properly consider how to judge our sense impressions (1.28.28-33). Philosophy, then, has its beginning in the search for a means to distinguish the truth about what is good and bad from mere opinion and convention (2.11.13ff.).

The solution to this problem is education: For Epictetus, the educated person is one who knows how to make proper use of impressions and adjusts their desire and aversion accordingly so that they desire only what is genuinely good and are averse only to what is genuinely bad: "Instruction [or 'education,' τὸ παιδεύεσθαι] consists precisely in learning to desire each thing exactly as it happens" (1.12.15, LCL). The truly knowledgeable person will not desire what is outside their control or be averse to things beyond their power. Since the universe is determined, and the only thing really "up to us" is our own judgments, nothing aside from our use of impressions and our judgments is truly good or bad. Our judgments are good if we adjust them so that we allow ourselves to be swayed by nothing that is outside our control; they are bad if we allow externals to negatively impact our judgments so that we let those externals affect our happiness. If one is properly trained in the use of impressions, in proper desire and aversion, then and only then will true happiness result:

> What, then, is the fruit of these doctrines? Precisely that which must needs be both the fairest and the most becoming for those who are being truly educated: tranquility, fearlessness, freedom. For on these matters we should not trust the multitude … but rather the philosophers, who say, "Only the educated are free." (2.1.21-22, LCL)

---

[39] As noted by Gill in Hard, ed., *Epictetus*, 317 n.1.28.7, what the Stoics, and Epictetus, oppose in reading the passage this way is the notion that Medea displays here "weakness of will," which we discussed above in connection with the *Memorabilia*. Epictetus apparently follows Chrysippus in interpreting Medea's words this way.

And the truly educated person will be able to face with equanimity even the kinds of trials and torments that societal convention would judge unbearable:

> Let others practice lawsuits, others problems, others syllogisms; do you practise how to die, how to be enchained, how to be racked, how to be exiled. Do all these things with confidence, with trust in Him who has called you to face them ... in which having once been placed you shall exhibit what can be achieved by a rational governing principle when arrayed against the forces that lie outside the province of the moral purpose. (2.1.38-40, LCL)

This, then, is the gist of Epictetus's teaching in the *Discourses*: He exhorts his students to understand what is and is not under their control, encourages them to pay careful attention to their desires and aversions, and rebuts common opinions about the necessity of wealth, fortune, or social status to happiness. His teaching is not about "Stoicism" writ large, for although he sometimes discusses physics and logic, the two other major concerns of ancient philosophy and of earlier Stoicism, the overwhelming focus of the *Discourses* is ethics or the way to a happy life. Stoic physics is largely presumed rather than argued, although occasionally alluded to (e.g., 2.1.18). As for logic, Epictetus discusses it from time to time but most often to put in its proper place as a sort of companion of ethics. Epictetus heaps scorn on students who take pride in their "book learning," their knowledge of logical arguments or the classic works of Stoic authors like Chrysippus, but neglect training in desire and aversion and in making proper use of impressions (2.16.34-35; 2.17.27-40; 3.2.6). At one point, Epictetus declares that only those who are already well along in training their desires and aversions, and in understanding right action, should busy themselves studying logic and arguments, but that many would-be students of philosophy have a bad habit of focusing on logic to the detriment of other, more basic tasks (3.2).

So far, everything we have described of Epictetus's ethical teaching is more or less in line with standard Stoic doctrine. But as mentioned earlier, recent scholarship has also identified aspects of the *Discourses* that mark out Epictetus's individuality, in contrast to older work that viewed Epictetus as a slavish summarizer of earlier Stoic ideas. Epictetus introduces a number of innovations that, while not repudiating earlier Stoicism, do lend particular uniqueness to his interpretation of Stoic ideas. Here we mention Epictetus's innovation in terms of the *content* of his teaching; the *manner* of his teaching, which has its own unique qualities, will be discussed shortly.

With respect to content, the chief innovation of Epictetus's ethics is his reframing and fleshing out of earlier Stoic conceptions of "role ethics."[40] Stoic philosophy traditionally argued that human beings should behave as befits their nature as rational beings with a share in the divine reason or governing principle, and Epictetus does not disagree (i.e., 2.8; 2.14.11-13; 3.9.11). However, Epictetus goes a step further. Behaving as befits a general human nature is only one part of the picture, for Epictetus also holds that each person ought to behave in accordance with what is appropriate to their own "role" as dictated by their specific place in society (3.23.4-5).[41] In one passage (2.10), he begins by exhorting, "Examine who you are." As he unpacks this advice, he suggests that the student ought to consider not just their nature as a rational human being but their specific place in society:

> Next, if you sit in the town council of some city, remember that you are a councillor; if you are young, remember that you are young; if old, that you are an elder; if a father, that you are a father. For each of these designations, when duly considered, always suggests the acts that are appropriate to it. (2.10.10ff., LCL)

The point of the fact that people have different "roles" is that what is appropriate behavior for one person or another can depend on their role. As Brian Johnson observes, for Epictetus the idea of "roles" serves as a concrete alternative to the traditional Stoic focus on abstract virtues:

> In Stoicism (and in ancient ethics more generally), ethical goodness is understood as the expression of character virtues such as justice or courage, but Epictetus holds that ethical goodness is the proper expression of one's roles, such as mother or teacher ... Through the concept of ethical roles, Epictetus reformulates the abstract and forbidding virtues of Stoicism ...

---

[40] For what follows, see Brian E. Johnson, *The Role Ethics of Epictetus: Stoicism in Ordinary Life* (Lanham, MA: Lexington Books, 2013).

[41] Johnson, *Role Ethics*, 12. Epictetus was not actually the first Stoic to put forth ideas like these, although his version of them is certainly the most fleshed out in our extant literature. This idea that each person has a specific role in addition to their general human nature is also found in Cicero *Off.* 1.107, dependent upon the earlier Stoic Panaetius. See the discussion in Robert F. Dobbin, trans., *Epictetus Discourses Book I* (Oxford: Oxford University Press, 1998), 79–80.

into the concrete obligations that ordinary individuals recognize as associate with their roles.[42]

Because different people have different roles, what can be described as reasonable or unreasonable for a given person can vary depending on that role. "To the rational being only the irrational is unendurable, but the rational is endurable" (1.2.1, LCL). But at the same time, "it so happens that the rational and the irrational are different for different persons," and education is needed precisely so that one may learn to discern what is or is not rational and irrational in their own case (1.2.5-6, LCL). In other words, to return to Epictetus's favorite topics of desire and aversion, each person should train their desires and aversions differently. For instance, it is reasonable for one person to be averse to menial labor, while for another their role makes performing such labor the most reasonable thing (1.2.8-9).

One practical upshot of Epictetus's concern with individual roles above and beyond each person's status as a generic human being is that he has very little to say about the classic Stoic notion of the "sage."[43] Earlier Stoics were known for their "division of human beings into two absolute classes: perfectly rational, virtuous, knowing and happy sages, and unequivocally irrational, imperfect, ignorant, and miserable fools."[44] No one is truly wise except the sage; even those who are progressing toward virtue are no more actually virtuous than those who have made no progress at all.[45]

By contrast, Epictetus does not use the figure of the sage as a representative of the end goal of Stoic education. And he rejects the notion that the one who progresses is just as removed from wisdom as any other nonsage. Instead, "he urges on his students the importance of what they can do to make progress *now*."[46] And one of the chief means by which one may measure one's progress is how well one adheres to the *role* that one has. "Sage" is not a "role" for Epictetus. Instead, Epictetus's exemplars for his students are famous politicians, athletes, and military leaders—and above all the ideal philosopher, Socrates,

---

[42] Johnson, *Role Ethics*, 3.
[43] On which concept see René Brouwer, *The Stoic Sage: The Early Stoics on Wisdom, Sagehood and Socrates* (Cambridge: Cambridge University, 2014); Tad Brennan, *The Stoic Life: Emotions, Duties, and Fate* (Oxford: Oxford University, 2005), 36–45.
[44] Long, *Epictetus*, 32.
[45] Brennan, *Stoic Life*, 36–7.
[46] Ibid., 33 (emphasis original).

the paradigm of wisdom for Epictetus.⁴⁷ "For Epictetus, ordinary individuals are ethically good if they perform those actions which can be reasonably defended as issuing from their roles in life."⁴⁸

Epictetus's innovations do not end with his twist on Stoic ethics. Just as important is his particular *style* of teaching, a style highly influenced by the Socratic tradition. Stoics in general revered Socrates as the archetypal wise man. Epictetus follows suit in this regard. The Stoics also endorsed Socrates's ethical position that only virtue was necessary for happiness. But Epictetus's reliance on Socrates goes beyond pointing to the Athenian philosopher's doctrines or moral example. A. A. Long has argued persuasively that in the *Discourses*, Epictetus does not simply use Socrates as a model or ideal figure to be imitated but actually bases his method of teaching on the principles of Socratic dialectic or *elenchus*.⁴⁹

The *elenchus* is the most distinctive feature of many of Plato's Socratic dialogues and, as many scholars also believe, the historical Socrates. In the Platonic dialogues, Socrates questions an interlocutor about a given subject—often the definition of a given idea or thing, such as piety in *Euthyphro*, or rhetoric in the first part of *Gorgias*. The interlocutor voices a provisional understanding of the subject, and then Socrates, through a series of questions, eventually convinces the interlocutor to assent to other beliefs that conflict with the view of the subject that the interlocutor proposed at the beginning.⁵⁰ Consider, for example, the titular interlocutor of Euthyphro: Euthyphro is confident he understands the definition of "piety" but eventually ends up arguing himself in a circle, back to the definition with which he originally began (that piety is "what all the gods love"), a definition that he had agreed with Socrates was untenable as it stood.

Thus, the *elenchus* may be understood as a method of discussion by which an interlocutor's conflicting beliefs are exposed in order to force a decision between irreconcilable opinions. This, at any rate, is the understanding of

---

⁴⁷ Johnson, *Role Ethics*, 76–9.
⁴⁸ Ibid., 3.
⁴⁹ Long, *Epictetus*, ch. 3.
⁵⁰ An alternate interpretation of the Socratic *elenchus* is Gregory Vlastos, "The Socratic Elenchus: Method is All," in his *Socratic Studies* (Cambridge: Cambridge University Press, 1994), ch. 1. Vlastos argues that the *elenchus* is meant to find truth, not just to expose contradictory beliefs.

the *elenchus* endorsed by Epictetus in the *Discourses*. He begins with the Stoic proposition, shared with Socrates, that no one willingly does wrong but rather is misled about what is right or good—recall his interpretation of Medea in Euripides's play. Since no one *wants* to be wrong (because no one ever considers being wrong to be good), neither is it the case that anyone other than a determined and thoroughgoing skeptic will continue to entertain a contradiction in his or her own beliefs once that contradiction is pointed out. This is why Socrates (and by extension, Epictetus himself) employs the elenctic mode of discourse (2.26). Epictetus hopes, by exposing his students' conflicting but mutually held beliefs about the right and good, to force self-examination that will lead to their greater understanding about the basic subject of Stoic ethics: What is and is not "up to" them. Indeed, Long argues that one of Epictetus's most notable deployments of Socratic method is his reframing of the *elenchus* as a method of self-examination, where the student becomes his or her own interlocutor regarding the rightness of the use of any given sense impression that might be judged good or bad:

> Just as Socrates used to tell us not to live a life unsubjected to examination, so we ought not to accept a sense-impression unsubjected to examination, but should say, "Wait, allow me to see who you are and whence you come ... Do you have your token from nature, the one which every sense impression which is to be accepted must have?" (3.12.15, LCL)[51]

From Epictetus's counsel to his students that they ought to engage in self-examination regarding sense impressions, a key difference can be discerned between the *elenchus* practiced by the Socrates of Plato's early dialogues and Epictetus's own use of the method. Unlike the early Platonic Socrates, Epictetus does not begin discussions with his interlocutors by professing ignorance on the subject under review.[52] Epictetus has a definite *program* to impart to his students, a strong point of view whose correctness he is convinced of. The *elenchus* is the means to impart his understanding of Stoic ethics.

In conclusion, then, we see that although Epictetus in the *Discourses* is heavily reliant on the earlier Stoic tradition as well as on Socratic ideas, he makes

---

[51] Long, *Epictetus*, 85–6.
[52] It is quite possible, of course, that the Socratic profession of ignorance—of knowing only that he knew nothing, as he puts it in the *Apology*—is ironic or rhetorical.

his own unique contributions in terms of both content and method: content, by expanding and nuancing Stoic "role ethics"; in method, by adopting the Socratic *elenchus* not only as a method of discourse with his students but also as a program of self-examination.

Philostratus's *Life of Apollonius of Tyana*

In or around the year 220 CE, the Sophist Philostratus, a member of the circle of the empress Julia, wrote a life (βίος) of the Pythagorean philosopher Apollonius of Tyana, who was active in the first century CE.[53] This work, the *Life of Apollonius of Tyana*, is one of the longest accounts of a philosopher-teacher, which has come down to us from antiquity. Moreover, it has frequently been the subject of comparison with the New Testament Gospels. For, like Jesus in the Gospels, Apollonius travels from place to place, gathers disciples, teaches, performs miracles, and provokes the ire of authorities. Stories are told about his miraculous birth. Comparisons between Apollonius and Jesus were drawn very early on, beginning in antiquity and continuing into modern scholarship.[54]

However, in most modern New Testament scholarship that discusses the *Life*, attention has been paid primarily to Apollonius's miracles and the issue of whether or not Jesus and Apollonius belong together as examples of a particular type of ancient figure, the "divine man."[55] Comparatively little attention has been paid by New Testament scholars to the teachings of Apollonius as opposed to his miraculous deeds. One gets the impression that the agenda for reading the *Life of Apollonius* has been set largely by the New Testament Gospels, where miracles are frequent. By contrast, the *Life* records

---

[53] Balbina Bäbler and Heinz-Günther Nesselrath, *Philostrats Apollonios und seine Welt: Greichische und nichtgreichische Kunst und Religion in der* Vita Apollonii, Beiträge zur Altertumskunde 354 (Berlin: De Gruyter, 2016), 1; Christopher P. Jones, introduction to Philostratus, *The Life of Apollonius of Tyana Books I-IV*, LCL 16 (Cambridge, MA: Harvard University, 2005), 1–3.

[54] See the discussion of the history of research in Erkki Koskenniemi, *Apollonios von Tyana in der neutestamentlichen Exegese*, WUNT 2. Reihe 61 (Tübigen: Mohr Siebeck, 1994), 6–11 and ch. 2.

[55] E.g., Koskenniemi, *Apollonios von Tyana*, 206–29. The notion of a "divine man" as a type in antiquity, and Jesus as belonging to it, was once a commonplace in New Testament scholarship but has fallen out of favor. See, e.g., Carl R. Holladay, *Theios Aner in Hellenistic Judaism: A Critique of the Use of this Category in New Testament Christology*, SBLDS 40 (Missoula, MT: Scholars Press, 1977).

relatively few miracles of Apollonius, while devoting considerable attention to his teachings and journeys.

The *Life of Apollonius* is divided into eight books. In an introductory section (1.1-3), Philostratus introduces the figure of Apollonius and gives his own reasons for writing the work as well as describing his sources. This sort of introduction, where an ancient writer introduces his subject, describes his sources, and discusses earlier writers' attempts at dealing with the same topic (often taking a dim view of those predecessors) is standard in Greco-Roman historical and biographical writing.[56]

From the beginning, it is clear that the *Life* is intended as an apologetic biography, that is, a defense of its subject against criticisms and misunderstandings that have arisen against him: "Some think [Apollonius] a sorcerer and misrepresent him as a philosophic imposter, but in this they are wrong," as Philostratus writes (1.2, LCL). He initially refutes these charges by comparing Apollonius to well-known and respected philosophers such as Pythagoras (whose doctrines Apollonius claimed as his own), Empedocles, Democritus, or Plato. (This section bears a striking resemblance to the opening of Xenophon's *Memorabilia*, where Xenophon defends his subject by claiming that all of Socrates's practices conformed to established precedent and convention.) He acknowledges that Apollonius possessed the gift of prophecy but likens this talent to the predictions of the oracle at Delphi (1.3.2). The apologetic tone for the work is set when Philostratus concludes,

> I have therefore decided to remedy the general ignorance and to give an accurate account of the Master, observing the chronology of his words and acts, and the special character of the wisdom by which he came close to being thought possessed and inspired. (1.3.1, LCL)

Unlike Xenophon and Arrian, Philostratus begins with an account of his subject's birth and youth. A quasi-divine origin is given to Apollonius, when we are told how his birth was preceded by his mother seeing a vision of the god Proteus (1.4) and was heralded by the cries of swans and a bolt of

---

[56] Compare, for instance, Josephus *J.W.* 1.1-5. The preface of Luke–Acts is also likely a (albeit greatly compressed) version of this convention (Lk 1:1-4). The Lukan prologue is discussed in the standard commentaries: e.g., François Bovon, *Luke 1: A Commentary on the Gospel of Luke 1:1-9:50*, trans. Christine M. Thomas, Hermeneia (Minneapolis, MN: Fortress Press, 2002), 17–18.

lightning: "No doubt the gods were giving a signal and an omen of his brilliance, his exaltation above earthly things, his closeness to heaven, and all the Master's other qualities" (1.5, LCL). An aura of wisdom and great destiny surrounds Apollonius in his youth: He is said to have had particular gifts of speech and memory from a young age and to have readily mastered the doctrines of all the philosophical schools before settling on Pythagoreanism, which he "absorbed by some mysterious faculty" (1.7.2, LCL). His prowess comes in spite of the total incompetence and laxity of his teacher Euxenus (1.7). After describing Apollonius's education in this way, Philostratus turns to an account of how the philosopher-teacher proceeded once he was on his own.

The material in book 1 that follows Apollonius's education and precedes his undertaking a journey to India sets both the tone and the content of Apollonius's teaching. His primary concern is with the gods and the correct ways by which human beings may worship and honor them. To this end, he promotes an ascetic lifestyle (1.8) and presses for reform at various shrines and sanctuaries according to his beliefs about the gods and appropriate worship. He rejects the idea that the gods welcome showy and extravagant sacrifices, or lengthy prayers, instead proposing that one ought only to pray: "O gods, give me what I deserve" (1.11.2, LCL). The introductory section displays Apollonius's virtues with various vignettes, including his rejection of sexual advances made by a lecherous ruler (1.12), his reconciliation with his irresponsible brother (1.13), and his prevention of violence in a city wracked by famine (1.15.2-3).

But while the introductory section introduces Apollonius and gives the basic gist of his teaching, the rest of the work is occupied not with recounting Apollonius's teachings, so much as showing how he puts them into practice during his journeys and his meetings with rulers and tyrants. Apollonius makes two great journeys in the *Life*, to India by way of Babylon (1.18-3.58) and to Egypt (5.43-6.23). In between the two, he confronts the power of Nero in Rome and, while never meeting Nero face-to-face, shames Nero's subordinates while defying the emperor's tyranny. He then meets Vespasian, who is portrayed as a good emperor in contrast to Nero, and his son Titus. After the trip to Egypt, he returns to Rome once again and escapes a death sentence at Domitian's hands by boldly defending himself before miraculously vanishing from the courtroom. The narrative ends with an account of different stories told about Apollonius's death, including some hint that he may not have died at all but was taken up by the gods (8.29-31). The portrayal of Apollonius and his teaching is consistent throughout the entire work, and it is to this that we should now turn, asking the same questions about the *Life of Apollonius* that we have asked about the works examined previously: What does the teacher in this work teach, and how does he teach it?

We have already alluded above to the primary subject of Apollonius's teaching: How human beings ought to correctly worship and honor the gods. When questioned by a consul during his first journey to Rome, Apollonius names his subject matter as "theology [θειασμός], and how to pray and sacrifice to the gods" (4.40, LCL). To this end, Apollonius is depicted proposing various reforms at shrines and temples of the gods:

> If the city was Greek and its cult was famous, he would call the priests together for a lecture about the gods, setting them right if they had deviated from any tradition. If the cult was exotic and peculiar, he would make inquiries about the founders and the purpose of the foundation. Then, after finding out the reason for the customs and suggesting any way that occurred to him of making the ritual more philosophic [σοφώτερον], he would go to his disciples and tell them to put any questions they liked. (1.16.3, LCL)

Notices about his proposed reforms at temples, and his lectures on appropriate worship of the gods, are particularly plentiful in book four (e.g., 4.1, 19-20, 24, 31-32).

Careful note should be taken in the above quotation of the difference drawn between Apollonius's activities at Greek sanctuaries as opposed to non-Greek ("exotic and peculiar") ones. The Greek sanctuaries are reformed in order to return them to tradition, while the non-Greek ones are made "more philosophic." This distinction is an indicator of another theme of Apollonius's teaching beyond proper worship of the gods generally considered: the restoration of traditional values and of classical "Greekness."

Many passages that take place during Apollonius's travels in Greek lands describe his dismay at the decline of traditional Greek virtues, particularly a moderate and "manly" temperament. His criticisms are often couched in highly gendered terms, such as in his critique of the Athenians for "effeminate" dancing and clothing at the Dionysia (4.21). He is particularly incensed at the Spartans for what he sees as their decline from the strength of their classical forebears, and several episodes in close proximity to one another show him rebuking Spartans, either individually as a group, for unmanly behavior and betraying the traditions of their ancestors (4.27, 31, 32). Philostratus shows that he considers Apollonius's "manliness" to be among his virtues, when at 7.1 he says that confrontation with tyranny shows a philosopher to be "a true man" (ἀνήρ). Wisdom, freedom, and virtue are part and parcel of a highly masculine "Greekness," and Apollonius's criticisms of Greeks are ultimately a conservative demand for a return to the traditions of the past, not a call for innovation.[57]

This casting of wisdom and virtue as Greek extends to the treatment in the work of non-Greek religious ideas and practices. Although we are told that Apollonius sought to make foreign cults "more philosophic," what this means is not defined. However, when Apollonius visits the Indian Wise Men, they describe their doctrines to him in primarily Greek terms.[58] Not only are they familiar with Greek ideas, they approve them heartily and know Greek traditions about the Homeric heroes, among other things (3.19). Apollonius is said to have "absorbed all their doctrines" (3.50, LCL) during his time with them, but their teachings more or less conform to the Greek ideas he already holds, for the Indians are even said to have been the source of Pythagoras's ideas (6.11-12). Given that Apollonius has a highly positive view of the Hellenized Indian Wise Men's teachings but a highly negative and judgmental one of the Egyptians' ideas during his second journey, it is probable that for a foreign cult to be "more philosophic" means that it is more Greek-like.

Not only are the Indians' ideas Greek, but Apollonius's conversations with them also afford an opportunity for further, oblique criticism of Greek decline from hallowed tradition and virtue. For instance, the Indian king Phraotes, whom Apollonius meets prior to his visit to the Wise Men, expresses admiration for Greek ideas but laments that so many Greeks who take the title of philosopher pervert the very notion of philosophy, while Indian philosophers are fewer but more dedicated (2.29.2-2.30). The Wise Ones

---

[57] Jaap-Jan Flinterman, *Power, Paideia, and Pythagoreanism: Greek Identity, Conceptions of the Relationship between Philosophers and Monarchs and Political Ideas in Philostratus'* Life of Apollonius (Amsterdam: J. C. Gieben, 1995), 92–4.
[58] Erkki Koskenniemi, "The Philostratean Apollonius as a Teacher," in *Theios Sophistes: Essays on Flavius Philostratus'* Vita Apolonii, ed. Kristoffel Demoen and Danny Praet (Leiden: Brill, 2009), 325.

also have their own criticism of the Greeks, despite their knowledge of Greek philosophy and culture, which they regard as superior to all other peoples' (3.32.2). Specifically, their leader Iarchus criticizes the Greek practice of choosing officials by lot (3.30.3). Thus, even when Apollonius is in other lands, Greek ideas and practices are always under examination.

The basic subjects of Apollonius's teaching—"theology" and the restoration of Greek virtues—are established clearly and early on in the work. The same is true of his *method* of teaching. 1.16.3, quoted above, indicates that he would question priests and offer them advice on cult reform and then give a "general lecture" later in the day—to whom, we are not informed (1.16.4). At other times, he will give discourses as circumstances dictate (6.3).

Philostratus also describes Apollonius's style and manner of speech. He did not engage in Socratic *elenchus*: When Apollonius spoke, "he was never heard being ironic or argumentative with his listeners" (1.17, LCL), and, when he lectured in Ephesus, "he did not use the Socratic method [διελέχθη οὐχ ὥσπερ οἱ Σωκρατικοί], but drawing his listeners' minds away from all other subjects, he advised them to study only philosophy" (4.2, LCL). In other words, Apollonius engaged in exhortation, or *protreptic* rhetoric, rather than in the question-and-answer style utilized by the Socrates of Xenophon or the true *elenchus* of the Epictetus of the *Discourses*. This is confirmed by another remark in Philostratus's description of Apollonius's speaking style:

> In answering he spoke as if *ex cathedra* [ὥσπερ ἐκ τρίποδος], saying "I know," "I believe," "Where are you off to?" "You ought to know." … [A]nd his sayings had the ring of commandments issued from a throne. When some quibbler asked him why he did not engage in inquiry [ζητόιη], he replied, "Because I inquired in my youth; now it is my duty not to inquire but to teach what I have found." And when the man asked him next, "How will a wise man converse?" he replied, "Like a lawgiver, for a lawgiver must make his own convictions into ordinances for the many." (1.17, LCL)

Apollonius is thus said to have taught through pronouncement, not dialectic. This rule is not strictly followed throughout the whole work. There are some passages, particularly his conversations with the Wise Men of India, where a more conversational form is adopted, but even there the change is only slight. The conversations with the Wise Men mostly consist of the Wise Men expounding their beliefs, which happen to look quite Greek in nature, and Apollonius agreeing (e.g., 3.18, 41). There are also a few other instances of such questioning (e.g., 5.21.2-4), but even in those, Apollonius tends to make dramatic pronouncements to persuade his listener after establishing their views, rather than trying to lead the dialogue partner to the realization of internally conflicting beliefs, as with the *elenchus*.

In discussing Apollonius's method of teaching, we must be cognizant of the fact that Philostratus places a great deal of focus on how Apollonius *acted*, not only what he said. Indeed, his actions are held to be a primary means by which he teaches his students: "Their chief aim in philosophy was to follow whatever he said or did" (5.21.1). He teaches, in other words, by deed and not only by word. Philostratus holds this to be the ultimate distinguishing mark of a true philosopher. The philosopher must not only expound his beliefs with conviction but also carry them out in practice. This point, that the philosopher is proven by his acting in accordance with his beliefs, is nowhere made more explicit than in the descriptions of Apollonius's confrontations with Nero and Domitian.

The theme of a philosopher's encounter with "tyranny" has a long history in ancient philosophical thought. Socrates, once again, is the archetype. His condemnation and execution by the Athenian state were taken as an example of how a philosopher could demonstrate fealty to his vocation even in the face of death, with his refusal to give up practicing philosophy in exchange for clemency serving as a model of commitment to one's principles. Later philosophers took note. The *Enchiridion* of Epictetus, for example, closes with Socrates's words (in the *Apology* of Plato) that his accusers cannot harm him even by killing him, a sentiment that accords with the Stoic insistence that the truly wise man is wholly unaffected by external circumstances.[59]

Plato also contributed to the theme of the philosopher as opponent of the tyrant when, in the *Republic*, he labeled the tyrant the unhappiest and most miserable of all people, the most unjust of all individuals, just as a state ruled by a tyrant is the most unjust of all kinds of states. Whereas the just person demonstrates complete harmony of soul, with desires kept firmly in check

---

[59] *Ench.* 53. Compare Apollonius's declaration (*VA* 4.38.2) that nothing on earth can make a wise person afraid.

by the rational part of the soul, the tyrant is a brute led entirely by his base appetites.[60] Thus, in subsequent philosophical thought, "tyranny" functioned not only as a concrete example of the kind of extreme duress that might tempt a philosopher into acting inconsistently with his beliefs but also as the very opposite of philosophy itself.

The first "tyrant" Apollonius faces is Nero, although the two never meet face to face. When, in book four, Apollonius decides to go to Rome in spite of Nero's violence against philosophers, his bravery and fortitude are contrasted with the timidity of others and their willingness to bend to the tyrant. First, fellow philosopher Philolaus, described as "cowardly," advises Apollonius to flee (4.36). Then, most of Apollonius's students desert him, fearing Nero (4.37). Apollonius, on the other hand, views Nero's disgraceful conduct and violence as an object lesson for budding philosophers (4.36.2). The decision whether to continue on to Rome in spite of Nero's threats against philosophy is a demonstration of which of the students is truly devoted to philosophy (4.37). After Apollonius's cadre of followers is reduced from thirty-four to eight, Philostratus says of those who departed that they "ran as fast as they could away from Nero and philosophy" (4.37.2). The philosopher who avoids openly acting in accordance with his beliefs, then, is no true philosopher. Apollonius's refusal to be cowed by Nero represents part of his "teaching," since, as noted above, Apollonius's students are depicted as hoping to emulate not just the great man's words but also his deeds.

The denouement of the Nero episode is relatively brief. While never meeting Nero himself, Apollonius is eventually brought before Nero's lackey Tigellinus after mocking Nero's musical pretensions. After explicating his origin and his purpose in practicing philosophy, Apollonius speaks only words of defiance against Tigellinus's threats, saying that no one can imprison him. Tigellinus takes Apollonius's boldness as a sign of supernatural authority and lets the philosopher go. The repeated references during this first visit in Rome to individuals who take Apollonius to possess supernatural power indicate that it is the philosopher's boldness and courage in proclaiming philosophy in spite of danger which vindicate him as a truly wise man (4.44).

---

[60] For Plato's views on tyranny, see Roger Boesche, *Theories of Tyranny from Plato to Arendt* (University Park: Pennsylvania State University Press, 1996), ch. 1.

After numerous other adventures, including a less-than-satisfactory journey to Egypt, Apollonius once again resolves to return to Rome, under a new emperor: Domitian. (He had earlier enjoyed cordial relations with Vespasian and Titus.) At the beginning of book seven, introducing the long section concerning Apollonius's dealing with Domitian, Philostratus makes plain his view of the tyrant as the opposite of the philosopher. Tyranny, he says, is the most convincing test of a true philosopher (7.1, LCL). He goes on to compare Apollonius's stand against tyranny to how other famous philosophers faced similar circumstances. In his remarks, he shows the existence of a long tradition of philosophers confronting tyrants, a tradition approaching the status of an archetype. Apollonius's feat in opposing Domitian, however, is held to surpass all these, because he confronted a tyrant who was the most powerful ruler in the known world, much stronger and more cunning than the crazed Nero had been (7.3.3-7.4.1). And this time around, Apollonius does not venture to Rome merely to make an object lesson of the tyrant but is deliberately sought out by the emperor on the charges of conspiring with Domitian's enemies and of sacrificing a young boy to gain auguries of success for the conspirators (7.11.3).

As with his first visit to Rome, the confrontation with Domitian is preceded by a section where others try to convince Apollonius to flee from danger and avoid the tyrant. The Cynic philosopher Demetrius tries to persuade Apollonius to remain safely away from Rome, arguing that it would be a terrible thing for Apollonius to die on account of false charges rather than in doing something that truly befits the wise man, such as defending family or city (7.12.2). He urges Apollonius that it would be easy enough to escape Domitian's wrath and live peacefully in some obscure place (7.12.5). The scene is quite reminiscent of Plato's *Crito*, in which Socrates's friends urge him to escape from prison before his execution.

Damis, Apollonius's chief student, whom Philostratus names as a chief source for the work (1.2.3), is greatly affected by Demetrius's argument and joins in the call for Apollonius to flee. He makes the comparison between the situations of Socrates and Apollonius explicit: "There is many an Anytos, many a Meletos waiting for us" (7.13.2, LCL).[61]

---

[61] He is referring to the individuals who are supposed to have brought the charges against Socrates, according to the Platonic dialogues.

In response, Apollonius gives a long speech explaining why he will not try and escape Domitian. After suggesting that Damis is afraid because of his Assyrian heritage (Assyrians "kowtow to tyrants, and [Damis] has no lofty ideas of freedom" [7.14.1, LCL]), he speaks against Demetrius's claim that Apollonius's confrontation with tyranny is not a worthy end for a wise man. On the contrary, he says, there is no better cause than philosophy:

> For the wise it is more proper to die on behalf of their beliefs. If someone attacks practices that they have followed not from legal ordinance or natural affinity, but out of their own strength and courage, then let fire, let the axe, assail the wise man, but none of these will overcome him, or induce him to say anything untrue. (7.14.2, LCL)

His own conscience would accuse him of disloyalty to truth if he were to flee now in the face of Domitian (7.14.10-11).

Hearing Apollonius's speech, Damis recovers his nerve: "He praised what [Apollonius] had said and assented to it ... and blessed Philosophy too for whom Apollonius showed such endurance" (7.15.1, LCL). With that, Apollonius and Damis continue on to Rome.

After a lengthy stay in prison awaiting trial, where he continues to teach and dispense advice to a variety of interlocutors (7.22-26), Apollonius is finally brought before Domitian in book eight. Although Philostratus provides Apollonius's defense speech (8.6-7), the philosopher never delivered it, he says, for after rebuking Domitian's attempts to frighten him into acquiescence, Apollonius simply vanishes from the courtroom, reappearing outside the courtroom in the flesh to Damis and Demetrius (8.5.4; 8.10-13). The philosopher's friends are amazed and delighted, and thereupon Apollonius resumes his travels in Greece, continuing to lecture and discuss religious reform at shrines and temples. The narrative then ends with a discussion of Apollonius's death, although Philostratus suggests that Apollonius may never have died at all and reports various tales about Apollonius being taken up by the gods (8.29-30).

The point of this summary of Apollonius's confrontations with tyranny is to emphasize one of the key themes of the *Life*: that Apollonius's deeds are as much a part of his "teaching," in Philostratus's view, as his words. Philostratus himself makes this clear in his remark, already quoted, that tyranny is the philosopher's greatest test, and his note that Apollonius's disciples were concerned not only with their teacher's words but his deeds as well.

Teaching Literature and the Gospel of Mark

There are strong formal similarities between the texts reviewed here and the Gospel of Mark. As with Socrates, Epictetus, and Apollonius, teaching is a central part of the Markan Jesus's career, and his teaching is mentioned at key points in the story: at its beginning (Jesus's first public appearance), at crucial turning points (the parables chapter and the passion predictions), and its last act (the temple incident).

Mark and the other three texts all frequently make use of the situations their protagonists encounter as "teachable moments": That is, the texts frequently depict the teacher-protagonist presenting his teaching in response to a situation he encounters or a person who approaches him. Socrates in Xenophon remarks on his students' love lives, offers advice on his acquaintances' financial prospects, and gives clever retorts to the challenges of rivals. Epictetus converses with strangers and uses newcomers who walk into his classroom as object lessons. And Philostratus uses vignettes from Apollonius's travels, particularly his journeys to India and Egypt, as occasions for the hero to present his views on gods and human beings.

Mark offers parallels to all these devices. Jesus remarks upon situations he encounters, as in the case when he observes the widow's offering (12:41-44). Strangers approach him and he responds—both friendly inquirers like the rich man (10:17-31) and an anonymous "teacher of the law" (12:28-34) as well as rivals like the Pharisees (7:1-23) and Sadducees (12:18-27). And summary statements throughout the gospel mention his teaching the crowds who follow him from place to place.

On the other hand, surface differences between Mark and the other texts are also clear: the differences in style and form, in particular. Mark's Greek is decidedly pedestrian in comparison with the classical prose of Xenophon, for instance. In terms of form, Mark does not utilize long discourses as do all three of the other works to some degree (with the exception of Mk 13). Further, Mark almost wholly refrains from offering obvious editorial or narrative comment on the action in the voice of the implied narrator, in contrast to Xenophon and Philostratus, who regularly interpret the teacher-protagonist's actions for the reader, or to Arrian, who prefaces the *Discourses* with an explanation of how and why he came to publish the words of Epictetus in just this form.

There are other, more drastic differences as well. First, Mark lacks either the apologetic or didactic purposes of our other texts. And second, the teachings of the Markan Jesus are not strongly unified by any central concept independent of the teacher himself but concentrate around the portrayal of Jesus himself as an authoritative figure. Both of these claims require further comment.

We begin with the differences in purpose. We proposed above that both the *Memorabilia* of Xenophon and Philostratus's *Life of Apollonius* have an apology for (defense of) their subjects as their primary purpose. This is made clear from the way both authors introduce their teacher-protagonists. Xenophon begins with a "defense" section that precedes the recorded conversations and teachings of Socrates. And Philostratus begins in a similar fashion, defending Apollonius against the charge of being a mere magician or wonder worker. On the other hand, in the case of our third text, the *Discourses* of Epictetus, an apologetic purpose is not in sight but, rather, Arrian states in his introductory preface his hope that the *Discourses* will accomplish the same goal as Epictetus's own spoken teachings: "to move the minds of the hearers toward what is most excellent" (*Diss.* 0.5, author's translation). The purpose, then, is to preserve Epictetus's teachings for those who did not hear the philosopher during his lifetime.

Neither of these purposes—apology or preservation of great teaching—is adequate to describe the Gospel of Mark's portrayal of Jesus's teachings. To begin with the second, which is easily rejected, Mark is not the kind of document we would expect were its purpose to preserve Jesus's teachings for future readers. There is simply not enough of Jesus's teaching in Mark to make the preservation of this teaching the purpose of the Gospel. We would expect something more like Q, Matthew, or Luke, if the Gospel had preserving Jesus's teaching as a chief purpose. And what teaching it contains is often quite opaque. For instance, "the kingdom of God," one of the highlights of the Markan Jesus's teaching in Mark, is never really explained, but knowledge of it is assumed throughout the Gospel. And those teachings of Jesus that *are* relatively clear, such as the prohibition of divorce (10:2-12) or the declaration that all foods are clean (7:18-23), are few in number. In Mark, the teachings of Jesus are shrouded in mystery.[62]

Now, to return to the first possibility, is Mark an *apology*? Consider again the two works we have examined, which are clearly apologetic in nature: the *Memorabilia* of Xenophon and Philostratus's *Life of Apollonius*. At the beginning of each of these works, we find clear statements attempting to refute various charges made against their subjects.

Xenophon begins with his "defense" section, where he tries to rebut the charges made against Socrates at his trial. Importantly, his defense of Socrates rests on his appeal to highly conventional values, such as piety and "usefulness" to the Athenian youth: In response to the charges that Socrates was impious, Xenophon asserts that Socrates was a model of conventional piety, indeed that he outdid his fellow citizens in piety because he held that the gods were entirely beneficent toward human beings and have knowledge of all things (*Mem.* 1.4.18). And the charge of corrupting the young is shown to be false by the fact Socrates benefited or was "useful" to his young companions by exhorting them to self-examination and virtue. In other words, Xenophon's defense of Socrates rests on his showing that Socrates shared conventional Athenian values, values that the average well-to-do citizen would rank as of considerable importance.

The same is true, similarly, of the *Life of Apollonius*. The opening of the work begins not with Apollonius himself but with his great predecessor and model, Pythagoras (*VA* 1.1). The purpose of this is explicitly to compare Apollonius favorably with Pythagoras, for after recounting Pythagoras's deeds and wisdom, Philostratus writes, "The practices of Apollonius were very much like this, and he approaches wisdom and overcame tyrannies in a more inspired way than Pythagoras" (1.2, LCL). He then goes on to refute the charge that Apollonius was a magician, since he consorted with Babylonian and Indian Wise Men, by pointing to traditions that other revered figures such as Democritus and Plato did the same thing (1.2). The tone is very much the same as Xenophon's

---

[62] Robert H. Gundry, *Mark: A Commentary on His Apology for the Cross* (Grand Rapids, MI: William. B. Eerdmans, 1993), 1023, similarly points out how the lack of emphasis on Christian doctrine and morality in the Gospel makes it unlikely that Mark has any sort of catechetical purpose in mind.

remark that Socrates's divine foreknowledge should be considered no different than common Athenian practices of augury (*Mem.* 1.1.2-4). Like Xenophon, Philostratus defends his subject by claiming that Apollonius acted just as much in accordance with a recognized set of virtues and was just as free of vice as other, more generally recognized authorities, if not more so. That is not to say that the values these figures conform to were *universally* shared, rather simply that such apparently divinely inspired wisdom and virtue would have been acceptable to an educated, philosophically literate audience.

This kind of appeal to widely shared values is a critical component of these apologetic texts. Both Xenophon and Philostratus rely for their persuasive effect on the fact that their audience will share certain values with their works' protagonists: Xenophon, for instance, counts on the fact that his audience shares a common concern with piety or "the pious" and thus will accept the presentation of Socrates's piety as a mark in the philosopher's favor. Philostratus counts on the reputation of figures like Pythagoras, Democritus, and Plato when he compares Apollonius to them in order to defend Apollonius.

The need for shared values as grounds for persuasion was recognized in antiquity at least since Aristotle. In his *Rhetoric* (1.3.5), Aristotle proposed that the different categories of speech he was propounding—judicial, deliberative, and epideictic—appealed to different values held by the audience: respectably, "the just," "the expedient," and "the honorable." Later, writers of the rhetorical handbooks of the Hellenistic period compiled various lists of values or categories to which arguments could appeal.[63]

Mark is not an apologetic text after the manner of the *Memorabilia* or the *Life of Apollonius* because the Gospel does not appeal to any such shared values: That is, Mark does not attempt to create common ground with those who might be skeptical of Mark's claims about Jesus. For instance, no explicit comparisons are made between Jesus and other figures more universally acknowledged as great teachers. Although there are strong allusions to figures of the Hebrew Scriptures such as Elijah, Elisha, and the later prophets, Jesus is never directly compared to any of these individuals.[64] Nor

---

[63] The point about Aristotle and the rhetorical handbooks is made by Mack and Robbins, *Patterns of Persuasion in the Gospels*, 38.

[64] Or, more accurately, Jesus is never *correctly* identified as being like a great figure from Israel's past. Though Herod identifies him with John the Baptist (6:16) and the disciples say that some people think Jesus is like John or Elijah or one of the prophets (8:27-28), none of these identifications are

does the Gospel care to stress that Jesus conformed to specific virtues that might be expected of him in his cultural context. In fact, one of the striking things about Mark is its total lack of concern with Jesus's reputation among outsiders to the early Jesus movements. At no point are apologetic demurrals or explanations offered for the dramatic claims the Markan Jesus makes for himself. Whereas, for example, Xenophon offers explanations for Socrates's religious practices that would be acceptable in society at large, Mark seems to positively revel in the offense that Jesus causes to his contemporaries in the narrative and potentially causes to those who are not Jesus followers. Jesus's words and deeds are simply authoritative declarations, to which characters in the story (and readers or hearers of it) must react. Mark appeals to no authority other than Jesus's extraordinary self-claims, and the implication, developed beginning at Jesus's baptism (1:9-11), that Jesus's words and deeds are authorized by God.[65] This argument about Mark's nonappeal to outsiders will be supported frequently in the exegesis of Mark contained in the following chapters.

However, at least one modern scholar has argued forcefully that Mark is indeed an apology: Robert H. Gundry, who has devoted an entire commentary on the Gospel to making the case.[66] It is particularly important to consider Gundry's work here because, unlike many commentators on the Gospel, he takes careful note of the way the teaching of Jesus is portrayed in Mark and has a clear thesis on how it relates to the rest of the Gospel.

Gundry begins by rejecting many of the better-known theses about Mark's purpose proposed in earlier scholarship, particularly those that see a coded or allegorical theological agenda behind Mark's portrayal of Jesus or the disciples. None of these proposals is feasible, says Gundry, nor is it necessary to peer behind the text and imagine the author's motivations:

> Mark's meaning lies on the surface. He writes a straightforward apology for the Cross, for the shameful way in which the object of Christian faith

---

affirmed by Jesus or any other character with reliable knowledge. Rather, Jesus is Messiah (8:29) and Son of God (1:1, 11; 15:39).

[65] The observation that Mark's Gospel takes its persuasive force solely from appeal to the authoritative figure of Jesus is made by Burton L. Mack, *A Myth of Innocence: Mark and Christian Origins* (Philadelphia, PA: Fortress Press, 1988), 197–99, and ch. 7.

[66] Gundry, *Mark*.

and subject of Christian proclamation died, and hence for Jesus as the Crucified One.[67]

This thesis rests on Gundry's observation that there are roughly two types of material in Mark. One strand of the Gospel describes Jesus as a successful teacher, wonder worker, and prophet; the other strand describes his persecution, rejection, and shameful death. The difficulty in the interpretation of Mark, then, is to explain how these two strands relate to one another. The dominant view in Markan scholarship has been "that Mark corrects the theology of glory with the theology of suffering."[68]

> This regnant view hypothesizes that Mark wrote for a Christian audience, that his audience held to a tradition which glorified Jesus as a thaumaturgist and teacher, that the audience expected to see in their own lives evidence of similar power and authority and saw weakness, failure, and persecution instead. ... To resolve this problem of cognitive dissonance, Mark incorporated the tradition containing the theology of glory, but corrected that theology by putting it in the framework of the theology of suffering, the theology of the Cross.[69]

Gundry apparently has in mind here those scholars who have proposed that the Gospel was written to combat some sort of heresy or theological error, particularly of the Christological variety. The most famous of these is Theodore Weeden's proposal that Mark intends to counter a "divine man" Christology.[70]

Gundry, for his part, thinks the matter should be put the other way around. Rather than correcting a "theology of glory" with a hard-headed look at Jesus's suffering and death, Mark wants (so Gundry argues) to offer a defense of a shamefully crucified Jesus by highlighting the glorious aspects of his life and death.[71] Furthermore, this "apology for the cross" is directed not to fearful or hesitant Christian insiders facing troubles and persecutions but to skeptical outsiders who count it against Jesus and the claims made about him that he

---

[67] Ibid., 1.
[68] Ibid., 2.
[69] Ibid., 2–3.
[70] Theodore J. Weeden, *Mark: Traditions in Conflict* (Philadelphia, PA: Fortress Press, 1979). On the many different proposals for a "corrective Christology" as the key to interpreting Mark's Gospel, see Joel Marcus, *Mark 1-8: A New Translation with Commentary*, Anchor Yale Bible 27 (2000; paperback ed., New Haven, CT: Yale University, 2005), 75–9.
[71] Gundry, *Mark*, 3.

died a shameful death on the cross.⁷² Directly pertinent for our topic is the fact that Gundry sees the way Mark portrays the teaching of Jesus as directly relevant to this apology. Referencing Mk 1:21-28, for example (a passage that will much occupy us later), he says,

> The crowds hang on Jesus' words because he teaches them with authority. The teaching of Christ God's [sic] Son is bound to carry supreme authority, but Mark goes further by remarking the effect and recognition of that authority. "They were knocked out at his teaching, for he was teaching them as one who had authority and not as the scribes" (1:22) … He does not tell what Jesus taught.⁷³

Gundry argues that *all* of the material in the Gospel, including Jesus's teachings, is intended to convince nonbelievers of Jesus's greatness by magnifying his glory, showing how that glory overshadowed and overcame the shameful end to which Jesus came.

Space here does not permit a full engagement with Gundry's massive (1,051-page) commentary. But a few basic remarks make it plain that Gundry has vastly overstated his case. As Joel Williams says, Gundry's argument that *all* the material in the Gospel is directed toward reluctant outsiders rather than community insiders runs afoul of many passages in Mark where the most straightforward reading is that the material is meant to exhort, warn, or persuade insiders.⁷⁴ Among various examples that could be offered, we take particular note of Mk 13. The majority of scholarship holds that Jesus's predictions of trials and tribulations (13:4-13) and his direction that those in Judea should flee (13:14) are *ex eventu* prophecy about the audience's own circumstances, placed on the lips of Jesus.⁷⁵ If Gundry were more nuanced in his thesis—for example, if he argued that the Gospel was intended *both* for outsiders *and* insiders—then finding instances of material that clearly addresses insiders would not be problematic. His determination to argue that

---

⁷² Ibid., 1026.
⁷³ Ibid., 6–7.
⁷⁴ Joel F. Williams, "Is Mark's Gospel an Apology for the Cross?" *BBR* 12, no. 1 (2002), 97–122.
⁷⁵ E.g., M. Eugene Boring, *Mark: A Commentary*, New Testament Library (Louisville, KY: Westminster John Knox), 358–59; Robert H. Stein, *Mark*, BECNT (Grand Rapids, MI: Baker Academic, 2008), 593; Francis J. Moloney, *The Gospel of Mark: A Commentary* (Grand Rapids, MI: Baker Academic, 2009), 259. Even though many scholars would also contend that the Olivet discourse of chapter 13 has some roots in predictions made by the historical Jesus, the consensus is that this tradition has been shaped by the concerns of the Markan community.

the Gospel was written *only* as an apology for the cross directed to outsiders, however, means that a lone instance like Mk 13 is sufficient to cast serious doubt on his case.

More generally, Gundry overestimates the degree to which the portrayal of Jesus's "glory" overwhelms or corrects the portrayal of Jesus's suffering and shameful death in the Gospel. Can we really say that a reader who did not already share Mark's primary convictions would be sufficiently impressed by Jesus's authority, miracles, and prophetic powers to ignore the fact that the figure to whom the community devoted himself practically broke down in fear in the face of his impending death?[76] Or that he was abandoned by his disciples? Or that his last devoted followers fled his empty tomb in fear? Obviously, this is a subjective impression, but a more plausible reading is that the Gospel does not "correct" the view of Jesus as a suffering and defeated figure but rather holds it in provocative tension with the view of Jesus as both suffering Son of God and authoritative Son of Humanity.

Gundry has therefore argued his case forcefully but unpersuasively. Mark is not first and foremost an "apology for the cross." That said, some of Gundry's observations about the teachings of Jesus in Mark are quite in line with the arguments to be put forth in our following chapters. In particular, he is one of only a small number of scholars who has taken seriously the way the teachings of Jesus in the Gospel connect with the issue of Jesus's "authority."

The second major difference between Mark and the texts examined earlier in this chapter deserves careful attention, for it leads us to one of the central conclusions to be drawn from the analysis of Mark in what follows: It is not a major feature of the Markan Jesus's career that he passes on a definite program, philosophy, or set of ideas for consideration independent of his own identity as the teacher. We are in full agreement with the remarks of M. Eugene Boring on Jesus's teachings in Mark:

> Despite its frequency, the term "teacher" is not for Mark Jesus' fundamental identity. He is not basically a teacher in the Hellenistic sense; his mission is

---

[76] Cf. the remarks of Williams, "Is Mark's Gospel an Apology for the Cross?", 116: "Mark's portrayal of Jesus in Gethsemane does not support an apology for the cross, since Jesus himself anticipates his crucifixion with dread."

not to teach his disciples his system of thought or way of life as a body of teaching independent of his own person.[77]

Consider again the texts of Xenophon, Arrian, and Philostratus—or rather, the literary figures of Socrates, Epictetus, and Apollonius. Each of these figures has a clear *program* of teaching: That is, their teachings are organized around a definite end goal toward which the words they speak and the actions they recommend are directed, and this end goal is clearly explained. The teachings of Socrates in the *Memorabilia*, for instance, have as their end goal happiness and good citizenship, and the means to their achievement is self-control and usefulness. The *Discourses* of Epictetus also have human happiness as their end goal, and all of Epictetus's words and counsels about "proper use of impressions," right judgment, and so on have this aim in mind. And Apollonius of Tyana in the *Life* propounds a theology of divine providence, embarking on an organized campaign of cultic reform and teaching to explicate his ideas about the gods—ideas that, if taken seriously, will lead the mind away from the debased desires of the tyrant and toward virtue and philosophy.

What is more, each of these figures presents their "program" as speaking for itself, in distinction from their own person. The validity of the teaching is not dependent upon the person of the teacher. The audience is exhorted to accept the teaching because of its intrinsic wisdom, not because the teachers are great figures (although they certainly are in the minds of our three authors).

By contrast, the teaching of Jesus in Mark is not independent of the teacher himself. Further, it takes some effort to describe what the central focus of Jesus's teaching actually *is*. At Mk 1:14-15, we are informed in a summary statement what the chief topic of Jesus's ministry supposedly was: the kingdom of God, in view of which Jesus called people to "repent and believe in the good news." But immediately, questions arise.

First, what exactly is the "kingdom of God?" The "kingdom" is referred to in a number of different ways in the Gospel. It is something that is coming or is near (1:15). It is like a seed sown haphazardly or secretly (4:26, 30). It is something that people can enter (9:47, 10:23) or be "not far from" (12:34). The first and last are particularly noteworthy. To say that the kingdom is "near"

---

[77] Boring, *Mark*, 253.

or "at hand" makes it seem like the kingdom is coming of its own volition, without human action. But to say that a person can "enter" or be "not far from" the kingdom suggests that the kingdom is something human beings reach or attain. Whatever it is, "the kingdom of God" is never, strictly speaking, given a definition in the Gospel. The Gospel seems to assume that the audience knows what the kingdom is. Jesus in Mark does not "teach the kingdom," in the sense of explicating the kingdom as a concept or program.

Second, Jesus teaches about things other than the kingdom in the Gospel. How do the rejection of purity regulations (7:1-23) or the prohibition of divorce (10:2-12), for example, connect with the kingdom? And what about the predictions of the passion, which are clearly called "teaching" (8:31)? Or Jesus's words and actions in the temple (11:17)? These disparate topics are difficult to connect directly with a single, unified understanding of "the kingdom of God," if we want to posit that the kingdom is the central focus of Jesus's teaching in Mark. For none of them give definition to the kingdom, instead appearing as though the kingdom itself were already a clear concept.

Although Mark draws upon Jewish traditions about God's kingly rule in describing the "kingdom of God," the Gospel's use of these traditions is inextricably linked with the identity of Jesus himself as teacher and divine emissary. The Markan "kingdom of God" cannot be understood without also understanding the person of Jesus. This is what distinguishes the "program" of the Markan Jesus, if we want to call it that, from the systems of thought prescribed by Socrates, Epictetus, and Apollonius: While the ideas the latter texts impart are independent of the teacher's authority and are expected to speak for themselves, as it were, Mark places all the persuasive weight on the overwhelming authority of Jesus.

To put it differently, the solution to the problem of what Jesus teaches in Mark, and why he teaches it, is to recognize that, despite the fact that Mark so frequently refers to Jesus as a teacher, the Gospel is not actually much interested in Jesus's teachings, at least not in and of themselves. This may seem like a paradoxical statement. Its defense will require an examination of the Gospel itself. But to explain briefly, we suggest that the Gospel of Mark arranges and presents the teachings of Jesus in a way that draws attention not to the teachings themselves but to Jesus himself: his divinely given authority and his ordained suffering as Son of Humanity and Son of God. The teachings of Jesus in Mark ultimately teach about Jesus himself, not about a system of thought external to Jesus as an individual. The lack of detail presented about Jesus's teachings in Mark results from the fact that the Gospel's concern is with Jesus's identity, not his program or system of thought. This distinguishes Mark significantly from the other texts studied in this chapter. The similarity in formal terms to other Greek or Greco-Roman literature about teachers and teaching conceals deep differences in both content and function.

2

Teaching and Authority in the First Half of Mark

In the previous chapter, we studied three important Greek and Greco-Roman texts featuring "teachers" as their protagonists. We also observed the key differences between those texts and the Gospel of Mark. Combining this comparison with the observations in the Introduction about the oddities of the way the Gospel presents Jesus's teaching activity, we are left with the question: How do we explain Mark's portrayal of Jesus the teacher in a way that pays due heed to both the literary characteristics of Mark and the Gospel's sociocultural context?

The present chapter, and the one following, will provide the data for our interpretation of the teaching motif in Mark. We will analyze individual passages, pointing out salient themes and consistent ideas that appear throughout the Markan text. We will see in our examination of individual Markan passages that no single overarching purpose unites Mark's various material about Jesus's teaching. Rather, there are several purposes at work. By means of the portrayal of Jesus's teaching, the Gospel (1) advances its plot, (2) creates its Christological depiction of Jesus, and (3) speaks to the concerns of the Gospel's audience.

Before turning to the individual passages, we begin by examining a key term or motif that, so it will be argued, is the guiding theme of the Gospel's picture of Jesus as teacher. That theme is the idea of Jesus's ἐξουσία, his "authority." We contend that one of the main purposes of the way Mark portrays Jesus's teaching is to depict Jesus as a figure who has extraordinary authority. We begin by examining the meaning of the term in Greek, Greco-Roman, and Second Temple literature, in order to establish a relevant background for the study of Mark. This will include a return to the texts of Xenophon, Arrian, and Philostratus, with an eye on the ways each text does (or does not) utilize the idea of ἐξουσία. Following this will be a brief overview of the use of the term in the Gospel of Mark.

Then, finally, we will take up the task of examining the Markan text in-depth. The goal will be to explain how Mark deploys the image of Jesus as teacher, posing to the text the same questions we asked of the texts of Xenophon, Arrian, and Philostratus: What does the teacher teach, and how does he teach it? We will see, among other things, that ἐξουσία plays a key role in how Mark portrays Jesus's teaching.

The Background of the Term ἐξουσία

From its earliest usage in Greek, the term ἐξουσία is used in several senses.[1] In the broadest possible sense, connected to its derivation from the verb ἔξεστιν, it can denote simply having the ability or power to perform an action. It is in this sense that we find the word used, for instance, in the myth of the ring of Gyges in Plato's *Republic*. Glaucon challenges Socrates's contention that justice is superior to injustice by arguing that every person, were he or she able, would choose to commit great injustices undetected rather than conform to standards of justice:

> Imagine giving to each of them ... the power [ἐξουσίαν] to do whatever they wish, and then following each of them, watching where their desire will lead them. We should then catch the just person red-handed going after the same thing as the unjust man, which everyone naturally pursues as a good thing because of his greed but is forcibly deflected by the law into respect for equality. (*Resp.* 359c, LCL)

This power or ability of committing injustice freely is compared to the power granted to Gyges by his magical ring (359d). Although in the myth proper this power comes from the ring, in the general statement about the nature of just and unjust people in 359c, no higher authority is said to be the source

---

[1] For what follows, see *TDNT*, s.v. "ἐξουσία."

of this power: Remaining hidden while committing injustice is just a trait or ability that Glaucon wants Socrates to imagine that people could theoretically possess.

Further examples of this usage are found in the works of Aristotle. In the *Nichomachean Ethics*, Aristotle suggests that different social units in the city-state resemble forms of government: Democracy is denigratingly compared to "households without a master" or a household in which "the ruler of the house is weak, and everyone is allowed to do what he likes [καὶ ἑκάστῳ ἐξουσία]" (1161a, LCL). Aristotle also employs the term in this sense regularly in his *Politics*: for instance, when referring to the basic ability of a person to achieve the happiness that everyone desires (*Pol.* 1332a).

Although this broad understanding of the term dominates classical literature, we also begin early on to see another, more specific meaning. In other contexts, ἐξουσία is used to denote the power or ability granted by legal or political entities to perform an action—that is, it means that someone has the "right" or "privilege" to carry out an action. It is in the overall sense of "political power" that we find ἐξουσία employed in certain fragments of Euripides:

> Many fine men have no way of proving themselves, because of the power [ἐξουσία] wielded by worthless ones. (frag. 738, LCL)
>
> I judge this among the follies of men, if one hands a father's property over to sons who lack good sense, or again authority [ἐξουσίαν] to citizens. (frag. 775, LCL)
>
> Never indulge your power [ἐξουσίᾳ δὲ μήποτ'ἐντρυφῶν], my son, by pursuing shameful desires for commoners; this brings in its train cold steel and knotted cords, when someone shames the children of the worthy poor. (frag. 362, LCL)

In each fragment, ἐξουσία is used to refer to specifically political power: power held over the institutions of the *polis*.

Beyond political power understood as legal authority, we can also find the term used to refer to wealth or status that affords opportunity—another sort of "institution," but one not really separable from other civil institutions, since wealth grants political privilege. In the *Politics*, Aristotle uses the word at one point to refer to the power that the wealthiest individuals have to avoid having to manage their slaves, delegating the task to another while they themselves pursue a life of leisure (*Pol.* 1255b). And in the Oxyrynchus papyri are found several instances referring to the rights afforded to parents or slaveowners.[2] Overall, then, this usage makes ἐξουσία more specific. It refers not just to a freely exercised ability or right but to the specific right located in the context of societal laws and traditions.

In contrast to the use of ἐξουσία to describe official societal permission, we also find the word used as the opposite of "law" or legal authority—either in the sense of "freedom," neutrally or positively understood, or in the sense of disobedience or licentiousness, the flouting of established law. This sense could also apply to the above-quoted passage of Aristotle from the *Nichomachean Ethics*, in which democracy is equated with anarchy, a state of affairs where everyone does what they want, in contrast to the established order of a household where a master's rule prevails.[3]

What about the use of the term in the three texts we examined in the previous chapter? In the *Memorabilia* of Xenophon, we find the term used mostly in the first sense examined—that which refers to the basic ability of an individual to do something unimpeded. For instance, in Socrates's recounting of the tale of Heracles's encounter with Vice and Virtue, the personified Vice, or "Happiness," declares that those who follow her ways will have "authority [ἐξουσίαν] to pluck advantage wherever they want" (*Mem.* 2.1.25, LCL). And, in a conversation with Glaucon, Glaucon's declaration that he would want to disband the city's garrisons were he in charge of military matters is met with Socrates's rebuke that the city's enemies "would be at liberty [ἐξουσίαν ἔσεσθαι] to rob us openly" (3.6.11, LCL). Elsewhere, Socrates describes as unjust persons who wish to have "power [ἐξουσία] to embezzle, to treat others with violence, to live in luxury" (2.6.24).

In the *Discourses* of Epictetus, we find an interesting shift that expands on the use of ἐξουσία understood as "freedom." While in some texts, it is understood in the sense of "licentiousness" or "lawlessness," the *Discourses* employ the term to describe the freedom that comes from proper understanding and acceptance of what is and is not under the individual's control:

---

[2] *TDNT*, s.v. "ἐξουσία," 562 nn.5–8.
[3] Ibid., 563.

> If all this is true and we are not silly nor merely playing a part when we say, "Man's good and man's evil lies in moral choice, and all other things are nothing to us," why are we still distressed and afraid? Over the things that we seriously care for no one has authority [ἐξουσίαν]; and the things over which other men have authority do not concern us. (*Diss.* 1.25.1-2, LCL)

The philosopher freely grants kings and rulers the things over which they have authority, ἐξουσία, such as the body and possessions, which are at the mercy of these temporal authorities. But this authority is nothing when it comes to the philosopher's own judgments (1.29.9ff).

In other words, ἐξουσία in the *Discourses* is an essential trait of the philosopher. It is what the Stoic has by virtue of their correct recognition that only their own judgments are truly under their control. The one who knows this recognizes the proper things over which they exercise "authority" and thus possesses an authority that cannot be harmed or diminished by temporal "authorities" or rulers. Epictetus turns the definition of ἐξουσία as lawlessness on its head: Rather than being lawless for disregarding the power claims of the king or ruler, the philosopher is in fact the only sort of person who lives in accordance with the (natural) law and thereby possesses true freedom, rather than the false freedom presented by worldly fixation with what is not under one's own control.[4]

Strikingly, ἐξουσία does not appear at all in the *Life of Apollonius of Tyana*. The examination can therefore now turn to the Septuagint, a key locus for understanding Markan usage of the term.

ἐξουσία in the Septuagint

The word appears in the LXX sixty-six times. However, it is quite rare in the books of the LXX that are translated from Hebrew. It does not appear at all in the Pentateuch and rarely in the historical books. It appears occasionally in the Writings but in the prophets occurs only in the book of Daniel.

---

[4] Cf. Epictetus *Ench.* 14.2: "Each man's master is the person who has authority over what the man wishes or does not wish, so as to secure it, or take it away. Whoever, therefore, wants to be free, let him neither wish for anything, nor avoid anything, that is under the control of others; or else he is necessarily a slave" (LCL).

In the case of 2 Kings 20:13 and in the examples from the wisdom books, ἐξουσία in the LXX translates the Hebrew מֶמְשָׁלָה ("rule, dominion, realm").[5] The term can refer geographically to the area that is ruled by a king, as in the 2 Kings example; King Hezekiah greets "envoys" from the king of Babylon by showing them all the riches he possesses: "There was nothing in his house or in all his realm (מֶמְשָׁלָה/ἐξουσία) that Hezekiah did not show them" (NRSV). The word can be used not only for that which is ruled by a human king but also for the territories or jurisdictions of others personified as rulers, such as God, as in Ps 114:2 (113:2 LXX), where the land of Judah is described as God's ἐξουσία. And in Ps136:8 (135:8 LXX), the sun and moon are respectively given "dominion" (NRSV) over the day and the night, respectively. In both psalms, ἐξουσία is once again translating the Hebrew מֶמְשָׁלָה.

In fact, the "political" meaning of the word seems to dominate in the LXX. The more generic sense of the basic ability or power to do something is rare. One of its only appearances is in Eccl 8:8:

> No one has power [LXX = ἐξουσία] over the wind to restrain the wind, or power over the day of death; there is no discharge from the battle, nor does wickedness deliver those who practice it. (NRSV)

In the case of Eccl 8:8, interestingly, the term ἐξουσία translates not מֶמְשָׁלָה but שַׁלִּיט, an adjective denoting the possession of "mastery," sometimes used substantively to describe the one who possesses said mastery.[6] So even here, the broad use of the term to denote ability or power overlaps with the "political" sense, applied to kings and rulers.

In other texts of the LXX, ἐξουσία means almost exclusively the power of a king, a ruler-like figure, or someone favored by a ruler to carry out an order or task. In the books of Maccabees, the word appears no less than twenty times across the four books, nine times in 1 Maccabees alone. In only one instance does it refer to anything else than the "authority" of a ruler or the authority granted by such a ruler to another person to do some action.[7] For example, the

---

[5] BDB, s.v. "מֶמְשָׁלָה".
[6] BDB, s.v. "שׁלט (I)."
[7] The exception is 4 Macc 6:33, where "reason" (λογισμός) is said to have ἐξουσία over the emotions (τὰ παθή).

word is used in the differing accounts in 1 and 2 Maccabees of how Antiochus gave permission to construct a Greek-style gymnasium in Jerusalem and to adopt other Greek customs:

> Some of the people were eager and went to the king, and he gave them authority [ἐξουσία] to observe the customs of the nations. So they built a gymnasium in Jerusalem, according to the ways of the nations, and made themselves uncircumcised, and departed from the holy covenant. (1 Macc 1:13-15; my translation)
>
> [Jason] promised to pay another one hundred and fifty [talents, to Antiochus] if he were allowed by the king's authority [ἐξουσία] to establish a gymnasium and an ephebe for it, and to enroll the people of Jerusalem as citizens of Antioch. (2 Macc 4:9; my translation)

The other usages of the word in 1-4 Maccabees similarly refer to the power of a ruler or the power granted by a ruler to perform a task such as raising an army or controlling a territory.[8] This pattern also continues in the Wisdom of Ben Sirach,[9] alongside occasional instances of other meanings, such as the more basic meaning denoting generic ability or power. For instance, a son should not be granted undue "freedom" in his youth (Sir 30:11), while the figure of Wisdom receives her "domain" in Jerusalem (24:11)—both these words are translations of ἐξουσία.

A particularly important book of the LXX for understanding the Gospel of Mark is the book of Daniel.[10] Daniel contains six chapters of "narrative" content and six "apocalyptic" chapters containing visions attributed to Daniel, who is presented as describing his visions in the first person. The narrative chapters that begin the book contain a number of uses of the term ἐξουσία. Since the narrative chapters focus on the situation of Daniel and his friends at the court of a foreign king, it is unsurprising that the usages of ἐξουσία that occur in these chapters follow the same pattern we observed in other late LXX texts like the four books of Maccabees and the Wisdom of Ben Sirach. In Dan 3:2, for instance, King Nebuchadnezzar summons a host of his elite subjects, including "those who held authority in the provinces" (τοὺς ἐπ'

---

[8] E.g., 1 Macc 10:8, 32, 35, 38; 14:4; 2 Macc 4:24; 7:16; 3 Macc 7:12; 4 Macc 4:5, 5:15.
[9] Sir 9:13, 10:4, 17:2, 45:17.
[10] See the enumeration of Mark's likely references to Daniel in James D. G. Dunn, *Christology in the Making*, 2nd ed. (Grand Rapids, MI: William B. Eerdmans, 1996), 67.

ἐξουσιῶν κατὰ χώραν). In 4:17, which recounts a vision of Nebuchadnezzar, God is spoken of in terms similar to that of an earthly ruler but as one who holds domain over all: "The Lord of Heaven holds authority over all things in heaven and on earth." And in 5:7, the king promises "authority over a third of the kingdom" (ἐξουσία τοῦ τρίτου μέρους τῆς βασιλείας) to whoever can interpret the mysterious writing that appears on the walls of his palace during a feast.

As for the second portion of Daniel, the sequence of visions (chs. 7–12), the word appears *only* in Dan 7. This is striking, since the chapter is extremely important for understanding the apocalyptic elements of the Gospel of Mark, especially the Markan use of the title "Son of Humanity" and the "little apocalypse" of Mk 13.[11] It is important to take careful note of the way the word ἐξουσία is utilized in Dan 7. For, although the term is used in a way that resembles the "political" meaning of the term we have already seen in Dan 1-6 and in other literature, it is in this chapter of Daniel that we find the most prominent example of "authority" being attributed, neither to a human ruler nor to God but to a figure whom later interpreters, including Mark, would regard as "messianic." The figure of the "one like a human being" who receives ἐξουσία in Dan 7 becomes a focal point for Markan ideas about the identity of Jesus as God's Messiah and chosen representative.

After a narrative introduction to the vision (7:1), "Daniel" narrates his own vision beginning in v. 2. Daniel sees four "great beasts" emerging from the sea: fantastical creatures that look like ordinary animals at first, such as a lion (v. 4) or bear (v. 5) but quickly take on grotesque characteristics such as wings, human-like features, massive teeth, and finally ten horns on the final creature. Then a final entity makes its appearance: a new horn, sprouting from among the ten horns of the last "great beast":

> I was considering the horns, when another horn appeared, a little one coming up among them; to make room for it, three of the earlier horns were plucked up by the roots. There were eyes like human eyes in this horn, and a mouth speaking arrogantly. (7:8, NRSV)

---

[11] On the Markan use of Dan 7, see Joel Marcus, *The Way of the Lord: Christological Exegesis of the Old Testament in the Gospel of Mark* (Louisville, KY: Westminster John Knox, 1992), 164–71.

Next, thrones appear, and an "Ancient One" dressed in white appears and takes a seat upon a throne of fire. He has attendants and a court, and "the books of judgement" are opened by the Ancient One's retinue. The last beast is destroyed, while the others have "their lives prolonged for a season and a time" (v. 12, NRSV).

Then, finally, the climax of the vision:

> I saw one like a human being
>> coming with the clouds of heaven.
> And he came to the Ancient One
>> and was presented before him.
> To him was given dominion
>> and glory and kingship,
> that all peoples, nations, and languages
>> should serve him.
> His dominion is an everlasting dominion
>> that shall not pass away,
> and his kingship is one
>> that shall never be destroyed. (7:13b-14, NRSV)

The "dominion" of the "one like a human being" (so the NRSV) translates the Hebrew שָׁלְטָן; the LXX renders the Hebrew as ἐξουσία.

This passage has been the site of an enormous amount of scholarly discussion, which is understandable considering its importance for understanding the use of the term "Son of Humanity" in the New Testament Gospels. Many of the issues that have been debated, such as the history of the passage's redaction or the exact contextual meaning and derivation of "one like a human being," need not concern us here.[12] What *is* important to note for our purposes is that the political meaning of ἐξουσία—the use of the term to mean the permission or authority exercised or granted by a king or ruler—has been extended to another figure, the "one like a human

---

[12] On the redaction of Dan 7, see John J. Collins, *Daniel: A Commentary on the Book of Daniel*, Hermeneia (Minneapolis, MN: Fortress Press, 1993), 278-80. On the importance of Daniel to early Christian eschatology, including the issue of the "son of humanity," see Adela Yarbro Collins's section on "The Influence of Daniel on the New Testament," in the same volume.

being," who is neither God nor, strictly speaking, a human ruler. Yet, as George Nickelsburg notes, this figure is "invested with authority that has its repercussions on the earthly level: all human kingdoms will be subservient to his authority."[13]

This figure in Dan 7 is an exceptional case of the application of the term ἐξουσία because he is granted authority not just over Israel but over the whole earth. Whereas in the Psalms it is God who is described as ruler of heaven and earth, in Daniel, at least part of this authority is delegated to the "one like a human being." Thus, not only is "authority" or ἐξουσία a primary trait of the "one like a human being," but in Daniel, this authority takes a decisively different turn than in the other texts we have examined, because the authority that is given is an authority to perform actions or functions typically reserved for God alone—particularly, the "authority" to rule not just Israel but all the nations, the whole world.

In the context of Dan 7 itself, it is most likely that the "one like a human being" is a personification of the elect community or the "holy ones of the Most High" (Dan 7:18, 22, 27).[14] However, regardless of the way one interprets the "one like a human being" in the context of Daniel, it is clear that in later Christian literature, not least Mark's Gospel, the phrase "one like a human being" becomes the name of a particular individual, the "Son of the Human One" or "Son of Humanity," a transcendental figure whose power stems directly from the divine realm.

This is in stark contrast to the way renowned or even "messianic" (anointed) rulers are portrayed in other Jewish texts, including both biblical and postbiblical texts. Consider, for example, the portrayal in Second Isaiah of Cyrus as God's "anointed" (i.e., Isa 44:28; 45:1-6, 13). The main thrust of Second Isaiah's portrayal of Cyrus is that God has chosen him for the liberation of Israel. There is no sense that Cyrus has taken a share of God's own rightful rule of the nations; he is simply a means by which Israel's return after the exile is to be accomplished:

---

[13] George W. E. Nickelsburg, *Jewish Literature between the Bible and the Mishnah: A Historical and Literary Introduction*, 2nd ed. (Minneapolis, MN: Fortress Press, 2005), 78.

[14] In agreement with J. R. Daniel Kirk, *A Man Attested by God: The Human Jesus of the Synoptics* (Grand Rapids, MI: William B. Eerdmans, 2016), 139–49, who critiques the view of J. Collins (*Daniel: A Commentary*) that the "one like a son of humanity" is an angelic figure.

> I have aroused Cyrus in righteousness,
>> and I will make all his paths straight;
> he shall build my city
>> and set my exiles free,
> not for price or reward,
>> says the LORD of hosts. (Isa 45:13, NSRV)

Or consider another example, *Psalms of Solomon 17*:

> See, Lord, and raise up for them their king,
>> the son of David, to rule over your servant Israel
>> in the time known to you, O God.
> Undergird him with the strength to destroy the unrighteous rulers,
>> to purge Jerusalem from gentiles
>> who trample her to destruction/ (17:21-22, trans. *OTP*)

As the passage goes on, the anticipated Davidic king is further described: The tribes of Israel will be gathered again, and foreigners will be expunged from the land. "There will be no unrighteousness among them in his days, for all shall be holy, and their king shall be the Lord Messiah" (*Pss. Sol.* 17:32). But as with the Isaiah passages concerning Cyrus, the Davidic king is not a "transcendental" figure who appears from the heavenly realm, as is the case with the Son of Humanity in Mark. God will "raise up" a king, but there is no sense that this king will, in spite of all his accomplishments, be anything other than an ordinary human being.

To conclude, in most texts of the LXX, the term ἐξουσία is most commonly employed to describe the right to rule and the ability to issue commands that are followed, possessed either by God or by human rulers. In Daniel, however, we find that ἐξουσία is ascribed to a figure who is more than a human ruler but less than God: the "one like a human being." The fact that Daniel makes this connection is extremely important for our reading of Mark. For Mark interprets the phrase as a title, applies it to Jesus, and thus gives Jesus the "authority" that the "one like a human being" receives in Daniel 7.

Ἐξουσία in Mark: A Preliminary Overview

Ἐξουσία appears ten times in the Gospel of Mark.[15] This compares to the ten uses in Matthew, sixteen in Luke, and eight in John. Given Mark's proportionally shorter length than the other Gospels, it is clear that this is an extremely important motif for Mark. Only Luke exceeds Mark in his attention to the subject. Further, virtually all of Mark's uses of the term, seven in total, refer directly to Jesus; that is, Jesus is the figure who is said to possess ἐξουσία. Two more instances refer to the disciples, who are granted this ἐξουσία by Jesus himself. Finally, there is an oblique use in the parable of the householder and his slaves in Mk 13:34: The slaves are said to receive "authority" when their master departs. In its context in Mark's Gospel, this passage likely refers to Jesus and his disciples as the master and slaves. Thus, the use of ἐξουσία in Mark specifically centers around the issue of *Jesus's* ἐξουσία. He is the one who either has it or gives it in all places where the term is used. By contrast, although Luke uses ἐξουσία twice as much (sixteen times), the Third Gospel is not only much longer than Mark (thus allowing more space proportionally for the use of the term), it also introduces a number of instances where the word is used to refer to the "authority" not of Jesus but of other figures, such as the devil (Lk 4:6), a Roman soldier (7:8), or "worldly" authorities (12:11, 20:20, 23:7). Mark's usage is much more restricted and precise in meaning than Luke's.

It is particularly noteworthy that, in Mark's Gospel, the theme of Jesus's ἐξουσία appears especially in scenes that are critical to the storyline and the Gospel's presentation of Jesus. The first appearance of the term occurs in 1:22 and 27, bookending the story of an exorcism that marks Jesus's first public appearance, the opening of his ministry. It is a central point at issue in the controversies with his opponents in Galilee. He passes it on to his disciples when he sends them out. And he is confronted with the question of the source of his "authority" following his dramatic demonstration in the Jerusalem temple. The only section of the Gospel noticeably bereft of any discussion of ἐξουσία is the passion narrative.

---

[15] Mk 1:22, 27; 2:10; 3:15; 6:7; 11:28 (twice), 29, 33; 13:34.

Both the frequency of the term ἐξουσία as well as its thematic importance at key points in the Gospel suggest that it is a worthy focus for our analysis. And, as we will see, it is combined at key junctures with the motif of Jesus as teacher, suggesting that the two terms have the potential to mutually illuminate one another. The insights to be gained by studying the two in conjunction will be made clear in the detailed study of key Markan passages, to which we must now proceed.

Jesus as Authoritative Teacher in Mark

We come now to the heart of this study: the examination of Mark's Gospel itself. We will proceed by interpreting passages from Mark's Gospel, which have to do with Jesus's teaching. Throughout the study of Mark, we will pay attention to the primary issue at hand: the portrayal of Jesus as a teacher. To that end, two questions will be kept in mind as we proceed. In each passage where Jesus is portrayed as teaching, (1) what is Jesus teaching and (2) how does he teach it? These are the same questions that we posed regarding the three texts examined in the previous chapter, and it is now time to ask them of Mark's Gospel. But to this we must also add a third question: How does the portrayal of Jesus's teaching connect with the Markan depiction of Jesus as possessing unique "authority" (ἐξουσία)? For to understand Mark, it is necessary to understand how the Gospel connects teaching with the issue of authority.

A New Teaching, with Authority (1:21-28)

We begin our interpretation of Jesus's teaching in Mark by turning to the very first passage in which said teaching is mentioned: Mk 1:21-28. And, in support of the proposed theory that Jesus's teaching in Mark is closely linked with the issue of his "authority," this is also the first passage in which the term ἐξουσία appears.

It has frequently been observed, from the perspective of form and redaction criticism, that the beginning and end of this passage are quite odd when compared to the main focus of the passage, which is an exorcism taking place in the synagogue at Capernaum. Therefore, it is a consensus of scholarship that Markan redaction is responsible for the framing of the passage, most particularly the notices about Jesus's teaching.[16] We read at 1:21:

> And they entered into Capernaum. And immediately on the Sabbath, Jesus entered the synagogue and taught. And they were astonished at his teaching, for he taught them like one who had authority [διδάσκων αὐτοὺς ὡς ἐξουσίαν] and not like the scribes.

One might expect, given that this introduction has posed the issues of Jesus's teaching and his authority, that it would be followed either with a description of what Jesus taught or with more detailed comparison between Jesus and the scribes. There is more conflict with the scribes later in the Gospel. But there is no description here of what Jesus actually taught in the Capernaum synagogue.

By contrast, consider the way in which the Gospel of Matthew, taking over Mark's material, deploys this notice about the crowd's astonishment and the comparison with the authority of the scribes: It is placed at Mt 7:28–29 and constitutes the conclusion to the large body of Jesus's teaching found in the Sermon on the Mount. The comparison with Matthew highlights the oddity of the Markan summary statement in its original context, for it does not fit well with the exorcism account that follows. It would seem to fit far better with an actual account of the content of Jesus's teaching (as in Matthew), but Mark does not proceed this way. Instead of describing Jesus's teaching, Mark introduces a new character, a "man with an unclean spirit" (1:23). The unclean spirit, or demon, recognizes Jesus as "the Holy One of God," a title not used elsewhere in Mark.

The oddity is compounded by the addition of the summary statement that *closes* the passage. The closing summary returns to the concerns of teaching and authority:

> And they were all amazed, so that they began to question among themselves, saying: "What is this? A new teaching, with authority! He even commands

---

[16] Rudolf Bultmann, *History of the Synoptic Tradition*, trans. John Marsh (Oxford: Basil Blackwell, 1972), 209; Robert A. Guelich, *Mark 1-8:26*, WBC 34A (Dallas, TX: Word Books, 1989), 55; Marcus, *Mark 1-8*, AB 27 (2000: reprint, New Haven, CT: Yale University Press, 2005), 190–1.

unclean spirits, and they obey him!" And at once, the report spread about him throughout the whole region of Galilee. (Mk 1:27-28)[17]

So the passage opens with the issue of Jesus's teaching and the manner in which he teaches it—with "authority." It then shifts abruptly to an exorcism account, before returning in its conclusion to a mention of Jesus's teaching that neatly melds together exorcism and teaching. The exorcism, curiously, is described as a "new teaching, with authority" (1:27).

To return to the first of our guiding questions: What does Jesus teach here? It is difficult to say at first glance. For, as mentioned, in the passage's opening, the "teaching" that evokes the amazement of the crowd is not explained, and in the conclusion, it is the exorcism itself that is described as constituting the "teaching." The former represents a significant gap in the narrative flow; the second is highly unusual. The only information about the teaching we are given is that it is in contrast to that of "the scribes."

Given that no content is given to Jesus's teaching here, how do we understand what happens in the scene and the reason for its inclusion at this juncture in Mark's Gospel? We note, first and foremost, that the emphasis, in both the opening and closing of the passage, is that the crowd is amazed at Jesus's "authority," and in 1:22 this authority is said to be the key element that distinguishes Jesus's teaching from that of "the scribes." This recognition of Jesus's authority is the sum total of the scene's import: The only plot development here is that the crowd recognizes Jesus's authority over and against the scribes. The crowd does not react to Jesus's teaching, whatever it was. Even if it were the case here, as Adela Collins suggests on the basis of a comparison with 7:1-23, that Jesus's teaching here concerns the interpretation of the Law, the people react not to superior legal insight or exegetical prowess on Jesus's part but to a specific quality of it: It is taught with ἐξουσία.[18]

To interpret the meaning of this "authority" of Jesus, we ought to return once again to the earlier discussion of the term in other literature. To recall, it does

---

[17] Given uncertainty about how to punctuate the Greek, the phrase "with authority" could be taken to refer either to the teaching ("A new teaching, with authority! He even commands") or the exorcism ("A new teaching! With authority he even commands"). Given that the *opening* summary statement links authority specifically with teaching, the author's preference is for the former option. That said, as we will see, the two activities, teaching and exorcism, end up closely linked together in this passage. See, for discussion of this issue, Marcus, *Mark 1-8*, 189.

[18] Adela Yarbro Collins, *Mark*. Hermeneia (Minneapolis, MN: Fortress Press, 2007), 165.

not refer to simple charisma or persuasiveness on Jesus's part. Some interpreters make this error, suggesting that Jesus's "authority" is his personal appeal, the conviction of his speech, and so on.[19] But ἐξουσία, as we have seen, refers to a quality that a person possesses due to external circumstances. It can be the "'ability to perform an action' to the extent that there are no hindrances in the way."[20] Or, more commonly, and especially in literature closer to the period of Mark, it refers specifically to the right to give commands or orders and have them carried out. Such a figure is either a king or ruler or someone who has been given the right to be in charge and issue orders by such a powerful figure.

In this context, the second of these two understandings of ἐξουσία is implied. What Jesus's teaching possesses here is not persuasiveness or forcefulness of speech. Nor does it make much sense to say that the crowd is marveling at the fact that Jesus is speaking unhindered, as though they are noting that no one or nothing is preventing him from talking. Rather, what the crowd recognizes is that Jesus has the kind of authority that either a ruler or a ruler's envoy might have.

The audience, of course, already knows whence this authority of Jesus comes: from God. It is God who is the "ruler" from whom Jesus has received his ἐξουσία. The opening of the Gospel declared Jesus to be χρίστος, "anointed," hearkening back to the anointing of Israel's kings or the anointed priests mentioned in the book of Leviticus.[21] And even more significantly, at Jesus's baptism the audience is privy to the words that God speaks to Jesus when the heavens are torn open: "You are my beloved son; I take delight in you" (1:11). The intertextual connections of this divine declaration are well-known to scholars. "You are my son," recalls Ps 2:7, in which God declares that Israel's king is his son. The use of "beloved" recalls Isa 42:1, where God indicates a "beloved" servant who receives God's spirit, just as Jesus does at his baptism.[22] Both the "king" of the psalm and the "servant" of Isaiah are figures chosen by God for special authority. Without delving too deeply into the questions of

---

[19] E.g., Walter Klaiber, *Das Markusevangelium*, BNT (Neukirchen-Vluyn: Neukirchener, 2010), 44: "Jesu Lehre is durch eine innere Kraft ausgezeichnet, die tief in das Leben der Mesnchen hineinspricht."
[20] Marcus, *Mark 1-8*, 191, quoting *TDNT*, s.v. "ἔξεστιν."
[21] *ABD*, s.v. "Christ."
[22] Adela Yarbro Collins, "Mark and His Readers: The Son of God Among Jews," *HTR* 92, no. 4 (October 1999), 394; Boring, *Mark*, 45–6.

the precise Markan nuances of the title "Son of God" for Jesus, it is clear that Jesus's status as an authoritative figure is made obvious to the audience when they "overhear" the words of God at Jesus's baptism.

Aside from the fact that Mark has already made Jesus's authority from God known in the baptism scene, that the "authority" of Jesus in Mk 1:22 is intended to be understood as a kind of "royal" authority granted by God is also made clear by the connections between Mark and Daniel, which we discussed earlier in the overview of the meaning of ἐξουσία. Recall that in Daniel, the "one like a human being" is in the LXX version given ἐξουσία over all nations of the earth.[23] Throughout Mark's Gospel, the "one like a human being" in Daniel is transformed into a title for Jesus, "the Son of Humanity."[24] Outside 1:21-28 in Mark, we find the notion of Jesus as Son of Humanity paired with the idea of his ἐξουσία, just as we find the two terms together in chapter 7 of Daniel. This strongly suggests that Mark derives both concepts from Daniel.

To return to our passage, then, what the crowd recognizes is that Jesus has a kind of royal authority, a right to rule or command that stems from his being a figure who has that right either by virtue of his position or by being sent by someone else—namely, God. But how does the crowd recognize this? The term "Son of God" is notoriously opaque in the narrative as the result of the Markan "secrecy motif" or what Wrede famously referred to as "the messianic secret."[25] There is no need to discuss the secrecy motif fully here, but suffice it to say that there is absolutely no reason given at this point in the narrative why the crowd should be able to recognize that Jesus is God's son. Among the characters in the Gospel, only Jesus knows it up to this point. The demons will recognize it too, later (3:11, 5:7). The high priest will seemingly recognize it at Jesus's trial when he demands to know whether Jesus is the "son of the Blessed One" (14:61). And at the foot of the cross, when Jesus dies, a Roman centurion will announce that Jesus was surely the son of God (15:39). Finally, the audience

---

[23] In the MT, by comparison, he receives "dominion and glory and kingship" (NRSV): וְלֵהּ יְהִיב שָׁלְטָן וִיקָר וּמַלְכוּ. The Greek translates the first Hebrew word, שׁלט.
[24] Dunn, *Christology in the Making*, 66.
[25] William Wrede, *The Messianic Secret*, trans. J. C. G. Greig (Greenwood, SC: Attic Press, 1971); see also the discussion in Jack Dean Kingsbury, *The Christology of Mark's Gospel* (Philadelphia, PA: Fortress), 1983.

is of course already privy to this knowledge, having "overheard" the words spoken to Jesus at his baptism.[26]

But the crowd in 1:21-28 knows none of this. There is, in fact, nothing in the passage that would explain how it is that Jesus's "authority" is recognized. We must recognize it as simply a brute fact of the narrative. This information is simply "meant" to be imparted at just this point. The rather arbitrary nature of the introduction of Jesus's "authority" further emphasizes the fact that it is this authority, and not the actual content of Jesus's teaching, which is the point of the passage.

It is not just that Jesus has "authority," however. The onlookers favorably compare Jesus's teaching to that of the "scribes," who apparently do not teach with such authority. The next step in understanding 1:21-28 is to understand who the scribes are.

Describing who Mark intends by "the scribes" is fraught with difficulty. The Gospel seems to assume that its audience knows who is meant, but we, not sharing the same cultural context, must reconstruct who the scribes were for ourselves. A particularly careful study of the identity of the scribes has been conducted by Anthony Saldarini.[27] On his reading of the evidence, "scribes" in the ancient world could perform a variety of functions and belong to disparate social strata: They could be anything from barely literate low-level village bureaucrats to high-ranking retainers of kings or priestly aristocrats. And what was true of the ancient world generally was also true in the land of Israel.

On the high end of the social spectrum, the most prominent example of a scribe in the Hebrew Scriptures is Ezra, a leader in the reestablishment of the Jerusalem cult after the Babylonian exile, who is "a scribe skilled in the Law of Moses."[28] This example is significant insofar as it is one of the few literary examples of scribes who are specifically said to be skilled in the interpretation

---

[26] Or possibly even earlier; one common textual variant in Mk 1:1 adds the note that Jesus is "son of God." But most scholars do not believe this was a part of the earliest text; one exception is Boring, *Mark*, 30, who argues that "the two words [υἱοῦ θεοῦ] could easily have been omitted by *homoioeleuton*" on account of the no less than thirteen words ending in -ου in vv. 1-3. This is certainly possible, but it seems unlikely that a scribe would make the mistake of omitting a well-known and common Christological title right at the start of a manuscript, before becoming tired and prone to mistakes: For discussion of this and other arguments, see Bart D. Ehrman, "The Text of Mark in the Hands of the Orthodox," *LQ* 5, no. 2 (Summer 1991), 149–52.

[27] Anthony J. Saldarini, *Pharisees, Scribes and Sadducees in Palestinian Society: A Sociological Approach* (1988; repr. Grand Rapids, MI: William B. Eerdmans, 2001), esp. ch. 11.

[28] Ezra 7:6; cited in Saldarini, *Pharisees*, 244.

of the Law. Closer to the period of the writing of Mark, the evidence for scribes as teachers of the Law, as they often seem to be in Mark, becomes less clear. Josephus follows the wide pattern of Greco-Roman usage in applying the term scribe to apply to figures from "all levels from village to royal court." Contrary to the portrayal in Mark and the other Gospels, Josephus's scribes do not appear to be an organized group with a coherent agenda; in the New Testament Gospels, meanwhile, they are depicted as almost single-mindedly determined to oppose Jesus.[29] Further, the scribes in Josephus are not depicted as teachers of the Law.

Other works do, however, associate scribes with knowledge of the Law. In 2 Maccabees, the martyr Eleazar is said to be "one of the most senior scribes" (πρωτευόντων γραμματέων; 2 Macc 6:18). He is killed for refusing to abandon the practice of the Law by eating pork. The fact that a scribe in particular is singled out for his piety *may* imply that some scribes were renowned for their knowledge of the Law. This is uncertain, however. More promising is the depiction of the ideal scribe in the book of the Wisdom of Ben Sira. In a well-known section, Ben Sira reflects upon the requirements for scribal training as well as the specific qualifications of the scribe (38:24-39:11). Notably for our purposes, the scribe is described as one "who devotes his life to understanding the Law of the Most High" (Sir 39:1 LXX, my translation). The scribe "will show forth the instruction of his teaching, and he will boast in the law of the covenant of the Lord" (39:8, my translation).

Ben Sira's ideal scribe is learned in more than just the Law, of course. To such a scribe is also attributed a generalized or universalized wisdom of which the Law of Moses is only a part. The scribe is also one who understands parables and proverbs, learns the secrets of foreign lands, and associates with rulers (Sir 39:1-4).[30] As Stephen Westerholm says, the "scribe" in Ben Sira seems to take on the attributes of a "sage" or wise man.[31] But nevertheless, we have in Ben Sira the unmistakable association of scribes with learning in the Law. However much of an idealized construct Ben Sira's picture of the scribe is, the text suggests that a link between scribes and learning in the Law was considered a plausible one in Jewish literature.

---

[29] Saldarini, *Pharisees*, 261.
[30] See John J. Collins, *Jewish Wisdom in the Hellenistic Age*, OTL (Louisville, KY: Westminster John Knox, 1997), ch. 3, for a discussion of the complicated relationship between the Law and wisdom generally speaking in Ben Sira.
[31] Stephen Westerholm, *Jesus and Scribal Authority*, ConBNT 10 (Lund: Gleerup, 1978), 26.

Ben Sira's ideal scribe, learned in the Law, seems to match quite well the scribes as depicted in Mark. They regularly challenge Jesus on matters concerning the Law (2:16, 7:1, 12:28). That they have knowledge in the Law is also suggested by the scene where Jesus says that it is an interpretation of "the scribes" that the Messiah is David's son, implying that the scribes have read the Law for an understanding of the Messiah's identity (12:35). Finally, there is the fact that the scribes in Mark are frequently associated with Jerusalem (i.e., 3:22, 7:1, 11:18, 11:27). Mark, then, seems to agree with Ben Sira that "scribes" are learned in the Law.

This presents a window on an apparent anachronism in Mark's story. As we have just seen, Mark typically connects his "scribes" with Jerusalem. Thus, even though the scribes evoked by the crowd's words in this passage are not specifically said to be from Jerusalem, Mark nevertheless seems to picture them as experts in the Law with connections to the temple establishment, rather than as the low- to middle-ranking functionaries that seem historically more likely to have been in residence in Galilee. On the basis of this, it is important for us to keep in mind that Mark's portrayal of the scribes is a literary device—one that has some basis in the historical reality, for some scribes were indeed experts in the Law but, nevertheless, anachronistic to a certain degree. The anachronism is repeated in the other scenes in the Gospel where scribes from Jerusalem are said to come to Galilee to debate with Jesus.

Why is the scribes' teaching viewed negatively compared to that of Jesus? That is, why does Jesus teach "with authority" and the scribes do not? Notice that it is not said that Jesus has *more* authority than the scribes or *superior* authority: Rather, he has authority and they have none: "for he taught them like someone who had authority, and not like the scribes" (1:22).[32]

If the argument presented earlier is cogent that Jesus's authority is the authority of the Son of Humanity, the authority that Daniel's "one like a human being" received, then the answer seems clear. Jesus's teaching has authority because he is

---

[32] Against Francis J. Moloney, *The Gospel of Mark: A Commentary* (Grand Rapids, MI: Baker Academic, 2002), 54, who interprets the remark about authority in 1:21 to mean that Jesus's authority was "different from that of the scribes." Rather, as stated, 1:22 ascribes *no* authority to the scribes. This interpretation is also supported by John Chijioke Iwe, *Jesus in the Synagogue of Capernaum: The Pericope and its Programmatic Character for the Gospel of Mark: An Exegetico-Theological Study of Mk 1:21-28*, TGST 57 (Roma: Editrice Pontifica Università Gregoriana, 1999), 62.

Son of Humanity—as well as Son of God, as the baptism scene made plain to the Gospel's audience. The scribes' teaching is not inferior because it misinterprets the Law, for example, much less because it lacks charisma or "genuineness." The issue has nothing to do with the *content* of their teaching at all, as a matter of fact. Rather, the issue is that Jesus, as God's messenger and Son, is superior to them simply by virtue of his "office." He is Messiah, Son of Humanity, Son of God; he has authority. As we will see later, throughout the Gospel, Jesus's arguments with the scribes (and other rivals) most often hinge upon the issue of authority, rather than the content of Jesus's teaching.

At this point in the argument, we have seen that Mk 1:21-28 sidesteps the *content* of Jesus's teaching to focus the discussion on Jesus's identity and person: the fact that he is God's authoritative agent, whereas the scribes are not. The fact that the crowd recognizes this in the Capernaum synagogue sets the stage for the "controversy stories" later in the Gospel. At this point, however, the scribes themselves are not actually present; they are mentioned but cannot speak for themselves here.

With this conclusion about the point of Jesus's "teaching" in this passage, we are better able to understand why the action of the scene includes, incongruously, an exorcism. Above all, the contest between Jesus as the "unclean" spirit is a demonstration of Jesus's authority, his right or ability to command and be obeyed. The spirit recognizes Jesus as "the Holy One of God," a title otherwise unattested in the Gospel. Although naming Jesus's title may be the demon's attempt to gain control over him, there is no depiction of a struggle for power between the spirit and Jesus. The spirit is doomed from the start, for the fact that Jesus is the "Holy One of God" gives him a power well beyond anything the spirit can hope to have. "In the present account 'Holy One of God' serves not as an attempt to gain control over Jesus but as a christological confession stemming from the supernatural insight and understanding of the demon."[33] The spirit has no choice but to acknowledge Jesus's superiority.[34] Its end is assured.

---

[33] Robert H. Stein, *Mark*, BECNT (Grand Rapids, MI: Baker Academic, 2008), 88, citing Ernest Best, *The Temptation and the Passion: The Markan Soteriology*, SNTSMS 2 (Cambridge: Cambridge University Press, 1965), 17.

[34] Wilfried Eckey, *Das Markusevangelium: Orientierung am Weg Jesu: Ein Kommentar* (Neukirchen-Vluyn: Neukirchener, 1998), 77.w.

Jesus does not actually teach anything in the body of the passage; he exorcizes an unclean spirit. Yet in 1:27, the crowd's response to the exorcism is once again to return to the subject of Jesus's teaching. Indeed, they specifically label the exorcism *as* a teaching: "And they were all amazed, so that they were saying to one another: 'What is this? A new teaching, with authority! He commands even the unclean spirits, and they obey him'" (1:27). The "teaching," the thing the crowd has learned, therefore, is the fact that Jesus has the power—the *authority*—to command unclean spirits. He "even" commands the unclean spirits, as they say—his authority does not just give him superiority to the scribes but even gives him command over spiritual forces.

We see, then, that despite the references to Jesus's "teaching," 1:21-28 does not actually focus on Jesus's teaching per se. Rather, the focus is on the sheer fact of Jesus's authority and the way in which it is noticed by the crowds and negatively compared to the (nonexistent) authority of traditional leaders like the scribes. The point is not that Jesus is a teacher. The point is that he is someone who possesses authority from God to issue commands even to unclean spirits and have them obeyed. Jesus speaks, and what he says happens. The theme of authority even pervades the exorcism itself: Whereas other extant accounts of ancient exorcism often include the detail that the exorcist calls upon a higher power to perform the exorcism, Jesus here does not invoke God or any other force by which the demon is to be cast out.[35] Rather, because Jesus is "Holy One of God," he has authority proceeding directly from God and does not need to manipulate other spiritual or heavenly powers to cast out the unclean spirit. There is, therefore, as Moloney observes, a unity between what Jesus says and what he does in this passage, even though the combination of "teaching" with exorcism does not seem at first to mesh particularly well.[36] In fact, once it is understood that Jesus's authority is the motif that provides the key to the passage, the combination makes sense. Jesus's authority is first announced by the crowd in 1:22, then demonstrated in dramatic fashion, which leads the crowd to reaffirm its earlier statement in 1:27.

---

[35] For examples of accounts where an exorcist calls upon a higher power, see Collins, *Mark*, 165–7, who cites Josephus *Ant.* 8.2.5 (an exorcism performed in the name of Solomon) and 4Q560 (an exorcism in the name of YHWH).

[36] Moloney, *Gospel of Mark*, 54–5.

It is worth noting that this Markan image of Jesus as an authoritative figure who makes things happen solely by his command is not entirely without precedent in the other texts we examined earlier. In the previous chapter, we noted that Mark, unlike the three texts we looked at in that chapter, did not appeal to common values as a basis for the acceptability of Jesus's teaching. There is, however, a strong affinity between the Jesus of Mark and Apollonius as depicted by Philostratus. The two are alike in that Apollonius, like Mark's Jesus, is depicted as a figure whose mode of address is one of command, rather than of argument or persuasion. This is particularly apparent in a number of stories about Apollonius's exorcisms. To give just one example, in the *Life* 4.20, Apollonius encounters a young man possessed by a demon, with a "reputation for shamelessness" (LCL) that causes him to continually interrupt Apollonius's teaching. Apollonius terrifies the demon with just a glance:

> When Apollonius looked at the spirit, it uttered sounds of fear and fury, such as people being burned alive or tortured do, and it swore to keep away from the youth and not enter into any human. (4.20.2, LCL)

The demon leaves hurriedly, knocking over a statue as proof of its exit, and the young man comes to his senses and adopts Apollonius's philosophical lifestyle as evidence that he is "cured." We see here that, similarly to Jesus in Mk 1:21-28, it takes only Apollonius's command to force the demon out; no struggle between Apollonius and the demon, or any invocation of a higher power on Apollonius's part, is necessary.[37]

Jesus, similarly, "teaches" in a way that demonstrates his authority and commands demons without even having to struggle with them. In Philostratus, Apollonius's teaching was distinguished by the fact that he did not employ dialectic or the Socratic method but made pronouncements. In Mark, Jesus does not appeal to the Law or established tradition but to his office as Son of Humanity and Son of God: Unlike the scribes, he has "authority."

In summary, although Mk 1:21-28 contains reference to Jesus's teaching, it does not portray Jesus as teaching a program of instruction to his disciples or to the crowd. The very fact that the focus is on "authority" cuts against Vernon

---

[37] This passage is cited by Wendy Cotter, *Miracles in Greco-Roman Antiquity: A Sourcebook* (London: Routledge, 1999), 85–6.

Robbins's thesis that the Markan Jesus is passing on a "system of thought and action" to his followers throughout the Gospel.[38] Instead, we are presented with the unelaborated theme of "teaching," paired with the much more pronounced theme of "authority." These two ideas, teaching and authority, occur together regularly in the rest of the Gospel, either explicitly or implicitly, as we shall see.

In the introduction, and at the beginning of this chapter, we spoke of three different goals accomplished by Mark's portrayal of Jesus's teaching. These were, we recall, (1) the advancement of the Gospel's plot, (2) the development of Mark's Christology of Jesus as a figure with authority, and (3) addressing the audience. It is clear from the foregoing analysis that the first two of these are particularly in view in Mk 1:21-28. First of all, the plot is advanced, for this is the first time the twin themes of Jesus's teaching and his authority are mentioned. Further, we also find the first reference to Jewish leaders with whom Jesus will come into conflict: the scribes. Even though the scribes themselves are absent from this scene, the way is prepared for their eventual confrontation with Jesus, because a negative contrast between Jesus and the scribes appears here for the first time. This means that the scene introduces the central conflict of the Gospel, the conflict between Jesus and the establishment that will ultimately lead to Jesus's death. The grounds for Jesus's eventual condemnation by his opponents are also signaled at this early juncture: his claim, here implicit but later explicit, to possess authority as God's Son.

The Authority of the Son of Humanity (2:1-12, 23-28)

Continuing the theme of Jesus's authority are two controversy stories (or "conflict stories," to use alternate terminology) that depict Jesus responding to criticism of his followers' practice. Just as 1:21-28 sidestepped the issue of Jesus's teaching to focus on his authority, so these passages, in spite of ostensibly focusing on issues of practice, ultimately have as their goal the depiction of Jesus as authoritative Son of God and Son of Humanity.

In 2:1-12, Jesus heals a paralyzed man, announcing to the man as he does so that "your sins are forgiven." "Some of the scribes" happen to be present and

---

[38] See the discussion of Robbins in the introduction.

are "questioning in the hearts" why Jesus pronounces forgiveness of sins when only God should be able to do so (2:6-7). Jesus's response is twofold. First, he responds with a counterquestion—as Bultmann observed, this is a common feature of controversy stories in the synoptic tradition.[39] Second, he responds by healing the paralytic as a demonstration that "the Son of Humanity has authority [ἐξουσία] on earth to forgive sins" (2:10-11).

Many scholars have held that this passage is a composite, and that vv. 5b-10 are a secondary addition to a story that originally focused solely on the miracle of Jesus's healing of the paralytic.[40] Whether or not one agrees with this view, the final form of the passage is our focus here. Treating 2:1-12 as a unit, therefore, we find several features of interest for our study of the themes of Jesus's teaching and his authority.

First, obviously, our key word ἐξουσία appears. This clues us in right away that in its current form, the story is not meant simply to resolve an issue of practice. Here the form-critical focus on the *Sitz im Leben* led Bultmann to overlook a crucial point. He traced the origin of this passage (and indeed all of the controversies as they stand in the Gospels) to the early church's disputes with outsiders about its practice—in this case, so Bultmann thought, the early church took upon itself the right to forgive sins and in this passage traced that right to Jesus himself, who possessed it by virtue of being Son of Humanity.[41] Regardless of the accuracy of Bultmann's claim that the early church claimed the right to forgive sins, this interpretation misses a key point: that the outcome of the dispute with the scribes is that Jesus's *authority* is once again magnified.

This is accomplished as follows. Jesus takes upon himself the right to forgive sins. Some commentators argue that Jesus in 2:5 does not actually take upon himself the right to forgive sins but announces that God has forgiven the paralytic's sins. The verb ἀφίενται functions, on this interpretation, as a "divine passive."[42] However, against this view, in the Markan context it is clearly *Jesus* who has the right to forgive sins, since he obliquely labels himself as "Son of Humanity" a short while later and demonstrates that this Son of Humanity

---

[39] Bultmann, *Synoptic Tradition*, 41.
[40] Arland J. Hultgren, *Jesus and His Adversaries: The Form and Function of the Conflict Stories in the Synoptic Tradition* (Minneapolis, MN: Augsburg Press, 1979), 106–7; Marcus, *Mark-18*, 218–19.
[41] Bultmann, *Synoptic Tradition*, 15–16, 48–9.
[42] Stein, *Mark*, 118.

has the authority to forgive sins. Further, as Stein notes, if Jesus had meant that God had forgiven the paralytic's sins, he could have just informed the scribes that they had misunderstood him.[43] The fact that he does not suggests that the narrator affirms that the scribes have the correct interpretation of Jesus's action, despite their hostility.

Therefore, the Markan Jesus magnifies his own authority by assuming the right to forgive sins. The scribes ask, "Who can forgive sins but God alone?" (2:7). Their question is rhetorical, but an answer is implied by what follows: Jesus, as the Son of Humanity, can forgive sins. He acts as God's agent, which the scribes do not know, but the Gospel audience does. Also, it is worth noting that the scribes' claim that Jesus is blaspheming foreshadows the charge of blasphemy at his trial in the Markan passion narrative (14:64). That moment, when Jesus declares his full identity openly for the only time in the Gospel, leans heavily on Jesus's claims about his authority, so it is notable that this much earlier declaration of authority by Jesus is also met with the charge of blasphemy.[44]

The passage also magnifies Jesus's authority by making Jesus's declaration about the authority of the Son of Humanity central to his response to the scribes. Jesus's response to the scribes' implicit accusation against him is twofold. He first asks a rhetorical question: "Which is easier, to say to the paralytic, 'Your sins are forgiven,' or to say, 'Rise; take up your mat and walk?'" (2:9). But he then immediately segues into a demonstration of power "so that you may know that the Son of Humanity has authority on earth to forgive sins." The answer to the earlier rhetorical question is obvious: It is easier to say that the paralytic's sins are forgiven than to pronounce him healed and have it occur—that is, it is one thing to speak and another to have the ἐξουσία, the ability to command that he be healed and have that command translate to action. This is, remember, the basic meaning of ἐξουσία as derived from ἔξεστιν: being able to perform an action without any hindrance.

But Jesus then preempts his own question by healing the paralytic with exactly the words used in the question. Therefore, it is immaterial what is

---

[43] Ibid., 118–19.
[44] The thematic link with Jesus's trial is noted by William R. G. Loader, *Jesus' Attitude toward the Law*, WUNT 2. Reihe 97 (Tübingen: Mohr Siebeck, 1997), 40.

easier, to forgive the paralytic, or to heal him, for Jesus has now done both. He has pronounced forgiveness *and* had his command for the paralytic to rise up and walk followed by just that action. Because he has the ἐξουσία to do the latter, he has it to do the former as well. Therefore, Jesus's question to the scribes can be seen as a kind of rhetorical trap: Even if the scribes admit that it is easier to tell the paralytic his sins are forgiven than to make him walk, Jesus responds by performing the far more difficult of the two. As Gundry says,

> The easier thing is to say, "Your sins are forgiven", for no human being can falsify that statement ... To give verifiable evidence of the invisible effectiveness of the easier statement and thus to belittle his silent accusers Jesus will proceed to say the less easy thing, "Rise and take up the pallet of yours and walk."[45]

The logical conclusion is that the scribes must acknowledge Jesus's authority, since he has accomplished both the easier task and the much more difficult one. And indeed, this is what they seem to do, rather incongruously, at the end of the passage: In 2:12, they join in the general acclamation by the crowd and the glorifying of God. God is glorified, but Jesus is recognized as authoritative.

Finally, note that the scribes do not speak their objection aloud: Rather, they are "questioning in their hearts," and Jesus "perceiv[es] in his spirit" their objection without them needing to voice it (2:8). Knowledge of the scribes' thoughts helps to characterize Jesus as a thoroughly extraordinary person, who possesses more than human insight into the world around him. As Robert Fowler notices, Jesus in Mark essentially shares the knowledge of an omniscient narrator.[46] Referring specifically to the story of the healing of the paralytic, Fowler writes,

> Rhetorically, verse [2:]8 reveals to the reader that Jesus knows something the reader already knows; if Jesus knows what the reader already knows, then what reader would not accept Jesus as a reliable, authoritative figure, worthy of the reader's trust?[47]

---

[45] Robert H. Gundry, *Mark: A Commentary on His Apology for the Cross* (Grand Rapids, MI: William. B. Eerdmans, 1993), 114; cf. Moloney, *Gospel of Mark*, 62.
[46] Robert M. Fowler, *Let the Reader Understand: Reader-Response Criticism and the Gospel of Mark* (Minneapolis, MN: Fortress Press, 1991), 73.
[47] Ibid., 74. Contextually, Fowler's overall point, from his reader-response perspective, is that the narrator's sharing omniscience with the authoritative character of Jesus enhances the *narrator's*

In summary, Jesus's authority is emphasized in 2:1-12 in three different ways: by his assumption of the right to forgive sins, by his actual healing of the paralytic, and by his "perceiving in his spirit" the secret objections of the scribes. The thing to notice is that the actual miracle is not the focus in the passage. Although it begins with the arrival of a person in need of healing and ends with the acclamation of the crowd, the substance of the passage is subtly shifted, by means of the three methods just enumerated, to the issue of Jesus's authority and its relation to the claims of the scribes. In 1:21-28, the scribes were not present and so could not speak for themselves about Jesus; in 2:1-12, by contrast, the scribes are present, providing another opportunity for Jesus's authority to shine forth in comparison to their lack of said authority.

We also see the same theme of Jesus's authority take center stage in Mk 2:23-28. In this passage, Jesus and his disciples are walking through grain fields on the sabbath, and the disciples begin "to make a path, plucking heads of grain" (v. 23). Some Pharisees happen to be present, and they object that the disciples are "doing what is not lawful on the sabbath" (v. 24).[48] In reply, Jesus gives two responses: first, a justification based on Scripture (vv. 25-26), and second, a saying about the nature of the sabbath that is said to show that "the Son of Humanity is lord also of the sabbath" (vv. 27-28).

Examined closely, the passage is extremely odd.[49] The situation to which the Pharisees object—namely the disciples' plucking grain—does not seem to fit at all well with the citation from Scripture that Jesus offers. Leaving aside the issue of the fidelity of Jesus's account to the original story in 1 Sam 21:1-6, such as the inaccurate claim that it occurred when Abiathar was high priest, the Samuel passage does not match what the disciples are doing. The disciples are not said to be hungry, as Jesus claims David and his companions were. The Pharisees' objection is most plausibly rooted in the fact that the disciples are "working" on the Sabbath, according to Pharisaic

---

authority as well as that of Jesus. But the point we make here stands: Jesus's authority is enhanced in the eyes of the audience by the fact that Jesus behaves as one who has the knowledge of an omniscient narrator.

[48] The presence of the Pharisees ought to underscore for us the fact that what we are reading is a composition for Markan purposes, not a straightforward historical account. As E. P. Sanders somewhat snidely but accurately puts it, "Pharisees did not organize themselves into groups to spend their Sabbaths in Galilean cornfields in the hope of catching someone transgressing" (E. P. Sanders, *Jesus and Judaism* [Philadelphia, PA: Fortress Press, 1984], 265).

[49] On the following difficulties, see Moloney, *Gospel of Mark*, 68-9.

interpretation.⁵⁰ Yet the Samuel passage does not really address the Pharisees' criticism: The justification for David's action according to Jesus is that he "had need and was hungry, he and those with him" (2:25). But the disciples are not said to be eating, nor does Jesus claim that David's action took place on a sabbath. Nor is it specifically said that the disciples are hungry.⁵¹

A further aporia is that the link between vv. 27 and 28 is unclear at first glance. The conjunction ὥστε that begins v. 28 is best interpreted as an inferential conjunction, inferring from the saying in v. 27, about the sabbath being made for human beings and not human beings for the sabbath, that "the Son of Humanity is lord also of the sabbath."⁵²

Given the above problems, it is best to interpret the passage not primarily as a dispute about sabbath practice but rather as another occasion where Jesus asserts his authority. We begin with the two concluding sayings about the sabbath being made for human beings and about the Son of Humanity being lord of the Sabbath. In what way does the second follow from the first—or, to put it differently, why does the Markan Jesus assert such a conclusion from the premise? Joel Marcus suggests that Jesus acts here as an eschatological Adam and acts as lord over the sabbath in this capacity.⁵³ This would link the two sayings together in such a way that Jesus is depicted as the archetypal "human being," or last Adam, to use a term from Pauline theology. However, this conclusion does not seem warranted: Marcus cites Gen 1-3, but in Genesis the sabbath is not a gift for human beings but represents the "seventh day" of Gen 1-2, on which God rested from the work of creation (Gen 2:3).

A more likely understanding of these sayings is presented in a careful study by Vernon Robbins of the various synoptic forms of this pericope.⁵⁴ Robbins sees the connection between v. 27 and v. 28 as arising from Jesus's identity as the Son of Humanity, already well-established at this point in the Gospel.

---

⁵⁰ Morna D. Hooker, *The Gospel According to Saint Mark*, BNTC (1991; repr. Grand Rapid, MI: Baker Academic, 2011), 102-3, notes, "Both reaping and threshing were included in the thirty-nine primary activities which were defined as 'work' (M. Shabbath 7.2)."

⁵¹ Contra Mary Ann Tolbert, *Sowing the Gospel: Mark's World in Literary-Historical Perspective* (Minneapolis, MN: Fortress Press, 1989), 133-4, who claims that the point of the story is that religious tradition is "subordinated" to the need of the disciples.

⁵² On the inferential conjunction: Daniel B. Wallace, *Greek Grammar beyond the Basics: An Exegetical Syntax of the New Testament* (Grand Rapids, MI: Zondervan, 1996), 673.

⁵³ Marcus, *Mark 1-8*, 246.

⁵⁴ Vernon K. Robbins, "Plucking Grain on the Sabbath," in *Patterns of Persuasion in the Gospels*, ed. Burton L. Mack and Vernon K. Robbins (Sonoma, CA: Polebridge, 1989), ch. 5.

Because God made the sabbath for human beings and not human beings for the sabbath, and because the Son of Humanity has authority from God to accomplish various tasks on earth, therefore Jesus, being the Son of Humanity, is lord of the sabbath—that is, has the right to interpret how the sabbath is to be observed.[55]

Robbins also proposes a way to understand how to interpret the presence of the David story along similar lines. What links the situation of Jesus and his disciples with that of David in the story cited by Jesus is not that the disciples are also hungry. Rather, it is the figures of Jesus and David who are the point of comparison. David claimed to be on an errand from the king when he asked for the bread, just as Jesus is sent on his mission by God, in his capacity as Son of God and Son of Humanity. By allowing David to take the bread,

> the priest accepted the principle that it is appropriate for a leader whom the king has sent on a special task to insist that regular procedures be bypassed in order to provide food for the men for whom he has responsibility. The priest accepted this principle when David used it with him, so the Pharisees should now accept the principle.[56]

Thus, both the example from David, which is common across the various synoptic versions of the pericope, and the sayings about the sabbath end up being connected to the person of Jesus, rather than being just a legal dispute. The David story is brought up to make the point that an authoritative figure such as David or Jesus should be yielded to in terms of deciding on the propriety of certain actions with regard to tradition and law. Seen in this light, the David story does not seem out of place, since this interpretation suggests that the issue at hand is not actually that the disciples are hungry, but that they are *Jesus*'s disciples—that is, followers of an authoritative leader whose word takes precedence.

Relating this line of interpretation to our earlier conclusions about Jesus's authority in 1:21-28 and 2:1-12, this passage provides another example of a situation that seems at first to be about teaching or legal issues but is actually about Jesus's claim to ultimate authority, an authority connected with his role as Son of God.

---

[55] Ibid., 126.
[56] Ibid., 116.

It may be asked how these two controversy stories we have discussed relate to the issue of teaching, for they do not specifically mention the subject. In fact, they are important for our discussion for two reasons. First, they both involve, as we have seen, the issue of authority, which we already saw in our discussion of 1:21-28 is tied strongly with the motif of Jesus's teaching. Second, the two stories are noteworthy precisely because they *do not* mention Jesus's teaching at instances where we might expect them to do so. It would be quite reasonable, for instance, for the scribes' accusation that Jesus commits blasphemy by pronouncing the paralytic's sins forgiven to be met with a response about the nature of forgiveness and how it is imputed. But this does not happen. Rather, Jesus simply poses a counterquestion that is implicitly answered by his miraculous deed and demonstrates his authority by performing said deed. There is no teaching or instruction about the subject of "forgiveness."

Similarly, in 2:23-28, there *is* what could be considered a "teaching" about the sabbath—the principle enunciated in 2:27 that the sabbath was made for human beings, not the reverse. But as we have seen, this verse is framed by two other responses from Jesus: the story about David and the saying that the Son of Humanity is lord of the sabbath. By framing the declaration about the sabbath this way, the Gospel directs attention away from the issue of what is or is not lawful on the sabbath to the authority of certain individuals—David and Jesus—to decide what does and does not count as violation of sabbath law. The passage ends with the declaration of Jesus's authority, not the enunciation of a legal principle.

To be sure, this focus on authority is not the focus of *all* the Markan controversy stories. In 2:13-17, the "scribes of the Pharisees" question Jesus's eating with "tax collectors and sinners" (2:16). Here Jesus does not refer to his own authority but makes an analogy with medical practice: "Those who are healthy have no need of a physician, but those who are sick do" (2:17). And in 2:18-22, the fact that Jesus's disciples refrain from fasting is justified by the analogies of the bridegroom and of shrunk and unshrunk cloth as well as an allusion to Jesus's own forthcoming death (2:20). The theme of authority is muted here.

Yet its prominence cannot be denied: It occurs, as we have seen, both during Jesus's initial appearance in Capernaum as well as during a number of dialogues with adversaries. It is also arguably at work when Jesus is repeatedly depicted healing and casting out demons, since the demons recognize his superior station (and thus, his authority) as Son of God (e.g., 1:34, 3:11). And we will see the authority theme continue to recur as the narrative proceeds.

The analysis of the controversy stories presented here is more or less in line with Burton Mack's similar study of what he calls "pronouncement stories," following the terminology used in a volume of *Semeia* edited by Robert Tannehill.[57] Based on his analysis of several such passages, Mack concludes that what sets the Markan stories of Jesus and his controversies apart from similar stories about other figures in the ancient world is that the Markan pronouncement or controversy stories are unusually fixated on the authority of Jesus as rationale for the conclusions drawn. The "arguments" presented make no sense unless one already accepts that Jesus is an authoritative figure whose word must be heeded. Mack cites Hultgren's statement about the Gospel controversies: "In the synoptic conflict stories the closing statements are generally merely *asserted*, and their authority is based on the fact that Jesus has made them."[58] Mack chose different "pronouncements" of Jesus to analyze for his study than the ones we have just discussed, but the foregoing analysis supports basically the same conclusion: The Gospel controversies are generally resolved, not by culturally conventional modes of argument but by blunt assertions of Jesus's superior authority.

This conclusion is also in line with Robert Fowler's view (see the Introduction) that much of Mark operates on the level of discourse, not story. Notice that there is no "uptake" in the controversy stories: Neither Jesus's opponents nor his disciples draw the conclusion that Jesus has great authority as a result of his pronouncements.[59] Only the audience draws this conclusion.

These two controversy stories, like the pericope of Jesus's appearance in the Capernaum synagogue, advance the Gospel's characterization of Jesus's authority as well as advancing the plot by developing the theme of Jesus's conflict with the established authorities. Here, unlike in the Capernaum scene, the establishment figures are actually present and challenge Jesus on multiple

---

[57] Burton L. Mack, *A Myth of Innocence: Mark and Christian Origins* (Philadelphia, PA: Fortress, 1988), ch. 7. The Tannehill-edited volume is *Semeia* 20 (1981).
[58] Hultgren, *Jesus and His Adversaries*, 33, cited in Mack, *Myth*, 203.
[59] Fowler derives "uptake" from J. L. Austin, and uses it to refer to the effect on the audience of a speech act. See Fowler, *Let the Reader Understand*, 18.

occasions. And to make clear the direction in which the relationship between Jesus and his opponents is going, Mark concludes this section of controversy stories with the following note about the result of Jesus's healing a man's withered hand on the sabbath: "And going out, the Pharisees immediately took counsel with the Herodians against Jesus, so that they might destroy him" (3:6).

The Disciples Receive Authority (3:13-19; 6:6b-13)

After controversy stories (2:1-3:6) and a summary statement about Jesus's interaction with the crowds (3:7-12), there follows a description of Jesus's calling of a special circle of disciples, the Twelve (3:13-19). It is somewhat similar in language to a later passage, 6:6b-13, so we will consider them together. In 3:13-19, Jesus ascends a mountain and calls to himself "those whom he wanted" (3:13) and makes them the Twelve, who are "to be with him, and to preach, and to have the authority [ἐξουσία] to cast out demons" (3:14-15). Similarly, in 6:6b-13, the previously named Twelve are sent out in pairs, with strict instructions about behavior and practice, bearing "authority over unclean spirits" (ἐξουσίαν τῶν πνευμάτων τῶν ἀκαθάρτων) (6:7).

In the former passage, the Twelve are initially constituted as a group, while in the second, they are formally sent out on a mission. This mission, however, is already alluded to earlier, in the former passage, where repetitive ἵνα clauses are utilized to describe the purposes for which Jesus calls the Twelve: They are to be sent out "in order that" they should be with him, preach, and cast out demons. They do not actually set out on any such mission, however, until 6:6b-13.

What is of interest for us is that in both passages, ἐξουσία is specifically mentioned (3:15; 6:7). In 3:15 the "authority" they are given is authority to perform the *action* of exorcism, while in 6:7, this "authority" is authority *over* something: over the unclean spirits, specifically. The two amount to much the same thing, each emphasizing a different side of the understanding of "authority" we have seen at work so far in Mark's Gospel. Up until 3:13-19, the only character who is described as having "authority" is Jesus. His authority consists in both his prerogative and his ability to perform certain actions simply by his proclamation: He teaches and is recognized as an authoritative teacher by what he says and does. He commands demons to depart, and they do so; he speaks only a command for the paralytic to be healed, and the paralytic is healed. Here, he passes on this same kind of "authority" to the Twelve. Unlike Jesus, however, in the case of the Twelve this authority is of only one kind: the authority to cast out the demons, authority "over" them—that is, the ability to issue exorcistic commands to the demons and have those commands obeyed. The fact that the "authority" of the Twelve is understood in precisely this way lends additional credibility to the contention already made, that Jesus's own "authority," which he here passes on to his closest followers, consists in being recognized as an agent of God and having his commands obeyed. Just as Jesus can command the demons because he is Son of God, so now the disciples are, by extension, granted authority to command the departure of demons as well.

A second feature of note appears in the follow-up to 6:6b-13, at 6:30, when the Twelve return from their mission: They report to Jesus "all that they had done and taught." This introduces a new element, for neither 3:13-19 nor 6:6b-13 specifically mentioned "teaching" as part of the mission on which Jesus sent the Twelve. The closest we get to this is a note at 6:12: "And going out, they proclaimed that all should repent." This is an appropriate place to remark upon another intriguing feature of Mark's portrayal of Jesus's teaching: the Gospel's free, almost interchangeable use of the verbs κηρύσσειν and διδάσκειν.

In 1:14-15, in his first reported words in the Gospel, Jesus "proclaims" the kingdom of God. But in 1:21-22 he "teaches" (διδάσκειν) in the synagogue in Capernaum. And in 1:39 he once again travels about "proclaiming" in synagogues. In 2:2 he is "speaking the word" to a crowd, which, while it is neither directly referred to as "teaching" or "proclamation," probably suggests proclamation of the Gospel. "The word" is a common technical term for Christian proclamation in the New Testament.[60] But in 2:13, as Jesus is "beside the sea," he is "teaching them" (i.e., the crowds who follow him from place to place).

When Jesus appoints the Twelve (3:13-19), the verb switches back to "proclaim," κηρύσσειν, once again: The Twelve are recruited not to "teach" but

---

[60] Boring, *Mark*, 131; Marcus, *Mark 1-8*, 308; Stein, *Mark*, 216–17.

to "proclaim" and to exorcize (3:14-15). The next we see of either verb is in chapter 4, the parables chapter, where Jesus is once again said to be "teaching" (4:2). But in a concluding statement (v. 33-34), the activity of Jesus in 4:1-32 is described as "speaking the word to them." Once again, this is likely a reference to proclamation of "the gospel," which indirectly links this "speaking the word" to the earlier use of κηρύσσειν in 1:14, where Jesus is "proclaiming the gospel of God." In 6:2 Jesus is "teaching" in the synagogue at Capernaum. In 6:12 the disciples are said to "proclaim that all should repent" (ἐκήρυξαν ἵνα μετανοῶσιν). But when they return from their travels, they are said to have "taught" (ἐδίδαξαν).

From this point on, in the remainder of Mark, there are no more references to the disciples or Jesus "proclaiming" during the events of the story. The remaining two uses of the term as applied to Jesus both have to do with his predictions about the future of the Gospel message: The Gospel will be "proclaimed to all nations" before the end of the tribulations foretold in ch. 13 (13:10), and the story of the woman who anoints Jesus will be told "wherever the gospel is proclaimed in the whole world" (14:9). The "proclamation" is now depicted as an event occurring in the future, rather than the time of the narrative itself. "Teaching," meanwhile, continues until the passion narrative and is particularly dominant during Jesus's activities in the temple (11:15-12:44).

The result of Mark's frequent switching back and forth between the two verbs, sometimes even in the same passage, has the result of blurring them together, making them basically synonyms for one another in the Markan context. What makes this subtle shading of the two verbs into one another so interesting is that, despite the fact that readers and commentators are inclined to go along with Mark's combination of them, this conflation of κηρύσσειν and διδάσκειν is relatively rare in extant literature.

Κηρύσσειν derives from κῆρυξ a messenger or herald.[61] It is in the sense of performing the role of a herald—delivering a message or summoning someone—that we find numerous prominent examples of the verb in Greek literature. In the *Iliad*, Agamemnon instructs a herald "to summon [κηρύσσειν] the long-haired Achaeans to battle" (*Il.* 2.443, LCL); Telemachus in the *Odyssey*

---

[61] For what follows, see *TDNT*, s.v. "κηρυσσω."

has a herald call the people to him (*Od.* 2.7); Athena in Aeschylus's *Eumenides* commands a herald to restore order in a crowd (*Eu.* 566). Among many other slightly different shades of meaning, κηρύσσειν can also refer to the giving of commands to an army (Xenophon *An.* 3.4.36), to the proclaiming of a person as having a certain status, such as that of free man (Pl. *Mor.* 197b) or criminal (Sophocles *El.* 606); or to the general spreading of a piece of news or a report, such as of a person's whereabouts (Sophocles *Tr.* 97, *El.* 1105). All in all, κηρύσσειν refers, in general, to the giving of messages and announcements.

In the LXX, κηρύσσειν can be used in this same sense of a command or announcement, especially that of an authoritative figure, such as a king or other leader: Both Moses and Aaron are said to give commands with this verb (Ex 32:5, 36:6), as are Jehu, Jehosaphat, and Cyrus of Persia (2 Kings 10:20; 2 Chron 20:3, 36:22). Surprisingly, it is used only rarely to refer to a prophet's declaration of "the word of the Lord" or the like (but see Jonah 1:2, 3:2). One partial exception, however, is a well-known passage from Isaiah: The prophet has been sent "κηρύξαι αἰχμαλώτοις ἄφεσιν" "to proclaim release to the captives" (Is 61:1).

The works of Josephus mostly follow the general trend of Greek literature. Although κηρύσσειν is used in two instances to describe the activities of prophets (on one occasion, a prophet whom Josephus considers a false one), it is otherwise almost always used to refer to the activities of "secular" heralds or messengers of rulers or to the giving of orders by military leaders.[62] In the corpus of Philo, meanwhile, the verb is virtually absent, although the noun describing the message the "herald" bears (κήρυγμα) is used a number of times.[63] In particular, Philo does not use κηρύσσειν even in places we might particularly expect it, such as the activity of Moses, which, as cited above, is sometimes used to describe Moses's activity in the LXX.

What about the three texts we discussed in the previous chapter? In the *Discourses* of Epictetus, the usage of κηρύσσειν sometimes resembles that in the Gospel of Mark. The verb can be used in an ordinary sense of "to cry aloud" (1.16.12). But it can also refer to the philosopher's presentation of Stoic

---

[62] The "false" prophet: *J.W.* 6.285; the proclamation of Jonah, *Ant.* 9.208. For the more "secular" usage: *J.W.* 1.295, 5.278 6.352; *Ant.* 6.98, 6.121, 10.235, 11.254, 11.258, 13.84, 14.402.
[63] I.e., *Mos.* 1.9, 2.22; *Gaius* 46. See also the use of κῆρυξ in *Gaius* 94, 100.

teaching (1.29.64) or to the Stoic's declaration to the world that he or she has found happiness despite material poverty because of the ability to make right judgments (4.6.23). More interestingly, at 3.22.70, in a discourse on the vocation of the Cynic philosopher, the would-be Cynic is advised to avoid the entanglements of civic and social life, lest he "destroy the messenger, the scout, the herald of the gods [κήρυκα τῶν θεῶν] that he is" (3.22.69, LCL). Finally, at 3.13.12, the philosopher can also be the person to whom something is proclaimed: The "peace" proclaimed by Caesar is negatively contrasted with the true "peace" that the person who accepts Stoic teaching has had "proclaimed" to her or him by "God through Reason."

An interesting point to note in connection with the use of κηρύσσειν in Epictetus is that we see in this literature a blurring, similar to that seen in the Gospel of Mark, between "teaching" and "proclamation." For the work of the philosopher in his role as teacher is compared to that of the herald, and Stoic doctrines are not only taught but "proclaimed" by the philosopher to others just as "Reason" proclaimed them to the philosopher. The blending of the two terms likely connects to the conception of the philosopher as a messenger of the gods, as in the portrayal of the Cynic in 3.22. The concept of the earthly messenger has been intertwined with the idea that the philosopher bears a certain stamp of divinity because he relates information about the gods and about the highest human happiness.

Strikingly, the same is *not* true of the other two texts we examined, the *Memorabilia* and the *Life of Apollonius*. Κηρύσσειν appears only once in the former and refers to the ordinary act of a decree made by a city-state (*Mem.* 2.1.15). The same usage occurs several times in the *Life of Apollonius*, but despite Philostratus's pains to depict Apollonius as divinely endowed, the protagonist is never said to "proclaim" his teaching, whether as a human or divine message.

To conclude this discussion of κηρύσσειν, we see that the usage in the Gospel of Mark, where the verb overlaps heavily with διδάσκειν as a description of Jesus's typical activity in his ministry, is mostly unprecedented in Greek and Greco-Roman literature. There are some precedents in the LXX. But one difference between Mark and the LXX examples, though, is that, unlike Moses in the scriptural traditions, Jesus is generally not portrayed as a lawgiver. Given that the verb most commonly refers, as we have seen, to the issuing of an order or proclamation by a ruler or city, its use to describe Moses, the archetypal lawgiver in Hellenistic Jewish tradition, is not surprising.

The use of the term in Mark actually most closely resembles, of all the texts studied here, that in the *Discourses* of Epictetus. Mark shares with the *Discourses* the tendency to blur together the roles of teacher and messenger so that the teacher's words are supported not simply by human wisdom but by divine authority. This is the most important conclusion to draw from our study of κηρύσσειν: Mark does not view Jesus as a merely human teacher but as in some way a messenger of God, just as Epictetus considers the philosopher a "messenger" and "scout" with a divinely supported mandate (*Diss.* 3.22.69). This possibly explains Mark's free interchanging between describing Jesus as "proclaiming," on the one hand, and as "teaching" on the other. The two have, in Mark, become essentially one and the same, for Jesus's teaching cannot be separated from his status as an authoritative messenger of God. This supports the point made at the end of Chapter 1: Jesus's message, his "teaching," does not occur in isolation from his person as God's agent.

The main point to draw here for the passages about the Twelve and their mission is that, taken together, the passages represent an example of a broader theme: the Markan tendency to blur the distinction between "preaching" and "teaching." The message of Jesus is "preached" or "proclaimed," as a divinely inspired message issued by Jesus as Son of God. But it is also described as a "teaching." We saw this at work in 1:21-28, where the "teaching" of Jesus became an indication of his divine authority, and in the controversy stories, where the practice of Jesus and his disciples was ultimately justified not just by rational argument or human wisdom but by the declaration that Jesus was Son of Humanity. The rationale for Jesus's message and methods, in fact, has far more to do with his authority than with his arguments. The same is true, vis-à-vis, of the disciples when they are sent out on their mission, during which they heal, exorcize, and teach: The "authority" of the disciples to exorcize is highlighted in both passages, while "teaching" is briefly mentioned only when they return to Jesus in 6:30, where we are told retrospectively that teaching had, in fact, been a part of what they had done on their mission. But, as with Jesus himself, the fact that authority and exorcism are mentioned repeatedly while teaching appears in a summary statement as an afterthought, suggests that in Mark's Gospel, "teaching" is being supplemented or even replaced by authoritative deed.

The Mystery of the Kingdom (4:1-34)

The "parables discourse" of Mk 4 has a strong claim to be the most important passage in the whole Gospel for understanding how and why Mark uses the motif of Jesus as teacher. As one of only two extended discourses of Jesus in Mark (the other being Mk 13), it is obviously of central importance in analyzing the "message" of the Markan Jesus. In the analysis here, we shall maintain our focus on the three questions that have guided us so far: What does Jesus teach? How does he teach it? And how does Jesus's teaching relate to the theme of his "authority" that we have already observed?

As with Mk 1:21-28 and 2:1-12, scholars have observed incongruencies in Mk 4, which have prompted questions about Markan sources and their redaction. For instance, after imparting the parable of the sower, Jesus retires to somewhere private at 4:10 and speaks with "those around him along with Twelve" about the meaning of the parable. But in the conclusion to the parables discourse at 4:33-34, he is suddenly once again in a public place, as though he were still teaching the crowd. Further, 4:10 and 4:13 suggest that Jesus is discussing *parables*, plural, with his followers, even though he has, up to this point, presented only the parable of the sower. And a third discrepancy has been detected between the "parable theory" of 4:11-12, which seems to assume that Jesus teaches in parables precisely *in order that* the crowd will not understand, and 4:33, which seems to presume that Jesus straightforwardly intended to teach the crowd by means of the parables.[64] However, as intriguing as these issues are, we will once again lay them aside and focus on the form of the passage as it stands, rather than on its sources and redaction.

The first thing we notice about 4:1-34 is that, for the first time in the Gospel, a notice that Jesus was teaching is accompanied by an actual description of that

---

[64] On the issues, see Adela Yarbro Collins, *Mark*, 239.

teaching. We recall that earlier mentions of Jesus's teaching were quickly left behind as the focus shifted to other activities of Jesus, such as his exorcisms, healings, and authoritative pronouncements.[65] Here, by contrast, we are told that Jesus taught (4:2), and the rest of the passage details what it is he taught. This detail alone confirms the importance of the passage for a discussion of the Markan Jesus's teaching.[66]

Interpreting Jesus's teaching here, however, is complicated by the fact that Jesus teaches not in plain declarations but "in parables" (4:2, 33-34). A wedge is thus driven between what Jesus *said* (the parables) and what he *meant* (the interpretation). All hear the parables, but only those closest to Jesus (and the Gospel's audience) hear the interpretation. It is also worth noting that only the first parable, that of the sower, is specifically interpreted; the other parables that follow the "parable theory" of 4:11-12 are not interpreted, even though we are told in 4:34 that "he explained everything privately to his disciples." A strong presumption, therefore, is that the parable of the sower and its interpretation are meant to function as a sort of interpretive key for the rest of the parables in the discourse.[67]

The parable of the sower depicts a "sower" who sows seed on various types of ground. The fates of four different groups of seed are detailed: The first three groups fall on various types of unsuitable soil and so do not prosper, but the final group of seed falls on "the good soil" (4:8) and leads to a bountiful harvest.

After Jesus presents the parable, the scene suddenly shifts from a public to a private one. Jesus retires to an unspecified place and "those around him with the Twelve" ask him about the meaning of his parables. His response is programmatic, applying not just to the parable of the sower but to all of the parables that follow:

> And he said to them: "To you the mystery of the kingdom of God has been given [δέδοται]. But to those outside everything comes in parables, in order that [ἵνα] they might see yet not perceive, and hear yet not understand, lest [μήποτε] they should turn and it be forgiven them. (4:11-13)

---

[65] Joachim Gnilka, *Das Evangelium nach Markus*, vol. 1, EKKNT 2.1 (Züruck: Benziger, 1978), 158.
[66] Jean Delorme, *L'heureuse annonce selon Marc: Lecture intégrale du deuxième évangile*, LD (Paris: Les Éditions du Cerf, 2007), 263: "Pour la première fois est rapporté un enseignement de Jésus plus consistant, du moins plus élaboré que quelques paroles brèves."
[67] So, e.g., Hooker, *Saint Mark*, 120.

These verses, the so-called Markan "parable theory," are among the most controversial in the entire Gospel. We will return to them below. For the present, it is to be noted that these words of Jesus should influence how we view the interpretation of the parable of the sower, which immediately follows. The interpretation sheds light on what is meant by the "mystery of the kingdom of God."

Jesus then turns to the interpretation of the parable already given. First, he chides his hearers (still the limited circle of "those around him with the Twelve") for not understanding the parable of the sower: "And he says to them: 'Do you not understand this parable? How then will you understand all the parables?'" (4:13). This constitutes Jesus's affirmation that understanding the parable of the sower is the key to understanding the other parables, including those which immediately follow.

Then Jesus interprets the parable for those listening. At first glance, the allegory is straightforward: The different groups of seed correspond to different types of people who hear "the word." But on closer inspection, his exegesis is confusing. For there is a subtle shift in the referent of the "seed" in the parable's interpretation. Jesus says that "the sower sows the word" (4:14), but when he interprets the fate of each kind of seed, the types of seed apparently represent not what is taught (the word) but those who are being taught: They are choked by the cares of the world, they shrivel up, and so on. Even in describing the fates of the seed, the referent is still not entirely fixed: The first group, the seed that falls alongside the path, is said to fail because "Satan comes and takes away the word sown in them" (4:15), which would suggest that the seed itself is the word once again. The Gospel seems unclear about which aspects of the parable are supposed to represent the teaching and which represent those taught: In general, it seems as though those taught correspond to the soil—as in 4:15 when the seed is the "word" taken away from the "ground" by Satan—while at the other times the seed seems to represent those taught, as in the other examples of seed.

Despite the ambiguity of the text here, the parable still leans in the direction of a deterministic interpretation of the "sowing": The seeds fail not because they themselves are bad but because of where they happen to fall during the sowing. The soil determines all; the fate of the seed has to do with nurture, not nature. The critical detail to note is that the parable is not about different types of "seed" but about different types of *soil*. The seeds succeed or fail not because of any intrinsic qualities or flaws but because of where they simply happen to land when they are sown.[68]

So the focus in the parable is on the soil, not the seeds. But the fact that the parable is not about seeds but soil creates a conundrum: Despite the fact that Jesus is "teaching" in his parables, the images he uses here are highly dubious from a parenetic standpoint. For, as just mentioned, the seeds do not succeed in and of themselves but rather because of the soil. The use of seed imagery in ancient discussion of teaching or parenesis was, of course, common. Adela Collins cites the following example attributed to Hippocrates:

> The learning of medicine may be likened to the growth of plants. Our natural ability is the soil. The views of our teachers are as it were the seeds. Learning from childhood is analogous to the seeds' falling at the right time on prepared ground. The place of instruction is as it were the nutriment that comes from the surrounding air to the things sown. Diligence is the working of the soil. Time strengthens all these things, so that their nurture is perfected. (*Lex* 3)[69]

Burton Mack similarly observes that agricultural imagery was a "standard analogy" for Greek *paideia* (understood as cultural ideals and their inculcation) in the Hellenistic world: "Ears acquainted with Hellenistic culture to any degree at all would immediately have recalled the stock image for offering instruction with a view to the inculcation of Hellenistic culture."[70]

One might be tempted, therefore, to think that Mark is just using a standard Hellenistic trope for teaching. But the issue is that, as mentioned, despite the use of seed imagery to begin the parable, the focus is ultimately not on the seed but on the soil. And soil is a decidedly unsuitable image for parenesis, for soil cannot change in response to instruction. As Boring says,

> The imagery does not particularly lend itself to parenesis; each type of soil cannot decide to change its character … The seed/word is good throughout. The soil is passive and cannot change.[71]

---

[68] As James R. Edwards, *The Gospel According to Mark*, PNTC (Grand Rapids, MI: William B. Eerdmans, 2002), 129, remarks, the parable is not a metaphor for "wrong or right discipleship." That would imply that the seeds themselves have something to do with their own respective fates.
[69] Collins, *Mark*, 245.
[70] Mack, *Myth of Innocence*, 159.
[71] Boring, *Mark*, 132.

This is why the parable and its interpretation do not function well as an instance of parenesis or moral exhortation. There is nothing that either the crowd or the inner circle is instructed to *do*. They are not meant to hear the parable or the interpretation and resolve to become "good soil" or obey the word more steadfastly. If that were the case, the parable would be nonsense, because the "seed," the word, fails or flourishes irrespective of its own qualities. But this is not what we find. Jesus simply outlines the reasons why so much of the sown seed fails; there is no sense that he is instructing his hearers to make any kind of change. There is no exhortation.

What *does* this "teaching" teach, then? The answer is to be found by paying attention to the *apocalyptic* nature of the parable's discourse. By this is meant that the parable shares a number of key themes with Jewish apocalyptic literature, and that these characteristics shed light on the function of the parable in Mark's Gospel.[72]

The imagery of the parable is, like much apocalyptic literature, dualistic. Although there are four types of seed in the parable itself, in the "parable theory" of 4:11-12, these correspond to only two types of hearer of the word: those who have received the mystery of the Kingdom of God and "those outside." This is reminiscent of other known forms of Jewish and Christian apocalypticism. A well-known example of similar dualism is found in the Community Rule of Qumran (1QS):

> From the God of Knowledge comes all that is and shall be. Before they ever existed He established their whole design, and when, as ordained for them, they come into being, it is in accord with His glorious design.
>
> He has created man to govern the world, and has appointed for him two spirits in which to walk until the time of His visitation: the spirits of truth and injustice. Those born of truth spring from a fountain of light, but those born of injustice spring from a source of darkness. All the children of righteousness are ruled by the Prince of Light and walk in the ways of light, but all the children of injustice are ruled by the Angel of Darkness and walk in the ways of darkness. (1QS 3.13ff.)[73]

---

[72] The apocalyptic connection is well-described by Gnilka, *Markus*, vol. 1, 165.
[73] The translation is that of Geza Vermes, *The Dead Sea Scrolls in English*, rev. and extended 4th ed. (London: Penguin, 1995). It is worth noting that it has been questioned whether the cosmic dualism of this "Treatise on the Two Spirits" was as significant a part of the Qumran sectarians'

There are, of course, obvious differences between Mark's parable and 1QS: In Mark, the fates of the good and bad seeds are not ascribed to separate good and evil agents; rather, the sower is the only agent in sight. It is the soil that determines what happens, not the conscious activity of any agent—although this pattern is, as mentioned, made somewhat inconsistent by the allegorizing of the seeds beside the path as the word devoured by Satan before it has a chance to grow.

In both Mark and 1QS, however, the dualism is deterministic in nature: The division between good and bad is not only absolute, it is preordained by prior circumstances. In 1QS, God has preordained the ways of both the "children of righteousness" and the "children of injustice"; in Mark, the soil is there prior to the sowing, and it is the pattern of the sower's casting about of the seed that determines what happens. Boring correctly notes that this absolute division into "insiders" and "outsiders" that we find in Mark is present also in other early Christian literature, especially the letters of Paul and his followers.[74] But the Pauline examples generally lack the deterministic outlook of Mark and 1QS: That is, although the division between insiders and outsiders is stark, it is not held to have been determined by either inalterable circumstances or the act of God. Indeed, insofar as Paul does make use of the concept of God's predestination, he does so in the conviction that this predestination will work for the good of all, not the condemnation of outsiders (see esp. Rom 11).

More similar to Mark and 1QS is the dualism of the Johannine literature: Consider, for instance, the stark division between the audience and the world (1 John 2:15-17) or the explanation of those who have departed from the community as "not of us" (1 John 2:29).

The point is this: The parable of the sower incorporates a dualistic logic of predestination that makes it difficult to read as parenesis. Whatever Jesus is saying to his audience in the story, it does not have anything to do with an exhortation for them to change their behavior. Commentators often seem unwilling to concede this point. Many writers, even those who recognize the logic of dualism and predestination at work in this parable, often claim that it

---

views as has sometimes been asserted: see Charlotte Hempel, "The *Treatise on the Two Spirits* and the Literary History of the *Rule of the Community*," in *Dualism in Qumran*, LSTS, ed. Géza G. Xeravits (London: T&T Clark, 2010), 102–20.

[74] Boring, *Mark*, 123, citing 1 Thess 4:12, 1 Cor 5:12-13, Col 4:5.

nevertheless serves a parenetic function. For instance, Moloney opines that, in the parable, "hearers of the word are challenged to make their response to the teaching of Jesus." The parable is a "call to decision."[75] This is in spite of the fact that Moloney does recognize the fatalistic attitude toward outsiders expressed in the "parable theory" of 4:11-12.[76] The sentiment is echoed by other writers: Klyne Snodgrass interprets the overall thrust of Mk 4 as a challenge to right hearing on the part of the audience.[77] Morna Hooker also views the parable as a call to decision for or against Jesus.[78] And even Boring, who places significant emphasis on the apocalyptic overtones of the chapter, allows that the section retains some parenetic potential.[79]

This interpretation of the parable of the sower is mistaken. There is no parenesis, in the sense of instruction or exhortation. The focus on the soil in the Markan parable makes it unsuitable for use as an exhortation to change one's life or attitude. The soil cannot change what it is. The specific configuration of Mark's agricultural imagery in the allegorical interpretation of the parable makes the fate of "the word" inevitable rather than contingent.

There are, of course, certain aspects of Mk 4 that do lend themselves to the parenetic interpretation. In particular, Jesus's repeated call for his audience to "listen," and to pay attention to their listening, would incline in this direction (Mk 4:3, 9, 23-4).[80] However, in the overall context of the Gospel, these exhortations to listen appear highly ironic. They are directed in the first place toward the disciples, "those around him with the Twelve" (4:10) and to the crowd. However, neither group, in the long run, will show any signs of having heard, let alone understood, Jesus's message. The disciples famously desert him during the passion narrative, and the crowd turns on him before Pilate, at the behest of the temple leaders. Therefore, the repeated calls to listen fall on deaf ears.

Mark's interpretation of the parable is both dualistic and fatalist, two traits that it shares with apocalyptic literature. These characteristics make it unlikely that the parable is to be interpreted parenetically.[81]

---

[75] Moloney, *Mark*, 88.
[76] Ibid., 90.
[77] Klyne Snodgrass, "Between Text and Sermon: Mark 4:1-20," *Int* 67, no. 3 (2013), 284–86.
[78] Hooker, *Saint Mark*, 120.
[79] Boring, *Mark*, 132.
[80] Tolbert, *Sowing*, 150.
[81] In agreement with the conclusion drawn by Joel Marcus, *The Mystery of the Kingdom of God*, SBLDS 90 (Atlanta, GA: Scholars Press, 1986), 60–2.

Then what is the actual point of the parable and its interpretation? The Markan Jesus himself says, "The sower sows the word" (4:14). The subject of the interpretation is the fate of the word, interpreted in apocalyptic terms. Jesus describes the fate of different types of people who hear the word. Sometimes, Satan takes the word away before it can take root. Other times, individuals fall away in times of trial. And in other cases, "the cares of the world and the love of wealth" (4:19) choke the word. But finally, sometimes the word does bear fruit, "thirty and sixty and a hundredfold" (4:20). We are justified in referring to Mark's interpretation of the parable as "apocalyptic" because it is dualist (the distinctions between the different types of bad seed are of no matter; the only the difference between good and bad is relevant) and fatalist (the "soil," that is, the nature of the hearers, is what determines the ultimate outcome).

Thus, the "teaching" of Jesus in the parable and its interpretation is not parenesis but rather a description of what inevitably happens to "the word." It is, in Morna Hooker's words, a "teaching about teaching."[82] In the midst of apparent failure, the "teaching," the word, succeeds against all appearances to the contrary. In fact, this is occurring in the context of the Gospel plot itself. That the parable and interpretation are actually a commentary on the events of the Gospel of Mark has been noticed by both Joel Marcus and Mary Ann Tolbert. Marcus writes,

> The sower's experience in the parable corresponds to that of Jesus throughout the Gospel. As the sower scatters seed everywhere, so Mark's Jesus teaches everyone (4:1-2, 33), even those who are vehemently opposed to him (6:6; 11:17; 14:49). The parable occurs in a section of the Gospel in which some people accept Jesus' word, while others reject it, just as in the parable one soil brings the seed to fruition, while others kill it.[83]

Tolbert goes further, arguing at length that the parable actually amounts to a typology of the different kinds of response to Jesus portrayed in the Gospel. Those from whom Satan plucks the word away, for instance, are Jesus's opponents, the scribes and Pharisees, who are hostile to Jesus from the start. Those who fall away on account of troubles and persecutions are actually

---

[82] Hooker, *Saint Mark*, 120.
[83] Marcus, *Mystery*, 38–9.

Jesus's disciples, who abandon Jesus once it becomes clear that his "way" leads to suffering and death. And those "choked" by the "weeds" of worldly concerns are those such as the rich young man (10:17-22), who let earthly desires and demands dictate their response to the word.[84]

Tolbert's typological proposal is mostly persuasive, with some caveats. In particular, she is able to adduce far clearer typological examples for the first two types of soil (representing Jesus's opponents and his disciples, respectively) than for the third (characterized by the rich young man and, dubiously, Herod). But she does correctly identify the fact that the parable and its interpretation are a commentary on the success and failure of the word as *fait accompli* and not parenesis meant to ensure the word's success. She recognizes the deterministic nature of what happens to the "seed":

> For the Gospel of Mark, it is simply the hard and painful truth that some people are in essence good and others are not. Those who are reveal their affiliation with God's good earth by the abundant fruit they bear; those who are far from God's kingdom risk becoming prey to Satan in their heard-hearted unfruitfulness. The seed, the word Jesus preaches, acts as the necessary catalyst to the process of transformation, but it can elicit growth only from good ground.[85]

It is recognition of the inevitability of what happens to the seed/word that allows us to understand the cryptic words of Jesus in the so-called parable theory, his statement that those close to him have received "the mystery of the kingdom of God."

On the subject of the "kingdom of God" itself, we may be brief. The subject has been studied in exhaustive detail since the beginning of critical New Testament scholarship as a discipline, and there is no need to examine it here. It is meant to call to mind the cluster of concepts, hopes, and predictions concerning God's rule over Israel, which are found in biblical and extrabiblical Jewish literature. In the classic statement of Norman Perrin, "The Kingdom of God is the power of God expressed in deeds; it is that which God does wherein it becomes evident that he is king."[86] The idea of God's kingship has

---

[84] Tolbert, *Sowing*, ch. 8, esp. 127–31, 153–61.
[85] Ibid., 163.
[86] Norman Perrin, *Rediscovering the Teaching of Jesus* (New York: Harper and Row, 1967), 55.

more to do with God's active involvement in world events than it does to do with a spatial notion of territory or kingdom; as Morna Hooker puts it, "The emphasis is on the rule of God, rather than on the territory where this rule is exercised."[87] Although there is no one stable conception of the "kingdom" that prevails in Jewish literature, there is no reason to adopt the view of Burton Mack that the "kingdom" in early Christian literature is an infinitely malleable symbol that each early Christian group manipulated freely as a self-referential cipher. Early Christian usage, including that in Mark, cannot be understood without an acknowledgment of its background in Second Temple Judaism—a background that Mack sidesteps with the technically true but rather pedantic insistence that the exact term "kingdom of God" does not appear in much Second Temple literature.[88] Even though the exact term does not often appear, the older view that the Gospels' concept of the "kingdom of God" has its background in a strand of traditional Jewish expectation about God's making known his rule over Israel in the world is still to be preferred.

A more difficult issue presents itself: What is the "mystery" (μυστήριον) about this kingdom, which "has been given" (δέδοται) to "those around him with the Twelve?"

Because the verb δέδοται, "it has been given," is in the perfect tense, it is tempting for the exegete to search backward in the Gospel searching for a prior point at which the "mystery" was disclosed to Jesus's inner circle. Adela Collins, for instance, suggests that the verb is meant to refer to previous episodes in the Gospel where the inner circle has already heard Jesus's teachings.[89] And Robert Stein sees the verb as referring to basically the entire chain of events in Jesus's ministry as portrayed in the Gospel up to this point.[90]

A better interpretation is that the "mystery" has been disclosed much closer at hand: in the parable of the sower itself. This does not exclude the possibility that the "mystery" also includes, more obliquely, the events of the rest of the Gospel, for, as we have seen, the parable functions as a kind

---

[87] Hooker, *Saint Mark*, 55.
[88] Mack, *Myth of Innocence*, 70–3. See also his "The Kingdom Sayings in Mark," *FF* 3, no. 1 (1987), 3–47. That the "kingdom of God" in Mark is to be related to the notion of God as king in Jewish literature is by far the scholarly consensus—see, e.g., Hooker, *Saint Mark*, 55–8; Moloney, *Gospel of Mark*, 49; Klaiber, *Das Markusevangelium*, 92; Collins, *Mark*, 154–5.
[89] Collins, *Mark*, 249. She cites 1:21-22, 39; 2:2, 13; 4:1-9.
[90] Stein, *Mark*, 207–9.

of commentary on the reception of Jesus's message throughout the Gospel. Nevertheless, the more direct reference of the "mystery" is to the immediately preceding parable.[91] This is demonstrated by the fact that Jesus contrasts the "insiders," his inner circle who have received the "mystery," with "those outside," for whom "everything comes in parables" (4:11). Thus, the parables are what distinguishes insiders from outsiders: Outsiders hear only the parables, while the "mystery," the actual *meaning* behind the parables, is given to the insiders. The only other candidate for what might be implied by Jesus's phrase "in parables" is the scene where Jesus is accused of being in league with Beelzebul (3:23). But since the most detailed use of parables is in this very chapter, immediately preceding 4:11-12 (although technically, Jesus has only spoken *one* parable in this scene so far), it is the parable of the sower itself that is most likely referred to when Jesus talks of how everything comes to outsiders "in parables."[92] This is made more likely by the fact that Jesus interprets the parable for the insiders while withholding the interpretation from "those outside."

As for the fact that the verb δέδοται occurs in the perfect tense, implying a past action with present results, Stein supplies the reason for this, which conflicts with his contention that the word refers to the entirety of Jesus's ministry: The verb is a "divine passive," that is, referring to an act of God.[93] As the careful reader will note, God's divine plan has been in view since the beginning of the Gospel, when an authoritative divine voice announces the arrival of John as forerunner by quoting the words of Scripture, and the "voice from heaven" declares Jesus to be Son of God. Therefore, we should view this "divine passive" not simply as referring to a specific event that has happened prior to this scene but rather as a declaration of an absolute, preordained state of affairs based on a divine decree. In this way, the use of δέδοται here is comparable to the verb often found introducing scriptural citations in the Gospels: γέγραπται, "it is written."[94]

---

[91] In agreement with Marcus, *Mystery*, 43–7.
[92] It is possible that Markan or pre-Markan redaction, placing 4:11-12 between the parable and its interpretation, is responsible for this discrepancy between the singular parable related by Jesus so far in chapter 4 and his reference on the other hand to "parables," plural, in 4:11. See Guelich, *Mark 1-8:26*, 199–200, and the references cited there.
[93] Stein, *Mark*, 207; cf. also Eckey, *Markusevangelium*, 139.
[94] See, e.g., Mk 14:27, Mt 4:6; Lk 2:23, Jn 8:17.

The "insiders" are Jesus's immediate audience in 4:10ff. But who are "those outside" (4:11)? The answer must be that "those outside" are the "crowd," those who hear the parables but are not privy to the interpretation that Jesus gives in private. Tolbert argues against this conclusion, on the grounds that "those outside" ought to have the same referent in 4:11-12 as it did in 3:31-35:

> In the immediately preceding episode "those outside" denoted Jesus' natural family, while those inside were his new family, people who do the will of God ... "Those outside" in 4:11, then, corresponds to that class of people who, for whatever reasons, do *not* do the will of God.[95]

But this interpretation overlooks the fact that the distinguishing feature of "those outside" in 4:11-12 is that they have heard everything "in parables." Therefore, it stands to reason that "those outside" must refer to persons who have heard Jesus speak in parables. In this particular scene, the only people who have heard the parables aside from those already identified as "insiders" are the crowd, which does not hear the interpretation of the parable of the sower. Thus, the crowd is indeed numbered among "those outside." The use of the spatial term "outside" to describe Jesus's family in 3:32 should not be confused with the use of the term in 4:11-12, which refers not only to physical space but also to an epistemological divide between those who understand because they have received the "mystery" and those who do not.

So the "mystery of the kingdom of God" is contained in the parable itself and by extension its interpretation. But what, exactly, does this "mystery" consist in? Recall that, formerly, we suggested that the interpretation of the parable of the sower allegorizes the parable so that it refers to the fate of "the word," that is, the message spread by Jesus in the Gospel. Further, as we also saw, the fate of the word as portrayed in the interpretation is more or less automatic: The fatalism of the interpretation suggests that the "seed" that represents the word is more or less predestined to its fate because of the various types of soil on which it happens to land. Therefore the "mystery" is precisely this: the fact that the word is, in many instances, doomed to failure. The "mystery of the kingdom of God" is the twofold recognition that, on the one hand, many people will inevitably reject Jesus's message, while, on the other hand, this failure is

---

[95] Tolbert, *Sowing*, 160.

only temporary and will not prevent the eventual arrival of the kingdom of God. Further, as Joel Marcus says, this state of affairs is the manifestation of Mark's apocalyptic cosmology, of a division between the old age of evil and the eschaton. At the latter, evil should disappear, but it has not:

> The new age has indeed arrived; the excellent yields pictured in 4:8, which *almost* strain credulity, bear witness to its advent for those who have eyes to see. Yet, contrary to what was commonly expected of the eschaton, evil has not evaporated from the universe. The bad soil, with its accompanying sterility and death, the signs of the old age, still exists.[96]

Marcus's interpretation focuses on the "cosmic" aspects of Markan apocalyptic as manifested in this chapter. But we ought to keep in mind that this cosmic conflict manifests in Mark's Gospel in the form of the reception and nonreception of the word. That is, the passage is fundamentally about Jesus's *teaching* and its fate. Therefore, an understanding of the passage is vital not just for understanding Markan eschatology but also for understanding Mark's presentation of Jesus as a teacher.

The fatalism that we saw in the interpretation of the parable reaches its apex in the quotation from Is 6:9-10 in Mk 4:12. This verse has incited a huge amount of debate, most likely because, on its face, it suggests something highly offensive to Christian theological sensibilities: that Jesus told parables precisely *in order that* [ἵνα] people would fail to understand his message. It is therefore not surprising that numerous commentators have sought for an interpretation that would avoid this conclusion. Most often, this is accomplished by arguing for alternative translations for ἵνα or μήποτε. However, as Craig Evans has demonstrated with references to numerous other scholars, it is highly unlikely that these conjunctions can be translated plausibly in a way that would remove the unwanted implication of the quotation. Therefore, the translations should be "in order that" and "lest," respectively—they are "final, or telic, in meaning."[97]

If Jesus is speaking his parables precisely so those outside the inner circle will not understand, this fits well with the interpretation of this passage that we have

---

[96] Marcus, *Mystery*, 49, emphasis original.
[97] Craig A. Evans, *To See and Not Perceive: Isaiah 6.9-10 in Early Jewish and Christian Interpretation*, JSOTSup 64 (Sheffield: Sheffield Academic Press, 1989), 91–9. The quotation is from page 95. On the final or purpose clause with ἵνα, see BDF §369.

been pursuing. Jesus "sows" the word. "Those outside" see only failure: Most people reject the word, and Jesus himself ends up on a Roman cross. But to "those inside," the interpretation of the parable shows that all is not lost, that the word will ultimately succeed in spite of all obstacles. The division between insiders and outsiders is furthermore given a scriptural warrant, which lends credence to the idea that the situation faced by the word is divinely ordained. Boring aptly compares the Markan answer to the apparent failure of the word to Paul's words in Romans 9-11: On the outside, it appears the word of God has failed because Israel has largely rejected the message of Jesus's followers (Rom 9:6), but a reading of Scripture suggests that this state of affairs was foretold beforehand and is merely temporary.[98]

What about the "parables" and sayings that follow the interpretation of the parable of the sower, contained in 4:21-32? If the parable of the sower and its interpretation emphasize the necessary fate of the word, and remark upon the fact that the word often goes unheeded, the sayings that follow emphasize that the word *will* succeed in time: Nothing is hidden except to be revealed; all will eventually come to light (4:21-23). The "mystery" will eventually be known widely, even though this is not happening at the present time. The additional parables in 4:26-32 lend additional support to this encouraging message. The seed is sown, and its growth is mysterious, but it will one day come to fruition and it will be time for the harvest. The mustard seed is small but eventually becomes great.

It is worth noting that the saying at 4:24 contradicts the overall emphasis of the passage on the preordained fate of the word. For it suggests that Jesus's audience can "hear" more or less well, depending on the "measure" that they give. This line of thought would lend itself more toward the parenetic interpretation of the parable of the sower, which we rejected above. But, also in accordance with what we said earlier, the overall storyline of the Gospel makes the saying highly ironic: Those being warned to pay close attention in 4:24 ultimately end up falling away: The disciples flee, and the crowds reject Jesus. No one from his inner circle save the women at the cross, who go unmentioned until the passion narrative (15:40-41), will remain, and even they will hurry away from the empty tomb in fear at the Gospel's

---

[98] Boring, *Mark*, 127.

conclusion. Therefore, given the ironic context of this saying, we cannot be particularly confident that the Gospel intends it as a straightforward encouragement to better listening. In fact, the juxtaposition of this saying with the actual outcome of Jesus's ministry—the crucifixion—renders the fatalism of the rest of this chapter all the more striking. Even Jesus's own words do not affect the "soil" into which the "word" is planted; he cannot force people to listen if their nature is fundamentally such that they are not meant to understand.

Our discussion of this passage has been long and involved. It is therefore worth making clear, in conclusion, the import of the exegesis of Mk 4 for our understanding of Jesus's teaching and, concomitantly, his authority.

First, we have learned that the "teaching" of Jesus in Mk 4 is about the kingdom of God or, more specifically, the "mystery" concerning it. But this teaching is not a summons to a new way of life or mode of behavior; it is not part of a "system of thought and action" (to refer once again to Vernon Robbins's preferred way of describing the activity of the Markan Jesus). There is little hint of exhortation; nothing is enjoined upon the hearer. For the teaching of Jesus here is ultimately a description: specifically, a description of the fate of the word and an assurance that the word will ultimately bear fruit. It is not a call to action but a message of comfort.[99] The only action called for is to take heart and persevere.

This "teaching" is undergirded with apocalyptic dualism and supported with reference to a quotation from Scripture (4:12). Both of these aspects of the passage indirectly emphasize the authority of Jesus still further. Raymond Brown's study of the meaning of "mystery" in the NT indicates many instances in Jewish literature where the term refers to divinely held knowledge that God grants to a chosen few.[100] As he puts it,

> It was recognized that occasionally God chooses to reveal his mysteries to men, and in the postexilic period there were individuals who professed to have been introduced in vision to the secrets of God.[101]

---

[99] Marcus, *Mystery*, 64.
[100] Raymond E. Brown, *The Semitic Background of the Term "Mystery" in the New Testament*, FBBS 21 (Philadelphia, PA: Fortress Press, 1968).
[101] Ibid., 7.

The purpose of the parable and its interpretation is to reveal a divinely ordained mystery: God keeps hidden from the majority of human beings the fact that the kingdom will arrive only amidst tribulation but has revealed it, through Jesus, to a select group. This knowledge does not have the character of something publicly available, open in principle to any observer. Rather, it can only be known if God, through Jesus, chooses to make it known. In this way, it is nothing like the teachings which Xenophon, Arrian, and Philostratus ascribe to their teacher-protagonists. In those cases, the knowledge imparted was discernable via human wisdom and reasoned argumentation. This is not the case in Mark. Despite the repeated invitations to "listen," the Markan Jesus forthrightly states in 4:11-12 that only a select few will, by divine decision, understand the truth about the coming kingdom.

Because Jesus is the one who does the revealing, his status as God's agent and his knowledge of the "mystery" that he imparts both enhance his authority. He is a figure with more-than-human knowledge, which he is able to pass on to whom he wishes. He further interprets Scripture along the same lines. Reading the passage as apocalyptic in tendency, we can plausibly suggest that Jesus, in his role as teacher, takes on the role of the "mediating" figure often found in Jewish apocalyptic writings. That is, in his capacity as interpreter of the parables and presenter of the "mystery of the kingdom of God," Jesus resembles, for example, the angelic figure who interprets the seer's visions in the book of Daniel (Dan 7:15-27, 8:15-26, 9:20-27, etc.). He teaches but only in the manner of a divine messenger interpreting strange and hidden things. His teaching is meant only for the ears of the few.

We note also that, although little in the way of plot development occurs in this chapter, the parables discourse nevertheless plays the critical role of setting up a key element of the Markan story: the theme of the misunderstanding of the disciples and their eventual falling away from him when Jesus is arrested. The contents of chapter 4, particularly Jesus's description of his inner circle as those to whom the "mystery" of the kingdom has been given, would lead the reader to expect that the disciples will faithfully learn their master's teachings. That this does not prove to be the case is one of the most distinctive features of Mark's Gospel. In any event, it is here that the setup occurs for the disciples' repeated misunderstandings that follow, such as their incomprehension of the feeding miracles and their squabbles over authority and prestige. In light of these later passages, the categorization of the disciples as privileged insiders can only be seen as ironic.

Mk 4 is also an extremely important chapter with respect to the third purpose suggested above for the Gospel's portrayal of Jesus's teaching: namely, the purpose of speaking to the concerns of the Gospel's audience. Here we move beyond the strictly intratextual, literary analysis of the text and preview the discussion of the text's relationship to its historical context, which will be addressed in the conclusion. Here, it suffices to say that the combination of secrecy and irony in the chapter means that the primary beneficiaries of Jesus's teaching in parables are the audience of the Gospel, rather than the characters in the story. The "outsiders" are fated not to understand, and even the "insiders" will be portrayed as fair-weather friends who fall away in the time of persecution that is Jesus's arrest and execution. Thus, there is no one left to understand Jesus's message except the last group that overhears his teaching: the audience. As Burton Mack observes,

> Those who are to be instructed by Jesus' teaching are not those to whom he speaks in the story, but those who read the story in Mark's time. Mark addressed his readers by attributing his message to Jesus and letting them overhear Jesus' instruction to others.[102]

From this point on in the Gospel, this third purpose of instructing the Gospel audience will play an increasingly important role in Mark's depiction of Jesus's teaching.

A Brief Note on Mk 7:1-23

Mk 7:1-23, the debate over handwashing, seems to cut against most of the tendencies we have observed so far in Mark's portrayal of Jesus's teaching. In the rest of the passages surveyed so far, we have noted Mark's tendency to avoid clear and direct presentation of the actual content of Jesus's teaching in favor of emphasizing his authority. Even when, as in Mk 4, the actual content of the teaching was presented, it was veiled in mystery and irony. This is at first

---

[102] Mack, *Myth of Innocence*, 169.

glance not the case in 7:1-23, which presents a debate between Jesus and the Pharisees on the issue of handwashing. The issue and the arguments are stated forthrightly.

It is a matter of great debate what the takeaway from Jesus's comments to the Pharisees and to his disciples is supposed to be. Traditionally, Mark's parenthetical comment that "Thus he cleansed all foods" (7:19) has been taken to mean that the Markan Jesus is taking the radical step of annulling parts of the Mosaic Law pertaining to food.[103] Recently, however, Daniel Boyarin has forcefully argued that this is not the case. Rather, according to Boyarin, Jesus opposes the Pharisaic innovation of observing "the traditions of the elders" in addition to the written Torah. Jesus's complaint against the Pharisees, Boyarin argues, is that the Pharisees have overextended the laws of purity by ruling that a person can be made unclean by eating foods that have come into contact with persons in a state of impurity:

> According to the Talmud itself, it was the Rabbis (or the legendary Pharisees) who innovated the washing of the hands before meals—which implies that the ingesting of defiled or polluted foods renders one impure. It was thus against those pharisaic innovations, which they are trying to foist on his disciples—that Jesus railed, and not against the keeping of kosher at all.[104]

Regardless of whether this interpretation is correct or not, we do need to ask how this passage fits in with the argument advanced so far.[105] To this point, Jesus's teaching, or mention of it, has been employed in Mark for purposes that are, paradoxically, nondidactic: Jesus's teaching in the Capernaum synagogue scene, the controversies, and the parables chapter is employed not to present

---

[103] E.g., Marcus, *Mark 1-8*, 457–8; Boring, *Mark*, 202–3; Hooker, *Saint Mark*, 179–80; Collins, *Mark*, 356.

[104] Daniel Boyarin, *The Jewish Gospels: The Story of the Jewish Christ* (New York: New Press, 2012), 118.

[105] As much of a tour de force as Boyarin's argument is, the majority opinion (that Mark's Jesus rejects kashrut) is to be preferred. The fact that Matthew (whose concern for matters of Torah interpretation is well known) deletes the note that Jesus "cleansed all foods" (cf. Matt 15:17) suggests that Matthew, at least, believed that Mark's Jesus was abrogating the Law and deleted that parenthetical because of his disagreement with this viewpoint. More importantly, in Mk 7:21-23, "what goes in" is contrasted not with "what comes out" in the sense of the biblical regulations of Torah (i.e., bodily emissions) but with moral failings. One would expect, if Boyarin's interpretation were correct, that "what goes out" would be more in line with the biblical laws—that is, if Jesus were upholding a conservative interpretation of Torah that rejected the "traditions of the elders," then the contrast would be between food and internal bodily things, not food and various sins.

a clear idea of what Jesus taught but to emphasize his authority and to relate that characterization to the Gospel's plot. Here, in 7:1-23, by contrast, we seem to have a specific teaching of Jesus on a particular matter: the interpretation of the laws of kashrut.

It is not as though this passage is completely bereft of the themes we have examined so far: M. Eugene Boring, in particular, has made a case that this episode is as invested in the issue of Jesus's authority as other parts of Mark's Gospel.[106] That said, noting the more straightforward, didactic approach of 7:1-23, we are not searching for a single interpretive key that will unlock the meaning of *every* passage in Mark that has to do with Jesus's teaching. Rather, we are on the lookout for the dominant *tendencies* contained in the material. The presence of a passage such as 7:1-23 does not turn Jesus into a straightforward teacher passing along ethical instruction; it does not nullify the patterns we have previously observed. Were numerous passages like this to occur, it might be necessary to call our working theory into question. But as it stands, 7:1-23 appears to be the exception, rather than the rule: a relatively rare example of a Markan teaching passage where Jesus does, in fact, impart a teaching, in this case about the interpretation of Torah, to the audience within the story, in the manner of a more usual teaching figure in Greco-Roman literature.

---

[106] Boring, *Mark*, 201–4.

3

Teaching and Authority in the Second Half of Mark

This chapter continues where the previous one left off, moving forward with our study of passages concerning Jesus's teaching and his authority. As we proceed, we will continue to note the same patterns at work in Mark's portrayal of Jesus's teaching: As in the first half of the Gospel, Mark deploys Jesus's teaching in order to advance the plot, characterize Jesus as authoritative, and address the Gospel audience.

"He Said This Plainly": The Passion Predictions

After the discussion of handwashing in Mk 7:1-23, which we briefly touched on at the end of the last chapter, our next mention of Jesus's "teaching" comes at a surprising point: the first passion prediction (8:31). The second such prediction (9:31) is also described as a "teaching." The third prediction is not described specifically as a teaching, but this can likely be inferred from the fact that the first two are called as such. We may discuss all three passion predictions and their "teaching" as a group.

The passion predictions have often been interpreted as a key weapon with which Mark wages a Christological battle with "opponents" in the community to which the Gospel is written. The most popular such interpretation suggests that Mark wants to emphasize Jesus's suffering and death, over and against Christologies that focus more on Jesus's exalted messianic status or wonder-working. In Theodore Weeden's influential formulation of this view, the Gospel is written to combat a "divine man" Christology, due to the evangelist's focus on the critical importance of Jesus's suffering and death.[1] Etienne Trocmé, too, writes that Mark criticizes an inadequate presentation of the Gospel that does not pay sufficient attention to Jesus's passion.[2]

The various theories of Christological conflict lying behind the Gospel, and the passion predictions in particular, tend to focus on how Mark interprets various Christological *titles*: in particular, how Mark understands the proclamation that Jesus is Messiah. Less often remarked upon is the *way* in which the passion predictions present Mark's Christology: the passion predictions are portrayed as part of Jesus's *teaching*. This suggests that we ought to interpret them in light of the overall portrayal of "teaching" in Mark. Accordingly, we ought also to look for hints that issues surrounding Jesus's authority are being referred to here.

The first passion prediction has as its context Peter's confession of Jesus's messianic identity at Caesarea Philippi (8:27-30). In response to Jesus's question about who people say that he is, the disciples offer various responses: People say that he is Elijah, or John the Baptist, or a prophet. When Jesus presses the question by asking who *they* think he is, Peter speaks on behalf of the group: Jesus is the Messiah. Jesus commands him to be silent about this. Then we read the first passion prediction:

> Then he began to teach them that it was necessary (δεῖ) for the Son of Humanity to suffer many things, and to be rejected by the elders, the high priests, and the scribes, and to be killed, and after three days to rise again (ἀναστῆναι). *He said this plainly* (παρρησίᾳ). (8:31-32, emphasis added).

Two significant features stand out. First of all, it is "necessary" for all these things to happen as Jesus says. Second, and critically, Jesus speaks this "plainly"—or, alternately, "boldly" or "openly."

That it is "necessary" for the Son of Humanity to suffer, die, and rise refers to the fact that it has been preordained or determined by God. The fact that Jesus knows God's divine plan lends further support to his authority—that is, the idea that he is God's specially chosen agent. For if he were not such an agent, how could he know that it was "necessary" for all this to take place?

---

[1] Theodore J. Weeden, *Mark: Traditions in Conflict* (Philadelphia, PA: Fortress, 1979).
[2] Etienne Trocmé, *La formation de l'évangile selon Marc*, Études d'histoire et de philosophie religieuses 57 (Paris: Presses Universitaires de France, 1963), 98.

Jesus is one who knows "divine things" or "the things of God" (τά τοῦ θεοῦ, cf. 8:33), even as others, even his followers, know only "human things." Gundry points, as well, to the authority and power associated with predicting one's own death as attested in Greco-Roman literature.[3]

The notion of "necessity" for these events puts one in mind of the futures foretold in apocalyptic literature.[4] Consider, for example, the later use of δεῖ in the Revelation of John:

> The revelation of Jesus Christ, which God gave him to show his slaves the things which must soon take place (ἃ δεῖ γενέσθαι ἐν τάχει). (Rev 1:1)
>
> And he said to me, "These words are trustworthy and true, and the Lord God of the spirits of the prophets sent his angel to show his slaves the things which must soon take place. (Rev 22:6)

The implication here is that all the events described in the visions, terrible as they are, take place according to a divine plan in which all things are working toward God's purposes. In Mark, use of δεῖ with this particular sense is to be found in Mk 13, the "little apocalypse," which leans heavily on the notion of sufferings and tribulations as part of a divine plan (13:7, 10, 14). Although we will discuss Mk 13 in greater detail later in this chapter, it suffices to say here that we find in Mk 13 the notion of divinely ordained catastrophe as a prelude to divine vindication. The disciples want to know what the signs will be that the end has come (13:4), and Jesus responds by enumerating the various terrible events that "must" occur before the coming of the Son of Humanity (13:26-27). In our current passage, Mk 8:31-32, we may read δεῖ in the same way. The first passion prediction shows what "must" take place in Jesus's lifetime, just as the events described in Mk 13 are in accordance with the same divine plan, except that they describe a later stage, the coming of the Son of Humanity.

Mark leans much less strongly on another use of δεῖ, found elsewhere in the New Testament: the use of δεῖ to describe a necessity preordained by the words of Scripture. In Matthew, for example, Jesus says that his arrest occurs in

---

[3] Robert Gundry, *Mark: A Commentary on His Apology for the Cross* (Grand Rapids, MI: 1993), 428.
[4] Joel Marcus, *Mark 8-16: A New Translation with Commentary*, Anchor Bible 27A (New Haven, CT: Yale University Press, 2009), 613; Joachim Gnilka, *Das Evangelium nach Markus*, vol. 2. Evangelisch-Katholischer Kommentar zum Neuen Testament (Züruck: Benziger, 1978), 6: "In apokalyptischen Texten bezeichnet δεῖ das notwendige Eintreffen jener Ereignisse, die zum Ablauf des Endzeitgeschehens gehören."

accordance with scriptural witness (Matt 26:54). In Luke, we find the incident where Jesus tells his followers to take swords with them when they leave on the journey that will result in Jesus's arrest so that Scripture will be appropriately fulfilled (Lk 22:36-38). Indeed, for Luke, fulfillment of Scripture is a major reason why Jesus suffers and dies the way he does:

> And he said to them, "These are the words which I spoke to you when I was still with you, that it was necessary (δεῖ) for all the things written about me in the law of Moses and in the prophets and psalms to be fulfilled." Then he opened their minds to understand the scriptures. And he said to them, "Thus it is written that the Messiah should suffer and be raised on the third day, and that repentance leading to the forgiveness of sins should be proclaimed in his name to all the nations." (Lk 24:44-47)

This use of δεῖ is also found in John and Acts.[5]

Mark, on the other hand, does not make use of δεῖ in this way, in spite of the fact that Scripture is constantly in the background of the Gospel. There is perhaps an allusion to this kind of thinking at the beginning of the Gospel: Mark says that the events of the Gospel take place in accordance with Scripture when "beginning of the gospel of Jesus Christ" is said to take place "just as it says in Isaiah the prophet" (Mk 1:1). But for the most part, the specific use of δεῖ to use corroborate the divine plan with the words of Scripture does not occur. The "necessity" that Mark applies to Jesus's predictions is therefore of a more generalized nature, more akin to the predictions found in apocalyptic literature than to early Christian scriptural interpretation. The use of Scripture to prove the "necessity" of events such as Jesus's death on the cross appears not to have been one of Mark's major preoccupations. This is an interesting detail, considering that we know from other early Christian texts—think of 1 Cor 15—that groups devoted to Jesus were already, before Mark's time, convinced that Jesus's life and death had happened in accordance with Scripture. Perhaps the Gospel avoids direct appeal to Scripture because it focuses more on the authority of Jesus as messenger and interpreter of God's will, rather than on proving via an external authority (Scripture) that Jesus has such an authority. The point for Mark is Jesus's self-claim to extraordinary status.

---

[5] I.e., Jn 12:34, 20:9; Acts 1:16; 17:2-3.

The next important aspect of these verses is that Jesus is said to predict all these things παρρησίᾳ. We could translate this as "outspokenly," "plainly," "clearly," or "boldly," among several possibilities. The word can be used to denote a boldness of speech or an unwillingness to hold back that which might offend or create danger: Demosthenes, in his *Second Philippic*, tells his audience that he "will speak the truth with boldness [παρρησίας] to you and will not hold back [ἀποκρύψομαι]" (Demosth. 6.31, my translation).[6] In Acts, Peter and John display παρρησία when they are brought before the Jewish leaders in Jerusalem (4:13).

The word can also be used in the sense of a boldness as opposed to timidity felt out of a lack of confidence in the strength of one's words or deeds. This is the sense in which we find it in in 2 Cor 3:12: "Having such a hope, we act with much boldness [πολλῇ παρρησίᾳ]." It is also used in this way in Peter's speech to the assembled people of Jerusalem in Acts 2:29.

However, neither of these senses of παρρησία particularly fits Jesus's situation in Mk 8:31-32. Jesus is apparently alone with his disciples, so there is no hint that Jesus is risking the wrath of authorities by speaking as he does about his upcoming suffering, death, and resurrection. The other sense, that in which "boldness" is opposed to timidity or fearfulness, makes slightly more sense: On such an interpretation, Jesus's boldness or openness about his upcoming fate would be contrasted with the fearfulness of the disciples, who do not want to accept that such things must happen to Jesus. This interpretation also seems unlikely, though. For if this were the case, one would expect Jesus's "boldness" to follow from the disciples' fearfulness, rather than to be the cause of it. That is, the disciples do not become reluctant and fearful about what will happen in Jerusalem until Jesus predicts the events for them. Jesus's παρρησία here is prompted not by the disciples' fear but by Peter's declaration that Jesus is the Messiah. And ironically, he speaks with παρρησία immediately after warning the disciples not to tell anyone that he is the Messiah, despite the fact that Peter has recognized this (8:30).[7]

---

[6] BADG, s.v. "παρρησία, ας, ἡ."
[7] This being said, Eugene Boring (*Mark: A Commentary*. New Testament Library [Louisville, KY: Westminster John Knox, 2006], 241) may be correct when he says that "Mark wants to portray Jesus as a model of those who forthrightly testify to the Christian faith in public rather than 'being ashamed'" (he refers to Mk 8:38).

A better interpretation is that Jesus's παρρησία is meant to contrast with *his own* behavior earlier in the Gospel: that is, with the essential secrecy of what he has been teaching his disciples. We already saw that, earlier in the Gospel, Jesus's teaching has gone mostly unremarked upon. It is not reported directly much, if at all, even to the audience. And even at the moments when his teaching might be made clear, such as when he interprets the parables in chapter 4, what he teaches is shrouded in secrecy: He teaches "the mystery of the kingdom of God" (4:11), which is never described directly but must, as we saw in our analysis in the previous chapter, be inferred from the content of the Gospel. Therefore, Jesus's earlier teaching has been secretive and mysterious; his "teaching" in the first passion prediction is, by contrast, open and clear: We might then translate παρρησία, then, as "plainly," as in the translation above. "Die Parrhesia ist die Offenheit in der Rede, die nichts verschweigt oder verhüllt."[8]

This is the first time in the Gospel, then, that Jesus has taught "clearly": Not only is what he is trying to say made plain to both the other characters (i.e., the disciples) and the Gospel audience, but we are actually told as much by the narrator: "He said this plainly."

The "plainly" refers not just to the manner of Jesus's teaching but also to the *content* of his teaching: that is, his suffering, death, and resurrection. For the first time, it becomes clear *what* Jesus has been teaching all along: that is, his own identity and destiny.

Looking back on our exegesis so far, we see this to be the case. In the Capernaum synagogue scene in 1:21-28, we concluded that the most salient result of Jesus's teaching in his opening appearance was that his authority as God's agent was recognized, both by the audience and by his hearers within the story. That scene also set up the clash between Jesus and the established leadership, by negatively contrasting the authority of Jesus with that of "the scribes." Further on, we saw that the parables discourse in Mk 4 positioned Jesus as an inspired messenger, equivalent to an angelic mediator interpreting a seer's visions in apocalyptic literature such as the later chapters of the book of Daniel. This, too, had the effect of enhancing Jesus's authority, for he is depicted

---

[8] Gnilka, *Markus*, vol. 2, 16.

as someone who knows "the mystery of the kingdom of God" and pronounces in absolute terms who receives it and who does not. He predicts the dualistic division of hearers into "insiders" and "outsiders." Finally, we also saw, in the brief discussion of the passages describing the mission of the disciples, how Jesus's authority was such that he was able to pass it along to his followers and send them out to proclaim to the kingdom and to challenge the rule of the unclean spirits over the people.

Here, beginning with the first passion prediction, we find for the first time a development of this focus on authority as part of Jesus's identity. Specifically, this identity is now qualified by a new prediction: the necessity of Jesus's suffering, death, and resurrection. Up until now, the theme of Jesus's eventual death has only been hinted at: in the murmurings of the Pharisees and Herodians, for example (3:6), or the analogy of the bridegroom, with its veiled reference to Jesus's death (2:19-20).[9] But in the first passion prediction, both the disciples and the Gospel audience have it straight from the mouth of Jesus himself that he must suffer, die, and rise. Because of the introduction of this new element to the plot, we are justified in thinking that this episode represents a major turning point in the Gospel.[10]

That said, it is *not* the case, as Weeden and others have thought, that the passion predictions represent a polemic against or rebuke of a different Christology. In particular, we should reject completely Weeden's view that turn to focus on Jesus's passion beginning in this chapter represents a polemic against a "divine man" Christology held by the disciples.[11] It is instead better to focus on Jesus's "teaching" here as a *development* of what has gone before, rather than a rebuke or correction of it.

While others have criticized "corrective Christology" approaches by pointing to Markan texts inconsistent with such interpretations, we take a different approach here, offering instead a coherent approach to Mark's

---

[9] This is also noted by Stein, *Mark*, 401.
[10] Cf. Darrell Bock, *Mark*. New Cambridge Bible Commentary (Cambridge: Cambridge University Press, 2015), 240: "This scene is the pivot in Mark's Gospel."
[11] Weeden's position is summarized in his article "The Heresy that Necessitated Mark's Gospel," reprinted in William R. Telford, ed., *The Interpretation of Mark*, 2nd ed., Studies in New Testament Interpretation (Edinburgh: T&T Clark, 1995), 89–104. See also the criticisms of "corrective Christology" approaches in Jack Dean Kingsbury, *The Christology of Mark's Gospel* (Philadelphia, PA: Fortress Press, 1983), 25–45.

portrayal of Jesus that unites the material about Jesus's suffering and death with the earlier teachings and miracles found in Mk 1-7.[12]

The problem with seeing the theme of Jesus's suffering, death, and resurrection as a corrective to a mistaken Christology is that such views tend to think of the theme of a suffering and dying Jesus as *antithetical* in some sense to the Christology implied by the earlier parts of the gospel, especially Jesus's miracles. That is, on such views, the authority that Jesus has displayed in the Gospel is challenged, all of a sudden, by the introduction of the passion themes. Gundry, in his commentary, has described this apparent dichotomy as the central driving conflict of Markan studies over the last century: The problem has been how to reconcile what commentators have seen as a "theology of glory," inherent especially in the miracles, with a "theology of suffering."[13] Whether or not this question has been as dominant as Gundry claims is open to debate, but it is certainly the case that many studies of Markan Christology have seen a disjunction between the material in the Gospel up to chapter 8 and the theme of Jesus as suffering and dying Messiah, which takes center stage in the second half of Mark.

But we ought to reject a dichotomy between Jesus's authoritative acts in Mk 1-7 and his passion in the second half of the Gospel. To put it plainly, the categories of "theology of glory" and "theology of suffering" are misleading when placed in opposition to each other. On this, we agree here with Gundry's rejection of the dichotomy, though for different reasons than he does.

To understand what is at work in the sudden revelation of Jesus's impending death in Mk 8:31-32, we need to recognize that what we find in the passage is a continuation of the theme of Jesus's *authority*. And once again, as in 1:21-28 and ch. 4, we find that Jesus's *teaching* is the vehicle for characterizing Jesus as someone who possesses this authority. In this way, we should speak not of two poles of "glory" and "suffering" but a single Christological idea, that of Jesus's authority, which unites them both. The Gospel presents Jesus as possessing authority throughout his life, into death, and beyond, even in his

---

[12] Problems with the view that Jesus's disciples embody a defective Christology are noted by Stein, *Mark*, 26-32; and Suzanne Watts Henderson, *Christology and Discipleship in the Gospel of Mark*, SNTSMS 135 (Cambridge, UK: Cambridge University Press, 2006), 7–15.
[13] Gundry, *Mark*, 2.

darkest moments. The passion predictions are where the Gospel first asserts the indissolubility of Jesus's authority even in face of his approaching death.

Jesus "teaches" here that he will suffer and die. But he also teaches that he will *rise*. This is what links the passion predictions with the earlier theme of Jesus's authority and his status as God's agent. All three of the passion predictions include the point that Jesus will rise from the dead after three days (8:31; 9:31; 10:34). It is true that the passion predictions devote increasingly more attention to detailing Jesus's suffering and death. But it is also the case that this suffering and death are not the last word. Jesus will rise from the dead. Even more, the suffering and death that are, by extension, foretold for his followers will also be followed by their vindication.

Each passion prediction is followed by instructions to Jesus's disciples, which enjoin a certain kind of behavior upon them. As analyzed by Vernon Robbins, the passion predictions each consist of a "three-step progression": First, the scene between Jesus and his disciples is established; second, Jesus predicts his suffering, death, and resurrection; and third, he summons his disciples to a new form of behavior as an implication of the "way" that Jesus is traveling to the cross.[14] This behavior is exemplified by taking up one's cross (8:34), becoming a servant (9:35), and sharing in the "cup" and "baptism" of Jesus's suffering and death (10:38-39), in contrast to the imperious rule of authorities among the "Gentiles" (10:42-45).

But amidst Jesus's calls to humility and acceptance of a suffering servant's path, we also find clear indications that this is not the end of the story for Jesus or his disciples. First of all, of course, there is the detail we have already noted: that Jesus's death will be followed by his resurrection. Second, we find, in the midst of this section of the Gospel, Jesus's promise of reward for his faithful followers, both now and in the age to come, which follows the saying about the difficulty the rich person faces in entering the kingdom of God:

> Peter began to say to him, "See, we have left everything and followed you." Jesus said, "Truly, I say to you, there is no one who has left house or brothers or sisters or mother or father or children or fields for my sake and the sake of the gospel, who will not receive a hundredfold, now in the present time,

---

[14] Vernon K. Robbins, *Jesus the Teacher: A Socio-Rhetorical Interpretation of Mark* (1984. Reprint, Minneapolis, MN: Fortress Press, 2009), 22–5.

houses and brothers and sisters and mothers and children and fields—with persecutions—and in the age to come, eternal life. But many of the first will be last, and many of the last will be first." (10:28-31)

While this passage follows not directly upon one of the passion predictions, but rather after Jesus's encounter with the rich young man (10:17-27), it nevertheless sets personal sacrifice in the here and now—including being persecuted, as foretold in the passion predictions and sayings about discipleship—against the possibility of reward, both now and in the future. This passage contradicts an interpretation of this section, which suggests that the primary purpose of the Gospel from here on out is to prepare disciples (and the audience) for the inevitability of suffering. This is certainly a part of it, but Mark's Jesus does not neglect to remind his hearers that suffering now will be followed by vindication later: Jesus himself will rise after three days, and his followers will receive "hundredfold" rewards and eternal life.

Nor is it only 10:28-31 that places present suffering alongside future vindication. The first passion prediction and the saying about taking up one's cross are followed by two sayings concerning the eschatological future. In 8:38, Jesus warns that the Son of Humanity will, at the judgment, "be ashamed" (ἐπαισχυνθήσεται) of those who are ashamed of him in this generation. The implication is that there are some, at least, who will be vindicated when the Son of Humanity comes because they were *not* ashamed "of me and of my words," as Jesus puts it.[15]

Further, Jesus also says, "Truly, I say to you that there are some standing here who will not taste death until they see the kingdom of God having come in power." When, exactly, they will "see" the kingdom having come in power is unclear. It could be a saying of the historical Jesus.[16] Or it could refer to an event beyond the bounds of the Gospel, that is, the final return of Jesus in the audience's own time.[17] Less likely is the notion that it refers to the

---

[15] See, for comparison, the positive affirmations in the Matthean and Lukan versions of the saying (Matt 10:32-33; Lk 12:8-10), as noted by Morna Hooker, *The Gospel According to Saint Mark*. Black's New Testament Commentaries. 1991. Reprint (Grand Rapids, MI: Baker Academic, 2011), 210.
[16] Hooker, *Saint Mark*, 211–13.
[17] Marcus, *Mark 8-16*, 630; Rudolf Bultmann, *History of the Synoptic Tradition*, trans. John Marsh (Oxford: Basil Blackwell, 1972), 121.

transfiguration,[18] or that it refers to the kingdom already being present in Jesus's ministry as it has unfolded in the Gospel so far.[19] The most plausible view is that it refers to an event beyond the bounds of the Gospel narrative: that is, the coming of the Son of Humanity at the parousia.[20]

Finally, we should recognize that the passion predictions do not, contrary to the way they are sometimes portrayed, change the entire tone of the Gospel. It is not as though Jesus suddenly announces his passion and then transforms immediately into a passive victim or thoroughly humble servant beginning in Mk 8. To the contrary, the image of Jesus we have seen earlier of an authoritative teacher who does extraordinary deeds continues essentially until Jesus's arrest—and even beyond that point, Jesus boldly confronts the religious authorities at his trial, and marvelous signs and portents attend the crucifixion itself. Jesus will conclude this section of the Gospel by healing a blind man (10:46-52). He will continue to display prodigious knowledge of the future, including the extraordinary apocalyptic discourse of Mk 13. He will silence all challengers to his authority in the temple and continue to leave the crowds spellbound with his teaching. We need not to overstate the degree to which the passion predictions change the persona of the Markan Jesus.

The point being made here is *not* that the passion predictions do not make the suffering and death of Jesus a central part of Mark's Gospel. They clearly do. The point, rather, is that despite this new dimension of Jesus's ministry, and the meaning of the "way" he embodies, which the passion introduces, the fact that Jesus is portrayed as a suffering and dying Messiah does not contradict the image of Jesus as a figure of divinely given authority and stature developed in the first seven chapters of Mark. There is no sudden reversal in Mark's portrayal of Jesus here, nor does anything that happens in the rest of the Gospel weaken the basic thrust of Mark's Christological portrayal: Jesus is God's authoritative agent who teaches with truth and performs mighty deeds. Jesus is a figure of authority before the passion predictions, and he will remain one after them.

It is clear, then, that in the passion predictions, the Gospel continues to fulfill the first of the aims we have seen at work in the Markan portrayal of

---

[18] Bruce D. Chilton, "The Transfiguration: Dominical Assurance and Apostolic Vision," *New Testament Studies* 27, no. 1 (October 1980), 115–24.
[19] C. H. Dodd, *The Parables of the Kingdom* (Glasgow: Collins, 1961), 43.
[20] Adela Collins, *Mark* Hermeneia (Minneapolis, MN: Fortress Press, 2007), 413.

Jesus's teaching: the depiction and exaltation of Jesus's authority as God's agent. It also hardly needs to be said that the three predictions also advance the Gospel's storyline (the second of the three aims), for it is at the beginning of the section of passion predictions that Jesus turns his attention toward the journey to Jerusalem, foreshadowing the Gospel's denouement. The entire section is, as we mentioned, a turning point in the Gospel by the reckoning of almost all scholars.

But most of all, we find compelling evidence for another claim that we made in the introduction: that, in Mark, attention is frequently paid to the instruction, not of the characters in the narrative but of the Gospel audience. This has of course been a part of the Markan Jesus's "teaching" from the beginning, as we have already seen. But here especially, the audience, rather than the characters who hear Jesus's "teaching," becomes the intended recipients.

That this is so is confirmed by the fact that the disciples continually misunderstand, and ultimately reject, what Jesus teaches here. Through all Jesus's warnings about the necessity of suffering, and all of his lessons about the importance of humility and leading as though one were a servant, the disciples fail to heed Jesus's teaching. As Vernon Robbins perceptively notes, this is the feature that makes Mark particularly stand out from other Greco-Roman narratives about itinerant teachers. An audience familiar with such narratives would expect, as a generic convention, that the teacher's students would be perceptive of their master's instruction and profit by it. But in Mark, the expectation is thwarted: Jesus teaches, but the disciples never understand. They flee from the scene of Jesus's arrest and, after Peter's threefold denial of Jesus, are never seen again.[21]

If the disciples fail to respond correctly to Jesus's teaching, then it is not an unreasonable surmise that it is for the benefit of the *audience* that this teaching is presented. To recall again Burton Mack's words concerning Mk 4 and apply them to a different part of the Gospel, the Markan audience "overhears" Jesus speaking to his disciples and is expected to absorb the teaching being presented.[22] Or, in Robert Fowler's terms, Jesus's teaching in the passion

---

[21] Robbins, *Jesus the Teacher*, 204–9.
[22] Burton Mack, *A Myth of Innocence: Mark and Christian Origins* (Philadelphia, PA: Fortress Press, 1988), 169.

predictions operates on the level of the discourse rather than the story, for it speaks to the implied reader rather than to Jesus's actual hearers in Mark.[23] This goes not only for Jesus's teaching itself but also for the portrayal of the disciples' negative response to it. The failure of the disciples in itself constitutes an object lesson for the audience, an example of how *not* to act in their own time toward Jesus and the claims made about his authority. As Robbins shrewdly recognizes, the failure of the disciples leaves the conclusion of the story, so to speak, in the audience's hands: How will *they* respond to Jesus? "Since no one in Mark's gospel fully adopts the system of thought and action taught and enacted by Jesus, the reader is the object of a special summons to perpetuate the system of thought and action 'to all the nations for the sake of Jesus and the gospel.'"[24]

It is this section of the Gospel, more than any other, which lends credence to Robbins's repeated insistence that Jesus in Mark teaches a "system of thought and action." As discussed in the introduction and in the previous chapter, this is an incorrect summation of most of the Gospel's content. At no point in Mk 1-7 did Jesus teach anything approximating a "system" that could be easily summarized, let alone adopted as a way of life. However, in the three passion predictions, and particularly in the sayings on discipleship that follow them, we *do* begin to see the outline of a kind of "program" enjoined upon Jesus's disciples, a certain way of living and acting toward others in the community. Here, then, lies the small amount of truth that lies behind Robbins's characterization of Jesus's "system of thought and action." It is here, *and only here*, in the Gospel that we find anything of the sort. Therefore, while we reject this characterization for most of the Gospel, Robbins's thesis may have some validity when applied to this particular section of Mark.

The passion predictions, then, support the thesis advanced so far: that the Gospel of Mark portrays the teaching of Jesus in such a manner as to advance the storyline, develop Jesus's authority, and speak to the Gospel audience.

---

[23] Robert M. Fowler, *Let the Reader Understand: Reader-Response Criticism and the Gospel of Mark* (Minneapolis, MN: Fortress Press, 1991), 249: "No uptake is ever demonstrated at the level of the story for any of Jesus' predictions of his death or resurrection. Such predictions are efficacious only for the reader."

[24] Robbins, *Jesus the Teacher*, 208–9.

Teaching and Proclamation in the Temple

Like the "parables chapter" of Mk 4, the incident of Jesus's disruption in the Temple (11:15-19) has generated a significant amount of scholarly discussion. Also like the parables chapter, much turmoil has resulted from the confusion of historical issues with exegetical ones. Just as, with Mk 4, scholars have often focused on what relation the "teaching in parables" and the "parable theory" have to the "historical Jesus," so the temple incident has often been considered a problem primarily for historical Jesus studies rather than Markan exegesis. However, our focus here will be on what the Gospel of Mark intends by the narration of this episode.[25]

We shall consider the temple incident both by itself as well as in relation to the entire complex of events occurring in Jerusalem in this portion of the Gospel. For it will be argued here that the aim of Mark's inclusion of the temple incident becomes clearer by an examination of the surrounding context.

The details of the temple incident itself are clear enough. In 11:15-17, we read,

> And they went into Jerusalem. And coming into the temple, he began to throw out the sellers and buyers in the temple, and overturned the tables of the money-changers and the chairs of those who sold doves. And he would not permit anyone to carry a vessel (σκεῦος) through the temple. And he was teaching (ἐδίδασκεν) them and saying to them: "Is it not written that 'my house will be called a house of prayer for all the nations?' Yet you have made it a 'den of robbers.'" And the chief priests and the scribes heard, and sought a way to destroy him. For they feared him, because the whole crowd was amazed at his teaching (διδαχῇ). And when evening came, they departed outside the city.

It is not often remarked upon that Jesus's words accompanying his action are said to be "teaching."[26] This makes the passage highly relevant for our topic.

---

[25] Even scholars who should know better make the mistake of reading Mark's narrative as historical report rather than narrative construct. Maurice Casey, *Jesus of Nazareth: An Independent Historian's Account of His Life and Teaching* (London: T&T Clark, 2010), 408–15, is a striking example of a well-known critical scholar who nevertheless accepts the Markan narrative as straightforward report, since he does not question any of its details.

[26] An exception is Boring, *Mark*, 322.

Several common interpretations of Jesus's action in the temple are severely deficient, insofar as they either overread the text or rely on dubious historical reconstructions as background in order to understand what Jesus is doing. Two interpretations in particular are highly problematic: (1) that Jesus rejects commercial or mercantile activity in the Temple and (2) that Jesus wants to "purify" the temple by forcing the buyers and sellers, or passerby in general, to a different area, leaving the temple as a more sacrosanct space.

First let us consider the proposal that Jesus is protesting against economic exploitation. This has been a popular understanding of Jesus's temple action in popular Christian piety but also has scholarly defenders as well, although these interpreters differ widely as to whether this portrayal is accurate or fair on the part of the evangelist. Richard Horsley, viewing Mark as a more or less accurate representation of the politically charged message of the historical Jesus, says that Jesus is

> pronouncing God's condemnation of the Temple because the high priests in charge have been exploiting the people in violation of the Mosaic covenant while seeking refuge and protection in their sacrosanct positions as heads of the Temple like bandits seeking refuge in their mountain strongholds/caves.[27]

Burton Mack comes at the text from the opposite perspective, viewing Mark as not only historically inaccurate but also anti-Judaic. Yet he too subscribes to the view that the Markan Jesus protests against commercial activity in the Temple. He thinks that this protest is a Markan invention, a questionable ad hoc narrative tactic meant both to emphasize Jesus's authority as one who has taken charge as God's Son and to explain why the earlier narrative thread of the plot to kill Jesus is suddenly resumed here:

> The [temple] act itself is contrived. Some gesture was required that could symbolize both casting out and taking charge with some semblance of legitimacy ... filthy lucre would do just fine.[28]

---

[27] Richard A. Horsley, *Hearing the Whole Story: The Politics of Plot in Mark's Gospel* (Louisville, KY: Westminster John Knox, 2001), 110.

[28] Mack, *Myth of Innocence*, 291. That Mark portrays Jesus as protesting economic injustice is also the view of Paula Fredriksen, *Jesus of Nazareth, King of the Jews* (New York: Alfred A. Knopf, 1999), 205–6. Like Mack, she views this as a Markan invention, believing that a real-life Jew like the historical Jesus would have had great respect for the temple.

Thus, although Horsley and Mack disagree on the historical reliability of the tradition, they nevertheless agree that Mark depicts Jesus as protesting against the very presence of buyers and sellers in the temple.

The fact that Mack views the protest against "filthy lucre" (in his words) as contrived does make an important point: namely, that the Gospel could contain an interpretation of Jesus's action that clashes with historical reality. This makes it unnecessary to probe whether a first-century Jew like Jesus would have been likely to oppose the temple establishment on economic grounds. It is no use, for instance, to argue that such an action on the part of Jesus would be inconceivable insofar as the buying and selling of sacrificial animals was a vital part of the operations of an ancient temple.[29] The whole thing could, as Mack suggests, be a Markan invention, written in the shadow of the temple's destruction and a long-running animus between the Markan community and the Jewish authorities.

That being said, the "protest against economic exploitation" interpretation should be entirely rejected. It is simply not attested by the text. It runs afoul of the fact that nowhere in Mark's Gospel up to this point does Jesus protest against economic exploitation by the temple or the authorities.[30] Further, the text itself actually provides positive evidence *against* this interpretation: Not just the "sellers"—the people doing the "exploiting" on this interpretation—are driven out but also the "buyers" (11:15). According to this interpretation, Jesus wants to protect the visitors to the temple from being economically exploited. So why is he driving them out along with the very people who are supposedly exploiting them? This would be an odd way of standing up for the rights of the oppressed common folk, to be sure. Timothy Gray correctly asks, "If … it was Mark's aim to show Jesus cleansing the temple from the abuses of those who sold to the people, then why does he show Jesus driving out both the πωλοῦντας and the ἀγοράζοντας?"[31]

The "economic exploitation" interpretation also fails to explain a very specific detail of the text: We are told that Jesus would not allow anyone to carry

---

[29] As does E. P. Sanders, *Jesus and Judaism* (Philadelphia, PA: Fortress Press, 1984), 64–5.
[30] The closest thing we get to an unambiguous attack on the authorities as economically exploitative comes after this pericope, at 12:40, where the scribes are said to "devour widows' houses."
[31] Timothy C. Gray, *The Temple in the Gospel of Mark*, WUNT 2. Reihe 242 (Tübingen: Mohr Siebeck, 2008), 26.

a "vessel" (σκεῦος) through the area. This refers either to the specific cultic instruments needed for temple worship, or to any kind of item whatsoever, depending on how one translates.[32] Regardless, neither translation helps the case that Jesus is protesting economic exploitation: Why would he oppose people carrying objects (cultic or otherwise) through the area if his ire was directed solely against commercial activity? The broader interpretation—reading the Greek as referring to any item whatsoever—would include cultic vessels, thus interfering with normal temple functioning, which Jesus would presumably not oppose on this reading.

Some scholars believe that Jesus was trying to *purify* the temple, not interfere with its operations in general. There are two main variants of this proposal. On the one hand, Jesus might simply be wanting to move the commercial activity in the temple elsewhere.[33] Darrell Bock, for instance, combines the "economic exploitation" interpretation with the further suggestion that "the crowding of this area with merchants prevented the opportunity for Gentiles who came to the temple to pray undistracted," and thus that Jesus's action was a matter of "spiritual priorities."[34] On the other hand, it has also been suggested that what Jesus opposes is the use of the temple precincts as a shortcut to the western city, an idea that supposedly finds precedent in the Mishnah.[35]

Regardless of whether these proposals make sense as an interpretation of the historical incident (if any) lying behind the Gospel story, they do not find their support from the actual Markan text, but rather from historical assumptions. The notion that Jesus opposed the use of a temple as a "shortcut" is supported only on the basis of the much later evidence of the Mishnah, which New Testament scholars now rightly approach with caution. On the other hand, that Jesus wanted the "buyers and sellers" simply to move elsewhere is based on several dubious assumptions. First, it requires that both Mark and his audience have a precise knowledge of the layout of the temple, and that this would have been of great importance to them. Second, the precise placement of the scene in the Court of the Gentiles (as Bock suggests) is based not on the text but on

---

[32] Collins, *Mark*, 530; BAGD, s.v. "σκεῦος, ους, τό."
[33] Hans Dieter Betz, "Jesus and the Purity of the Temple (Mark 11:15-18): A Comparative Religion Approach," *JBL* 116, no. 3 (Autumn 1997), 461–2.
[34] Bock, *Mark*, 293.
[35] Gnilka, *Markus*, vol. 2, 129; Betz, "Jesus and the Purity of the Temple," 457, 462; Hooker, *Saint Mark*, 268, references *M. Berakoth* 9.5.

an uncertain reconstruction of the temple layout and activities.³⁶ As Moloney points out, "No other location than the temple itself (v. 15) is given for this action."³⁷ The "purification" interpretation confuses exegesis of Mark with what could have "really happened" in the life of the historical Jesus given what is known about the temple. Finally, the notion that Jesus was concerned about whether the area was properly "spiritual" is an imposition of modern notions about "proper" religion upon the Markan text.

As with the "economic exploitation" interpretation, the textual evidence for these related proposals is also thin. There is no evidence whatsoever that Jesus simply wanted the commercial activity to be located outside the temple. If this were so, why would he prevent anyone from carrying items—whether cultic or otherwise—through the temple? In both the narrower reading of σκεῦος (the word refers only to cultic instruments) and the broader (it refers to "instruments" or items generally), the ordinary operation of the temple would be impeded. Further, this line of thought does not fit well with Jesus's words that accompany his action. Why, if Jesus calls the temple a "den of robbers," would he be content for the "robbers" to move just outside the temple? The robbers would presumably continue their robbing whether or not it takes place right inside the temple or just outside it.

The view proposed by Bock that Jesus opposes the fact that the buyers and sellers are crowding out the Gentiles for whom that area of the temple was meant also suffers from textual problems. While such an interpretation might be supported by Jesus's citation in v. 17 of Isa 56:7, it renders the conclusion of the passage, where the crowd is said to be captivated by Jesus's teaching, rather mysterious. For that would mean that the crowd in the temple both understood and approved of Jesus's action clearing the way for Gentiles, which does not seem likely (v. 18).

If these common interpretations of the temple incident fail to convince, how then should we understand this passage? Based not only on the evidence of the temple incident itself but also the surrounding context, both prior to and

---

36 E. P. Sanders, *Judaism: Practice and Belief, 63 BCE–66 CE* (London: SCM Press, 1992), 87–8, locates the selling of birds in the Royal Portico (cf. the diagrams on pp. 308, 312), while doubting that the selling of quadrupeds took place on the temple grounds, for reasons of purity.

37 Francis Moloney, *The Gospel of Mark: A Commentary* (Grand Rapids, MI: Baker Academic, 2009), 222.

following this passage, the temple incident is best interpreted as the climactic display in the Gospel of Jesus's authority as God's agent and his superiority to the established authorities and institutions of Israel. On the basis of this authority, Jesus foretells an event that the Gospel audience is already eminently familiar with: the imminent or already-occurred destruction of the temple during the war against Rome.

The destruction of the temple, not merely its reform or reorganization, is the logical interpretation of Jesus's actions in the Markan context. His actions result in a complete shutdown of temple activities: No one buys or sells, and no one can carry anything through. This would have brought temple operations to a standstill.[38] Once again, whether or not this would have historically been feasible for a single person to accomplish is beside the point: The point in any event is that *Mark* says that this is what happens in the context of the narrative, so we must accept the situation, however historically implausible, if we are to understand the text.

The thesis that Jesus's action symbolizes the destruction of the temple is also supported by the evidence of the cursing of the fig tree, which bookends the temple incident itself (11:12-14, 20-24). That the fig tree is symbolic of the temple is confirmed by the fact that Mark uses the technique of intercalation to postpone the effect of Jesus's curse upon the fig tree until after Jesus has pronounced judgment on the temple.[39] In that conclusion, Jesus gives a somewhat non sequitur response to Peter's observation that the fig tree has withered:

> And Jesus answering says to them: "Have faith in God. Truly I say to you that if you say to this mountain, 'Be taken up and thrown into the sea,' and do not doubt in your heart but believe that what you say will happen, thus it will be for you. For this reason I tell you, whatever you pray for and ask, believe that you will receive it, and it will be for you." (11:22-24).

The exhortation to "say to this mountain" that it be cast into the sea is not a general saying about faith. Rather, "this mountain" has a specific referent: The

---

[38] In agreement with Moloney, *Gospel of Mark*, 223-4; Boring, *Mark*, 322.
[39] Against Collins, *Mark*, 526, who argues that the fig tree symbolizes not the temple but its leadership. This seems unlikely, though, as Jesus's initial action in the temple is directed not specifically against the leaders but against the temple itself—he does not, for example, attack priests or scribes but brings *all* activity in the temple to a halt, as we have seen.

temple mount itself.[40] Jesus adds a note of finality to his symbolic destruction of the temple by dismissing the temple's worth in comparison with the faithful prayers that his followers are instructed to offer to God: Nothing more than prayer without doubt can simply lift up the entire temple edifice and hurl it into the sea.

Thus, the sayings about faith are not random or out of place: Rather, faith is the alternative that the Markan Jesus offers in place of the temple. The prayers of those who have faith are more effective than anything to do with the temple, the destruction of which Jesus has already foretold by his symbolic action. The disciples, and by extension the Gospel audience, are the new "house of prayer for all the nations."

This Markan response to the temple's destruction clearly operates not only from the perspective of the characters in the narrative but especially from the view of the Markan audience, who, to judge from Mk 13 (see below), either knows that the temple has been destroyed or expects that this destruction will occur shortly. The destruction of the temple is for Mark a fait accompli. Therefore, as Boring points out, it is necessary to read the temple incident not as a comment on the future prospects for the temple but as a reflection on its destruction and an argument about what should be done as a result of its demise:

> Mark is responding to a situation in which the temple no longer existed (or in which its imminent destruction is virtually certain). Thus Mark is not interpreting the present and ongoing function of the temple in God's plan, but is coming to terms with its destruction.[41]

---

[40] Boring, *Mark*, 324; William R. Telford, *The Barren Temple and the Withered Tree: A Redaction-Critical Analysis of the Fig-Tree Pericope in Mark's Gospel and Its Relation to the Cleansing of the Temple Tradition* (Sheffield: JSOT Press, 1980), 119; Hooker, *Saint Mark*, 270. James Edwards, *The Gospel According to Mark*. Pillar New Testament Commentaries (Grand Rapids, MI: William B. Eerdmans, 2002), 347, thinks that "this mountain" refers to the peak south of Jerusalem where was found a citadel of Herod the Great—"Herod's architectural ambitions had changed the face of Judea, yet whoever believes in God, says Jesus, can move mountains greater than Herodion." This interpretation fails to convince—Jesus has had nothing directly to do with Herod in the Gospel, and Herod or "Herodians" (cf. Mk 3:6) are not involved in the Jerusalem section of the narrative. Collins, *Mark*, 535, thinks the saying proverbial and that no specific mountain is in view. The problem with this interpretation is that it requires treating this cluster of sayings of Jesus as a rather haphazardly placed miscellany about "faith," with an uncertain connection to the preceding temple incident. The same can also be said of the interpretation that holds that the "mountain" in question is the Mount of Olives on which Jesus and his disciples are currently standing.

[41] Boring, *Mark*, 321.

The Markan response to the situation of the destroyed temple could not be clearer: The temple has been superseded by the faith of the community. But this is not the only conclusion the Gospel draws. Not only has the temple been superseded, it was insufficient and doomed to destruction even while it still stood. This is the meaning of Jesus's act in the temple. Jesus's words and actions are a projection of a conclusion about the temple drawn by the evangelist in their own time into the time of Jesus. The Gospel draws conclusions about the temple by reasoning "from solution to plight."[42] The logic goes: The temple was destroyed, therefore it must have been flawed.

Why, then, was the temple destroyed (or why is it about to be destroyed), according to the Gospel? The words of Jesus in the temple (11:17) are usually taken as the point of departure on this particular exegetical point. On the face of things, the sayings seem to make clear that the temple faces destruction because it was meant to be a "house of prayer" but has become a "den of robbers." And the fact that the chief priests and scribes want to kill Jesus upon hearing this (v. 18) suggests that his "teaching" is directed against them. This interpretation is supported by the fuller context of the passage from Jeremiah, which Mark alluded to with the reference to a "den of robbers." Continuing on from that phrase, contained in Jer 7:11, we read,

> Go now to my place that was in Shiloh, where I made my name dwell at first, and see what I did to it for the wickedness of my people Israel. And now, because you have done all these things, says the LORD, and when I spoke to you persistently, you did not listen, and when I called you, you did not answer, therefore I will do to the house that is called by my name, in which you trust, and to the place that I gave to you and to your ancestors, just what I did to Shiloh. And I will cast you out of my sight, just as I cast out all your kinsfolk, all the offspring of Ephraim. (Jer 7:12-15, NRSV)

The destruction of Shiloh, the site of the first sanctuary in Canaan built to honor Yahweh (Josh 18:1), is never directly narrated in biblical texts, but it is referred to both here in Jer 7:12-15 as well as in Ps 78:60.[43] Mark may also be distantly echoing a later passage in Jer 26, where the prophet is put on

---

[42] Adapting the famous conclusion E. P. Sanders drew about Paul's thought in *Paul and Palestinian Judaism* (Philadelphia, PA: Fortress Press, 1977), 47.

[43] Jack R. Lundbom, *Jeremiah 1-20: A New Translation with Commentary*, Anchor Bible 21A (New York: Doubleday, 1999), 468–9.

trial for prophesying that the temple will end up like the sanctuary at Shiloh—just as Jesus will be put on trial ostensibly for proclaiming the destruction of the second temple in the time of the Gospel's story (Jer 26). In any event, the implication of Jesus's words is that the temple is being destroyed because of the iniquity of the people.

But what, exactly, does this iniquity consists? We have already rejected the proposals that the Markan Jesus is upset at commercial activity in the temple or with the lax maintenance of the temple's purity. In fact, the full explanation of the temple's destruction is found not in Jesus's words or the temple action itself but in the *parable of the tenants*.[44]

The critical moment for our purposes comes at the end of the parable, after the wicked tenants kill the "beloved son":

> "What, then, will the lord [ὁ κύριος] of the vineyard do? He will come and destroy the tenants and give the vineyard to others. Have you not read this scripture: 'The stone which the builders rejected has become the cornerstone—this happened by the hand of the Lord [κυρίου] and is amazing in our eyes?'" (12:9-10)

Once again, we must bracket historical issues. Although multiple scholars have argued, on various grounds, that some form of the parable goes back to the historical Jesus, we focus on its place in the Markan narrative.[45] In the Markan context, the "beloved son" is clearly Jesus: "The Markan reader immediately identifies Jesus as the one, final emissary, the owner's beloved son ... Jesus has twice been identified by the voice of God as his beloved Son (ὁ υἱός μου ὁ ἀγαπητός, 1:11; 9:7)."[46]

The critical detail that ties this story together with the earlier temple incident is the notice that the "lord" of the vineyard will destroy the tenants as retaliation

---

[44] A recent treatment of the parable in its various attested forms is John S. Kloppenborg, *The Tenants in the Vineyard: Ideology, Economics, and Agrarian Conflict in Jewish Palestine*, WUNT 195 (Tübingen: Mohr Siebeck, 2006).

[45] E.g., Bernard Brandon Scott, *Hear Then the Parable: A Commentary on the Parables of Jesus* (Minneapolis, MN: Fortress Press, 1988), 237–53; N. T. Wright, *Jesus and the Victory of God* (Minneapolis, MN: Fortress Press, 1994), 497–501, 565–6; John P. Meier, *A Marginal Jew: Rethinking the Historical Jesus*, vol. 5, *Probing the Authenticity of the Parables* (New Haven, CT: Yale University Press, 2016), 240–53.

[46] Moloney, *Gospel of Mark,* 233. See also Kloppenborg, *Tenants,* 2–3, 220; Mary Ann Tolbert, *Sowing the Gospel: Mark's World in Literary-Historical Perspective* (Minneapolis, MN: Fortress Press, 1989), 236–7.

for the death of the "beloved son." What is the "vineyard," though? Although many commentators have thought that it refers to Israel, since this is what the "vineyard" imagery in Isa 5:1-7, Mark's source for the image, refers to, this interpretation has been called into serious question by Kelly R. Iverson.[47] One particularly strong argument against such a view, noted also by W. J. C. Weren, is that in Isaiah, the vineyard does not produce good fruit, and this is its fault; in Mark the vineyard is fruitful, but the tenants seek to withhold the crop from the landlord.[48] The upshot is that the Markan parable takes up no grudge against "Israel" writ large. Nor is the point of the parable that the "tenants," that is, the leaders, are guilty of great economic injustice, such as might be charged in Isaiah-like fashion. The sole crime of the "tenants" is their rejection of the messengers of the "landlord," up to and including his "beloved son."

Jesus in the parable looks ahead with prophetic foresight not only to his own death at the hands of the leaders but also to its aftermath: The destruction of the temple, which also lies in the future from the perspective of the narrative, is said to be the outcome of Jesus's death.[49]

Thus, the evil that necessitated the temple's destruction is, simply, that *the leaders of Israel* (aided and abetted by the compliant crowd, cf. 15:6-15) *killed Jesus*. The Markan Jesus voices a conviction that could only have made sense in the time of the evangelist and the audience, looking back on the events of Jesus's life and connecting them with the destruction of the temple, which for them has either already occurred or is confidently expected.

The explanation of the temple's destruction presented in the parable makes coherent sense in the context of the Gospel's overall narrative. For we are told in the parable that the "tenants" decided to kill the son out of greed and envy: They wanted his inheritance (12:7). They have no particular grudge against the son; they simply want what is his. This fits quite well with the

---

[47] Kelly R. Iverson, "Jews, Gentiles, and the Kingdom: The Parable of the Wicked Tenants in Narrative Perspective (Mark 12:1-12)," *BibInt* 20 (2012), 305–35. Mack (*Myth of Innocence*, 168) interprets the vineyard in the parable as Israel, as part of his broader contention that the Gospel of Mark is anti-Judaic (see, i.e., the pithy summary on p. 9).

[48] W. J. C. Weren, "The Use of Isaiah 5,1-7 in the Parable of the Tenants (Mark 12,1-12; Matthew 21,33-46)," *Bib* 79, no. 1 (1998), 12–13.

[49] Interestingly, the Markan parable does not mention that the son himself will be vindicated (i.e., resurrected). This is not, *contra* Wright (*Jesus and the Victory of God*, 501n.86), a mark in favor of the parable's historical authenticity. It simply means that the parable is meant as part of the Markan judgment on the temple more than a prediction of the resurrection.

portrayal of Jesus's opponents earlier in the Gospel. Recall, from the previous chapter that the issue at stake in most of the controversies over Jesus's "teaching" was not, in the final analysis, the teaching itself but, rather, Jesus's authority. The contest between Jesus and his opponents is one of the right to pronounce judgment; we found no coherent "program" of teaching on Jesus's part that clashed with an alternative advocated by the scribes and Pharisees. And the parable of the tenants brings back this theme in startling clarity. The "tenants" want to usurp the authority of the "son," without any motivation other than a greedy and rebellious desire to possess the vineyard. Indeed, from a logical perspective, the story is nonsensical, for no rebellious tenants in a "realistic" narrative could possibly have thought that the "owner" would leave them in possession of the vineyard if they killed his "son."[50] The parable, in its Markan context at least, is an allegory for the conflict over authority between Jesus and the Jewish leaders. Therefore, the parable of the tenants, as well as the overarching plot of the Gospel, suggests that for Mark, the authorities' animus against Jesus is the cause of the temple's destruction. Further, Mark consistently attributes the leaders' plot against Jesus to malicious, selfish motives.

This interpretation suggests that even though Jesus's words in 11:17 have usually been taken by scholars as the point of departure for understanding the temple incident, the clearest expression of the Gospel's views on the end of the temple is actually found in the parable of the tenants. The whole episode of the temple incident and its aftermath is most plausibly understood from the perspective of the third narrative purpose that we have already seen at work in Mark's portrayal of Jesus's teaching: the need of the narrative to speak to the concerns of the Markan audience.

Indeed, when we view the temple incident in the overall context of the Gospel, it is very difficult to view the incident as developing the narrative in any significant manner. The only such development is that the plot to kill Jesus is resumed, after having not been heard of since early in the Gospel. This functions more as a reminder to the audience that such a plot exists than

---

[50] As Kloppenborg (*Tenants*, 50) summarizes the view (without endorsing it), "The tenants' incredible belief that they could come to possess a vineyard through murder so thoroughly resists a realistic reading that it can only have been formulated on view of early Christian polemic against either the priestly rulers or against Israel in general."

anything else. Other than this, the temple incident has no effect at all on the plot. Although it sets the stage for the following series of sayings and stories in the temple where Jesus further displays his authority, no concern voiced by Jesus about the temple plays any role in the rest of his time there—he is not pictured as doing anything to "reform" the temple during his time in Jerusalem. Jesus is not immediately arrested—indeed, the Gospel explicitly says that the authorities feared to arrest Jesus (11:18). The incident does not even play a real role in Jesus's trial later on (14:53-65). Jesus's actual deeds in the temple are not used as evidence against him but rather the "false testimony" that he claimed he would destroy the temple in three days and build another (14:57-58). And ultimately Jesus is not even condemned for this but rather because of his claim to be the Messiah (14:61-62).

The reason the temple incident does not advance the narrative to any significant degree is that it, more than any other passage of the Gospel outside Mk 13, uses the characters and events of a time that is past from the perspective of the audience, to speak to that audience's present-day concerns. It is the Markan audience, not the characters in the story, who are addressed by the Markan presentation of Jesus's stance toward the temple.

The authoritative Jesus not only predicts the temple's destruction but also portrays that destruction as a result of his own death at the hands of the leadership, in the parable of the tenants. Jesus is depicted as not only knowing the temple will be destroyed but as actually *endorsing* this destruction as proper and deserved. In the discourse about faith that follows the temple act, Jesus sets aside the temple as nothing compared to the "faith" that can hurl the mountain into the sea. This is a rationalization of the temple's destruction for the benefit of the Markan audience, far more than it is an event in the storyline itself. Hence, we are justified in judging that it is the third of our three identified narrative purposes—that of speaking to the concerns of the audience—which is primarily at work in the temple incident and its surrounding narrative context. In fulfilling this purpose, the temple incident also continues to develop the narrative theme of Jesus's authority, which has remained consistent throughout the Gospel.

If we examine the rest of Jesus's activities in the temple, we become even more sure of our assessment that the purpose of the temple incident is to demonstrate Jesus's authority. Consider the passage that lies between the sayings on faith and the parable of the tenants: Jesus's confrontation with "chief priests, scribes, and elders" (11:27-33).

> And they came again to Jerusalem. And as he was walking in the temple, the chief priests, scribes, and elders came to him and said, "By what authority are you doing these things? Who gave you the authority to do them?" (11:27-28)

Jesus's response is to trap his interlocutors in an impossible dilemma. He retorts that they must earn an answer from him by answering whether the "baptism of John" was "from heaven or from human beings" (v. 30). They cannot answer him because they cannot bring themselves to admit that John had divine authorization for his baptism but also fear to incite the crowd by declaring John's baptism to be "from human beings."

This entire passage, obviously, is about Jesus's authority. The "things" that the leaders demand Jesus prove his authority for doing are his words and deeds in causing a commotion in the temple.[51] The very fact that Jesus turns the confrontation around by refusing to answer their question, but instead posing one of his own, demonstrates Jesus's own authority and its superiority to that of the leaders.[52]

Moreover, the scene plays up the theme of the leaders' animosity toward Jesus. Jesus perceives that their question harbors hostile intent. The temple leaders seek to have some legitimate charge against Jesus for usurping their authority.[53] That Jesus recognizes their animus against him is clear from the fact that once they fail to respond to his question, he follows up with the parable of the tenants. And the leaders know all too well what he means by it: "And they wanted to arrest him, but feared the crowd, for they knew that he had spoken the parable against them" (12:12). In other words, the parable is Jesus's interpretation of the conflict between himself and the temple leaders, which has just reached a new height in their demand that he prove the source of his authority. The use of the parable to interpret the actions of the chief priests, scribes, and elders provides a lens through which the narrative invites

---

[51] Craig A. Evans, *Mark 8:27-16:20*, WBC 34B (Nashville, TN: Thomas Nelson, 2001, 197: "In the present setting, the question put to Jesus is clearly in response to the temple demonstration in 11:15-17."
[52] Marcus, *Mark 8-16*, 799.
[53] Evans, *Mark*, 200.

the audience to view both the preceding discussion about Jesus's authority and the several scenes of conflict that follow, between Jesus and different establishment groups.[54]

Jesus is immediately shown to be correct in his assessment of the leaders' motives in what follows the parable of the tenants. "And they sent some of the Pharisees and Herodians in order to trap him by what he said [αὐτὸν ἀγρεύσωσιν λόγῳ.]" The "they" who send the Pharisees and Herodians are the chief priests, scribes, and elders who challenged Jesus about his authority and who were the audience for Jesus's parable responding to their question. They left the scene at 12:12 but have now sent others in their stead.[55] That they seek to "trap him by what he said" shows that their motives are disingenuous, that they act in bad faith. They do not seek a real discussion with Jesus about the matter they will raise but rather seek to have some legitimate grounds on which to accuse him. The verb ἀγρεύειν implies hunting or seizing prey, underlining the ill intent of the interlocutors.[56]

The bad faith of the Pharisees and Herodians, and their connection with the plot by the "chief priests, scribes, and Pharisees" to arrest Jesus, raises an important point about how this passage, and the other scholastic or controversy dialogues in this sequence of the Gospel, should be interpreted. The point of Jesus's confrontations with various leadership groups—Pharisees and Herodians, Sadducees, the scribes—is not primarily to record Jesus's opinion on the various matters under discussion but (1) to show him besting all opposition and (2) to insinuate that those who oppose Jesus do so for transparently wicked reasons. Therefore, we ought to view the various discussions in the temple (12:13-44) as an expansion upon the theme of Jesus's authority.

The logic goes like this. First, Jesus makes a powerful claim to authority by means of his demonstration in the temple. Then, the established leaders

---

[54] Timothy J. Goddart, *Watchwords: Mark 13 in Markan Eschatology*, JSNTSup 26 (Sheffield: Sheffield Academic Press, 1989), 119: "The parable functions as Jesus' answer to the authority question."

[55] Hooker (*Saint Mark*, 278) obscures the fact that the leaders with whom Jesus has been sparring are behind the sending of the Pharisees and Herodians, since she translates the verb passively ("Some of the Pharisees and Herodians were sent").

[56] LSJ, s.v. "ἀγρεύω". Cf. Edwards, *Gospel According to Mark*, 362: "The Greek word for 'catch,' *agruein*, occurs in the NT only here and connotes violent pursuit."

demand that he be clear about where his authority comes from so that they might have some political charge on which to arrest him. But Jesus turns the tables by demonstrating that he knows their disingenuous motives, telling them the parable of the tenants to make this plain. Then, finally, in a series of discussions with various groups and persons, he shows not only his positions on various "issues" (which are a rather random assortment) but also that his superior wisdom and cunning overcomes the opposition. As it says in 12:34, "no one dared question him"—and indeed, after this point, Jesus no longer receives challenges from others but instead completely controls the direction of the conversation. Moloney aptly describes the entire turn of events: "The reader moves steadily through a series of episodes that lead the leaders of Israel to silence and condemnation."[57]

This discussion of the temple sequence has been long, so it is worthwhile to summarize our conclusions. We saw, first, that the most common interpretations of Jesus's action in the temple are fraught with difficulties. We proposed instead that the Markan Jesus prophesies the temple's destruction as a divine punishment for his own upcoming death at the hands of the leaders, and that this is made plain in the parable of the tenants. Finally, we noted throughout that various aspects of the temple sequence in the Gospel support the narrative aims that Mark works toward throughout the Gospel, which we have already examined. The sequence supports the image of Jesus as possessing great authority, because he displays both incredible foreknowledge and authority in confrontations with various establishment groups. The plot is advanced, albeit subtly, by the sudden resumption of the plot to kill Jesus, which had not been mentioned since near the beginning of the Gospel, thus allowing for the passion narrative to proceed apace. And finally, the temple sequence spoke more clearly than any part of the Gospel so far to the concerns of the Markan audience, specifically to their need to interpret and rationalize the destruction of the temple, by linking this destruction to Jesus's own life and fate. Therefore, the "teaching" that Jesus expounds in the temple is not part of a program imparted to others but an interpretation of the past for the benefit of the Gospel audience.

---

[57] Moloney, *Gospel of Mark*, 229.

"I Am Foretelling All Things to You" (Mk 13)

Mk 13 is another heavily treaded locus in Markan studies. As with many of the other passages we have examined, a host of historical and redactional issues have been raised.[58] Particularly uncertain is the date for the Gospel's writing which ch. 13 implies: Arguments have been made for dates from the mid-30s CE to the period either right before or immediately after the temple's destruction in 70 CE.[59] For our purposes, it is sufficient to say that the Gospel is written with the destruction of the temple in view—either such a destruction is anticipated or it has already occurred and is a prophecy *ex eventu*.[60] This is demonstrated by the way the chapter begins: It is Jesus's declaration that "not a stone will be left on stone" of the temple (13:2), which prompts the disciples query to which the discourse responds: "Tell us when these things will be, and what will be the sign when all these things are about to be accomplished" (v. 4). In context, "these things" can only refer to Jesus's declaration that every stone of the temple will be torn down.

That this chapter must be considered under the rubric of a study of Jesus's teaching is suggested by the way the anonymous disciple proclaims to Jesus the grandeur of the temple in v. 1: This disciple addresses Jesus as "teacher" (διδάσκαλε). The question that must be asked is, what exactly does Jesus teach here?

In this chapter, the "teaching" is manifestly directed primarily at the Markan audience, *not* the disciples. That the disciples are not really the intended audience is clear from the fact that this chapter is, to put it bluntly, pointless in the context of the storyline of Mark's Gospel. Nothing whatsoever in the chapter influences the Gospel's plot. Its primary themes, such as the issue of false messiahs and prophets (vv. 6, 21–22) and the necessity of a mission to "all the nations" (v. 10), do not appear in the rest of the Gospel, either before or

---

[58] N. T. Wright (*Jesus and the Victory of God*, 339–68) makes the case for the substantial historicity of Mk 13 and parallels, as he does for much of the synoptic tradition; his argument has been answered by James G. Crossley, *The Date of Mark's Gospel: Insight from the Law in Earliest Christianity*, JSNTSup 266 (London: T&T Clark, 2004), 19–27. On the redactional issues, see, e.g., Frans Neirynck, "Le discours anti-apocalyptique de Mc. XIII," *ETL* 45 (1969), 154–64.

[59] Crossley, *Date of Mark's Gospel*, 29–43, discusses the various possibilities.

[60] Joel Marcus, *Mark 1-8: A New Translation with Commentary*. Yale Anchor Bible 27. 2000. Paperback edition (New Haven, CT: Yale University Press, 2005), 39: "It seems safe to say that [Mark's] Gospel was written in the shadow of [the Temple's] destruction."

after ch. 13. Jesus's words here are never recalled in the passion narrative, even though it might be considered particularly appropriate that the suffering of Jesus would be linked to the predicted suffering of the disciples, as in the three passion predictions. In fact, if Mk 13 were missing from all our manuscripts of the Gospel, we would likely never suspect its existence. The reader could still follow the Gospel's plot even if they skipped directly to ch. 14. Therefore, unlike many other passages we have examined, the discourse of ch. 13 is *not* meant to advance the Gospel's plot. Indeed, the plot grinds to a halt for all intents and purposes as the Markan Jesus instructs not the disciples but the narrative's audience.

But what exactly does Jesus "teach" here? One thing that is striking is that although the passage is often used to date the Gospel based on the prediction of the destruction of the temple, this destruction is not really the primary concern of the passage. The temple's destruction is only mentioned in Jesus's words that not one stone will remain on a stone (v. 2), and the mention of an "abomination of desolation," assuming that this term refers to some event in the proximity of the war, whether it be the destruction itself or the occupation of the temple by the Zealot faction.[61] Rather, the three most emphasized points in Mk 13 are (1) that the followers of Jesus will suffer and be persecuted, (2) that they must beware of being led astray either by false messiahs and prophets, and (3) that they ought not to draw false conclusions about the time of the end (cf. vv. 32–37). Thus, although it is the case that this discourse follows the prediction of the temple's destruction, and although it serves as the conclusion to the sequence of Jesus's teachings in the temple,[62] the temple itself is not the main subject of the discourse. Rather, the focus is on how the destruction should be understood in relation to the end of the age and the coming of the Son of Humanity.[63]

What unifies the predictions of persecution, the warnings about false prophets, and the statement about watchfulness for the end of the age? They all serve in this chapter to magnify Jesus's authority, just as has already been done throughout the Gospel. In Mk 13, however, this portrayal of Jesus as

---

[61] Marcus, *Mark 1-8*, 38; *Mark 8-16*, 890-91.
[62] Boring, *Mark*, 353.
[63] Moloney, *Gospel of Mark*, 253.

authoritative is no longer a two-level message meant both for the characters and the Gospel audience: Here, the full weight of Markan Christology is phrased in imperative terms to the audience.

Mk 13 first of all enhances the image of Jesus's authority by putting his knowledge of God's ultimate plan on display to the fullest extent seen in the Gospel. As in Mk 4, Jesus here functions like the angelic interpreters seen in apocalyptic literature, who make the coded meaning of the seer's visions plain. Although the events described in the chapter are not "visions" per se, the disciples in their query to Jesus at the beginning of the discourse nevertheless function like the confused apocalyptic seer who wants to know how to understand what he has seen. Throughout the Gospel, Jesus has been portrayed as one who has knowledge of God's plan by virtue of being Son of God, but it is in Mk 13 that this heavenly knowledge is most fully displayed. Jesus possesses great authority because the things he says will happen, do indeed happen: This will be particularly clear in the passion narrative, when Jesus predicts the disciples' abandonment of him and Peter's denial. But his foreknowledge in Mk 13 extends beyond the events of his own life and death to the end of the age and the fulfillment of God's divine purpose.

The chapter adds a new twist, however. Not only is Jesus's authority highlighted in a positive manner, but the importance of trusting in this authority is emphasized by the repeated warnings to beware of various pretenders (vv. 5–6, 21–22). Indeed, Jesus's discourse actually begins not with anything to do with the temple but with a warning to not be misled by deceivers. The struggle for authority is thus no longer on the level of the Gospel plot, between Jesus and the Jewish leaders, but between Jesus as portrayed in Mark and the "pretenders" who, it is feared, might mislead the Gospel's audience. The identity of these various so-called pretenders or deceivers is a historical matter that is relatively immaterial for our purposes. What is important is that the image of Jesus as authoritative, built up throughout the Gospel, is now being cashed out in terms of a command to correct obedience: believe not these pretenders but the (Markan) Jesus. And what does this obedience entail? Two things: first, the endurance of suffering and persecution; second, not being misled by false predictions of the end of the age, which claim to speak in Jesus's name. For the exact time of the end, no one knows; but followers of Jesus must remain vigilant until then (vv. 32–37).

This, then, is the function of Mk 13: The theme of Jesus's authority is moved fully from the level of the narrative to the level of the audience and its present situation. The Markan Jesus becomes the living, speaking Jesus who commands the audience to steadfast endurance and watchfulness until the end. Other claimants are to be rejected. The audience is exhorted to treat the Markan Jesus *as* Jesus himself, the living Lord. Although the distinction between the "earthly" Jesus and the Jesus who speaks to the community has been tenuous throughout the Gospel, here it is entirely collapsed: The evangelist assumes the authority of the risen and living Lord by speaking to the community in the voice of Jesus. The Markan Jesus stops being a character in the story and becomes to the fullest possible extent a prophetic voice whose words the evangelist proclaims. This is in line with the interpretation of the Markan "narrator" offered by Robert Fowler: The gap between the narrator, Jesus, and the implied author is largely nonexistent in Mark.[64]

In summary, then, not only is the authority of Jesus further enhanced—which is one of the three narrative aims of the Markan portrayal of Jesus's teaching we earlier identified—but also this authority is used to directly address the audience and exhort specific behavior. Namely, the audience is directed to demonstrate trust in Jesus's authority by identifying the words of the Markan Jesus with the words of Jesus as living Lord speaking to them in their own time.

To answer the question of what Jesus "teaches" in Mk 13, the answer then is that he demands recognition of his own authority. And he makes this demand not of the characters in the story—for as we have seen, Mk 13 is irrelevant on the level of the Gospel's plot—but of the audience. The aims of Jesus and the purpose of the Gospel's writing converge here. The Markan Jesus assumes fully the role of an authoritative figure not just for the characters but also for the Markan audience.

---

[64] Fowler, *Let the Reader Understand*, 73: "In the Gospel, Jesus speaks, but always with the narrator's voice. In other words, the narrator establishes his authority by establishing the authority of his main character, Jesus. The two become virtually indistinguishable." Further, "any characterization of the narrator as a personage separate and distinct from the implied author is absolutely minimal" (p. 77). Therefore, the implied author, narrator, and Jesus speak basically as one in Mark.

Conclusion

The analysis of Mk 13 concludes our discussion of Markan passages dealing with Jesus's teaching. Although not every passage that could possibly be considered under this heading has been examined, we have nevertheless offered a representative analysis of the most relevant sections of the Gospel. In the conclusion, we will present a synthesis of the results that makes plain the aims of Mark's portrayal of Jesus's teaching as a whole and attempt to place this portrayal in the historical and social context in which the Gospel of Mark was written.

Conclusion

Having studied numerous relevant passages in the Gospel of Mark, it is now appropriate that we summarize our results and offer a coherent summary of Mark's presentation of Jesus as teacher. We must also endeavor to place this portrayal of Jesus in its historical and social context, as best we are able.

Summary and Implications

The introduction laid out the goals of this study: to determine the function that the motif of Jesus as teacher plays in the Gospel of Mark. The project appeared useful because of the paradoxical fact that Mark frequently refers to Jesus as a teacher but does not often actually tell what Jesus taught.

The first chapter examined three non-Christian Greek and Greco-Roman texts: the *Memorabilia* of Xenophon, the *Discourses* of Epictetus, and the *Life of Apollonius of Tyana* by Philostratus. All three texts were carefully examined in order to establish what each teacher-protagonist teaches in the text and the manner in which each of them taught. This examination was included to provide a point of comparison for the claims later advanced about Mark: Specifically, that Mark's overall focus on the person of Jesus rather than his actual teaching makes the Gospel an outlier compared to other, outwardly similar texts about teachers and teaching from the Greco-Roman world. Our argument was that Mark differed from these texts in that it does not seek either to preserve the teacher's teaching in a readily comprehensible form or to defend the teacher against his detractors. The second and third chapters took up the task of defending these claims by means of an in-depth examination of the Markan text itself.

From the introduction onward, we suggested that no one single purpose lies behind Mark's portrayal of Jesus as teacher. Rather, the teaching motif is employed for three distinct purposes. First, Mark uses the motif as a catalyst for development of the plot at key points in the Gospel, where the narrative arc of Jesus's ministry, arrest, and death is advanced as characters react to Jesus's extraordinary teaching. Second, Mark develops a specific Christological motif, that of Jesus's *authority*, by making this concept a key part of many scenes concerning Jesus's teaching. By combining teaching with authority, Mark reconfigures Jesus's teaching so that the "teaching" portions of the Gospel no longer point to the teachings themselves but to Jesus himself as an authorized and authoritative teacher. And finally, Mark portrays Jesus's teachings in such a way that these teachings speak often far more to the audience in its historical situation than they do to the characters in the story. It became clear at several points, especially the parables chapter and the temple incident, that the story as it stands makes far more sense as an address to the audience than as a description of the "teaching" of Jesus to characters within the narrative.

From these observations, we suggest the following conclusions about Mark's treatment of Jesus's teaching:

First of all, the theme of Jesus's *authority* is crucial in Mark. In virtually every scene we examined, the issue of authority was either directly addressed, as in the Capernaum synagogue or the temple incident, or implicitly relevant, as in the controversy stories. Even in passages where it was not apparently present, such as the parables chapter, we saw that Jesus's authority was enhanced by his knowledge of future events and his direct address to the audience.

Second, we saw ample evidence for our claim in Chapter 1 that Mark's purpose is neither apologetic nor didactic. Jesus's teaching in the Gospel is not directed to outsiders and does not rest for its persuasiveness on cultural conventions held in common between Jesus and "those outside." As we saw most particularly in the controversies and the temple incident, the crucial issue in Jesus's teaching is the acceptance or rejection of Jesus's authority, not the use of reasoned argument or appeal to scripture or Jewish tradition. The parables chapter, in particular, cements the view that the majority of outsiders are *predestined* not to understand and obey Jesus's message: The "parable theory" invokes Isaiah to suggest that Jesus teaches in parables deliberately as a means of obfuscation. The parables become clear only to the audience that already knows the "meaning" of Jesus's teaching. Similarly, the temple incident serves not to teach about the temple but explains its destruction to an audience struggling to make sense of such a calamity. All in all, we can agree with George Kennedy's provocative assessment of Mark: The Gospel is "an example of what may be called radical Christian rhetoric, a form of 'sacred language' characterized by assertion and absolute claims of authoritative truth without evidence of logical argument."[1]

The Gospel is also not didactic. This may seem odd considering that Mark is so concerned with "teaching." But, as we have seen, the passages concerned with Jesus's teaching do not impart a system of thought. Mark does not intend to pass on a program of Jesus's teachings to readers, as we saw is the case with the *Discourses* of Epictetus. Only the three passion predictions concern anything that could be called a kind of program of Jesus, as they counsel the necessity of suffering in behalf of the kingdom. Even this, however, does not constitute a "system of thought and action" (to quote Vernon Robbins again), which Jesus's followers must enact in their own lives indefinitely: Mk 13 makes plain that their suffering will come to an end at the imminent turning of the age, and Mk 10:30 indicates that the followers of Jesus can expect reward both in the present age and the one to come, implying that the duration of the trials Jesus's followers must endure will not last long in the big picture.

From all this we may conclude that, paradoxically, Jesus's teaching is only an ancillary theme in the Gospel, at least in and of itself. In spite of the fact that, as we observed at the beginning of this study, Mark often mentions Jesus's teaching or describes him as teaching, the teaching motif is used not for its own sake but functions for other reasons in the Gospel. It serves, above all, to emphasize that Jesus is an authoritative figure.

The only "message" this authoritative Jesus imparts, then, is a counsel of endurance and perseverance. This message is backed up both by promises of reward and by threats of judgment—see, for instance, 8:38, where the Son of Humanity will be "ashamed" of those who deny him at the parousia. The "message," further, is confined to the passion predictions—Jesus's resurrection and the vindication of his followers are not the subjects of any of the other

---

[1] George A. Kennedy, *New Testament Interpretation through Rhetorical Criticism* (Chapel Hill: University of North Carolina Press, 1984), 104.

scenes we examined. Jesus does not truly teach but expounds his own authority. He teaches that he is an authorized teacher, and that he ought to be obeyed up to and until the turning of the age. This is why we may say that Mark's Gospel is not didactic in purpose. It demands obedience rather than exhorting a change in lifestyle backed up by arguments.

The Historical and Social Context

Throughout this study, we have alluded to the situation of Mark's audience. Following Robert Fowler, we have taken the standpoint that much of Mark operates on the level of discourse rather than story, and is addressed directly to this audience, with only secondary attention paid to the internal "logic" of the narrative or the characters' motivations. Since we have made this methodological move, it compels us to add a brief word about the historical and social circumstances of this audience and to make sense of the Gospel's use of Jesus's teachings in light of this. The following remarks are necessarily speculative but rely as much as possible on what we take to be the scholarly consensus concerning the provenance of Mark.

The majority view in scholarship is that the Gospel confronts a specific crisis: the destruction of the Jerusalem temple in 70 CE—Mark either views the destruction of the temple as imminent or writes in its aftermath. This is the view we have taken in this study. In making sense of the occasion for Mark's writing, we may draw on the suggestive framework for interpretation proposed by Merrill P. Miller, who in turns draws on the work of Steven Weitzman.

Miller proposes to view the creation of the Gospel as a product of two impulses: one toward "cultural persistence" and the other toward "social escape."[2] The first of these terms he draws from a fascinating study by Weitzman. Weitzman studies different strategies by which Jews in antiquity preserved their culture in the face of threats that might dissolve it, particularly the threats posed by foreign imperial powers.[3] Jews might

---

[2] Merrill P. Miller, "The Social Logic of the Gospel of Mark: Cultural Persistence and Social Escape in a Postwar Time," in *Redescribing the Gospel of Mark*, ed. Barry S. Crawford and Merrill P. Miller (Atlanta, GA: SBL Press, 2017), 207–399.

[3] Steven Weitzman, *Surviving Sacrilege: Cultural Persistence in Jewish Antiquity* (Cambridge, MA: Harvard University Press, 2005).

resist foreign domination, whether by strategically acquiescing, openly resisting, or fleeing (physically or symbolically) from the threat. Weitzman is interested not just in physical, historical strategies for cultural persistence but also in the ways they are portrayed in Jewish *literature*. This literature constitutes a use of the imagination to open up new spaces, new possibilities for various means of preserving Jewish cultural continuity: "This study stresses the role of the imagination in the struggle for cultural survival as a capacity that allowed early Jews to reshape the past to accommodate present needs, to transcend the constraints of visible reality, and to conjure invisible allies." Jews utilized "mythmaking, metaphor, magic, et cetera" as survival strategies.[4] Weitzman's examples include, for instance, stories of Jewish folk heroes such as Judith, who used cunning and bravery to turn the tables on a stronger foe when she slew Holofernes, or the various legends about the preservation of the ark of the covenant from the destruction of the first Jerusalem temple.

To return to Miller: He suggests that the narrative of Mark represents the same patterns of "cultural persistence" that Weitzman identified in various Jewish texts. While acknowledging that the aims of Mark are dissimilar from the aims of other Jewish literature—for Mark does not aim at "preserving Jewish ritual and some imagination of a still existing temple cult or its revival"—Miller nevertheless suggests that certain traits of Mark demonstrate the appropriateness of viewing the Gospel as an effort at Jewish cultural persistence: "Themes that are driven by the announcement of the kingdom of God and the coming of the Son of Humanity, the presence throughout Mark of scriptural idioms and texts, and mimetic writing drawing on biblical intertexts and figures of biblical lore are not superficial features of the gospel text."[5]

However, Miller quickly shifts to what he sees as the second purpose of Mark. This second purpose, which he contrasts with "cultural persistence," he terms "social escape."[6] By this he means an attempt by the Gospel to develop

---

[4] Ibid., 9.
[5] Miller, "Social Logic," 229. See also p. 379: "Like the Gospel of Matthew, the writings of Josephus, and the Jewish apocalypses and related writings after the war, the Gospel of Mark must be seen as an expression of a nativist Jewish cultural persistence."
[6] This term appears to be of Miller's own coinage.

a new social formation that survives the aftermath of the war with Rome by disassociating itself from the old order that had fought and been defeated by Rome:

> Mark's narrative project reconfigures in its plot and central subject the perception and reality of the loss of Jewish political and cultural capital … while at the same time attempting to immunize and exempt the kingdom of the God of Israel, an alternative symbol of social cohesion and power, from its consequences.[7]

Mark projects a strategy of cultural persistence because all the catastrophes of the war are explained as being a part of the plan and will of the God of Israel. We ourselves saw this to be the case in our examination of the passion predictions and the temple incident—both Jesus's death and the destruction of the temple are said to be ordained by divine will. Yet at the same time, Mark's hostility to the Jewish establishment, blaming the prewar Jewish leadership for both the death of Jesus and the temple's end, suggests to Miller that Mark is also engaged in a strategy of what Miller calls social escape. By reorienting the hopes of the audience around Jesus, and stressing the sufficiency of "faith" for the kingdom of God, Mark both preserves Jewish cultural continuity and at the same time isolates both Gospel and audience from Jewish society by laying claim to a different social formation: the movement that forms around Jesus and the kingdom.

> Mark's dual narrative was not only intended to project a different end to a biblical epic that had in view the building of a temple … or to appeal to certain readers attracted to the deeds of a marginal Jewish figure whose proclamation of divine rule survived the war … As a substitute story of humiliation and vindication, the beginning of the gospel of Jesus Christ is a story of leaving, evoking the fantasy of exemption and escape from self-identification as Jews subject to Rome.[8]

Weitzman and Miller's notion of "cultural persistence" is an extremely useful one for understanding the results we have found concerning Jesus's teaching in Mark. We observed that the Gospel repeatedly draws attention

---

[7] Ibid., 379.
[8] Ibid., 394.

away from the subject matter of Jesus's teachings as such and instead directs the audience toward the sheer authority of Jesus—his right to proclaim, to command, to speak things and have them occur. In the aftermath of the destruction of so much of Jewish cultural identity in the aftermath of the war, bound up as it was with the temple cult, such a redrawing of the cultural map makes eminent sense: Mark accrues to Jesus the authority that had formerly rested with the temple and its personnel. The Jewish scriptures also cede their erstwhile authority to Jesus: As we noted in Chapter 3, direct citation formulas of scripture are rare in Mark, and Jesus takes upon himself the authority to interpret the Law contained in the scriptures. Jesus claims this authority by being sent from God, by performing miracles to show his power, and by proclaiming judgment upon the old order, accurately "predicting" its destruction via prophecy *ex eventu*. The loss of Jewish culture is both explained and rationalized, while at the same time a remnant of that culture—the idea of God as sovereign, as king—persists in the figure of Jesus himself. Mark portrays faith in Jesus and the Gospel, and willingness to endure suffering to the end of the age, as the only things needful for Jewish culture to persist, for God to remain faithful to his people.

On the other hand, Miller's concept of "social escape" seems unnecessary. For escape implies total abandonment of a previous social group or culture. Miller describes social escape as a seeking of "exemption" from the consequences of the war with Rome. But what is seeking exemption if not another means of cultural persistence? What Millers calls social escape can be viewed as an example of one of the strategies for cultural persistence identified by Weitzman: a form of hiding or retreat.

Consider Weitzman's discussion of an important lacuna in biblical tradition concerning the destruction of Solomon's temple: the fate of the ark of the covenant. Weitzman notes that although the final fate of the ark is never narrated in biblical texts, a number of postbiblical writings try to fill this gap with various legends to the effect that the ark has been hidden until the time when Israel is restored. In one such tale, recounted in 2 Maccabees, the prophet Jeremiah hides the ark:

> Jeremiah came and found a cave dwelling, and he brought there the tent and the ark and the altar of incense; then he sealed up the entrance. Some of

those who followed him came up intending to mark the way, and but could not find it. When Jeremiah learned of it, he rebuked them and declared: "The place shall remain unknown until God gathers his people together again and shows his mercy" (2 Macc 2:5-7)[9]

In a similar story found in Syrian Baruch, an angel hides the ark and other items from the temple in the earth until Jerusalem is restored (6:7-9).[10]

Weitzman highlights this tradition as an example of the importance of the use of imagination as a strategy of cultural persistence:

> The telling of such a story created yet another opening in reality, imagining it in a way that makes the hiding of the ark a *possibility* ... In the hidden ark myth, a part of reality—the cave where Jeremiah hides the ark or the earth in which it is concealed by an angel—is outside, or underneath, the territory controlled by foreign rule, an unseen locale in which the core of the Temple cult can persist impervious to external surveillance and interference ... From the perspective of Jews who believe in this story, the Temple's contents survive, intact, inviolate, and potentially recoverable. In revealing their hiddenness ... the hidden ark story establishes yet another option for cultural survival, saving the Temple by keeping the knowledge of its continued existence a secret until the end of foreign rule creates an opportunity to recover it.[11]

To return to the subject of Mark, we suggest that the Gospel's shift toward locating all the authority previously vested in temple and scripture in the person of Jesus represents not social escape, as Miller would have it, but rather a form of the strategy of cultural persistence, which Weitzman identifies in the legends of the hidden ark.

It is well-known that secrecy plays a major role in Mark. Modern scholarship on the Gospel was launched by Wrede's identification of the "messianic secret" or what might more generally be called the "secrecy motif." Without delving too deeply into the scholarly quagmire that is the interpretation of the secrecy motif, it can be said that Jesus and his authority in Mark are as "hidden" as the ark and the cultic treasures of the legends. The Markan Jesus is "hidden" in multiple ways throughout the Gospel. His identity is a mystery

---

[9] Cf. Weitzman, *Surviving Sacrilege*, 25, and also n.26 and the research cited there.
[10] Weitzman, *Surviving Sacrilege*, 26.
[11] Ibid., 27–8 (emphasis original).

to his contemporaries, overlooked or outright rejected by all: No character proclaims Jesus as God's son except the centurion at the cross, at the Gospel's end (15:39). His teachings confuse insiders and intentionally mislead outsiders, as demonstrated in the parables chapter. His body is missing from the empty tomb (16:5-8). And his return will only be seen at the turn of the age when he comes as Son of Humanity—just as, in the ark legends discussed by Weitzman, the ark's hidden location will not be uncovered until Israel's restoration.

The point is that the figure of the authoritative Jesus accomplishes for Mark the same thing achieved by the stories of the hidden ark. Just as in the stories of the ark from 2 Maccabees and Syrian Baruch, artifacts of the first temple were placed beyond the reach of foreign domination by "relocating" them to an imaginative and conceptual space where they could be thought of as persisting, in Mark, Jesus himself is hidden beyond the reach of real-life forces that have devastated Jewish culture in light of the destruction of the second temple (whether for Mark that destruction is expected or already occurred). And the Markan narrative makes Jesus the sole locus for the continuation of Jewish belief and practice, because he has superseded the temple and seized control of the scriptures by becoming their sole correct interpreter. Therefore, the location of all authority in Jesus is Mark's strategy for cultural persistence: Jewish culture occupies an imaginative or conceptual space that can be preserved inviolate because it exists in the belief and social practice of the Gospel and its readers, and that space is the figure and authority of Jesus himself. Those who have faith enough to belong to the kingdom of God know the secret—that Jesus remains "hidden" until he comes again, but that his authority persists even in his apparent absence.

Thus, Miller's (correct) observations about Mark's focus on Jesus as the focal point of a new social formation can be explained without recourse to the additional concept of "social escape." Rather, such a tactic exemplifies the very strategies of cultural persistence identified by Weitzman.

This brief discussion of the historical and social context, drawing upon the work of Weitzman and Miller, completes our study of Mark's portrayal of Jesus as teacher. We have (1) examined the literary context for the portrayal of Jesus as teacher by examining other classical and Greco-Roman texts, (2) studied in detail relevant passages from Mark, and (3) described aspects of the historical and social context that make sense of Mark's peculiar emphases in his portrayal of Jesus's teaching. We have concluded that Mark portrays Jesus as a teacher, but that he focuses this portrayal not on the teaching itself but on the person of the teacher and his authority to teach as such. This focus on Jesus's authority also serves to advance the Gospel's plot, since the issue of authority is what propels the conflict between Jesus and the religious establishment. Finally, insofar as the Gospel's "message" about Jesus's authority works primarily at the level of discourse rather than story, it is also clear that the primary takeaway for Mark's audience would have been the necessity of accepting Jesus (as portrayed by the Gospel) as a new bearer of authority to replace the previous structures of leadership and cultural continuity lost with the end of the second temple.

Bibliography

Ahbel-Rappe, Sara, and Rachana Kamtekar, ed. *A Companion to Socrates*. Malden, MA: Blackwell, 2006.

Bäbler, Balbina, and Heinz-Günther Nesselrath. *Philostrats Apollonios und seine Welt: Greichische und nichtgreichische Kunst und Religion in der* Vita Apollonii. Beiträge zur Altertumskunde 354. Berlin: De Gruyter, 2016.

Beck, Fredrick A. G. *Greek Education: 450–350 B.C.* New York: Barnes and Noble, 1964.

Best, Ernest. *The Temptation and the Passion: The Markan Soteriology*. Society for New Testament Studies Monograph Series 2. Cambridge: Cambridge University Press, 1965.

Betz, Hans Dieter. "Jesus and the Purity of the Temple (Mark 11:15-18): A Comparative Religion Approach." *Journal of Biblical Literature* 116, no. 3 (Autumn 1997), 455–72.

Black, C. Clifton. *The Disciples According to Mark: Markan Redaction in Current Debate*, 2nd ed. Journal for the Study of the New Testament Supplement Series 27. Grand Rapids, MI: William B. Eerdmans, 2012.

Bock, Darrell. *Mark*. New Cambridge Bible Commentary. Cambridge: Cambridge University Press, 2015.

Boesche, Roger. *Theories of Tyranny from Plato to Arendt*. University Park: Pennsylvania State University Press, 1996.

Bonnette, Amy L., trans.. *Xenophon: Memorabilia*. Ithaca, NY: Cornell University Press, 1994.

Booth, Wayne C. *The Rhetoric of Fiction*, 2nd ed. Chicago, IL: University of Chicago Press, 1983.

Boring, M. Eugene. *Mark: A Commentary*. New Testament Library. Louisville, KY: Westminster John Knox, 2006.

Bovon, François. *Luke 1: A Commentary on the Gospel of Luke 1:1-9:50*. Translated by Christine M. Thomas. Hermeneia Minneapolis, MN: Fortress Press, 2002.

Boyarin, Daniel. *The Jewish Gospels: The Story of the Jewish Christ*. New York: New Press, 2012.

Brennan, Tad. *The Stoic Life: Emotions, Duties, and Fate*. Oxford: Oxford University Press, 2005.

Brouwer, René. *The Stoic Sage: The Early Stoics on Wisdom, Sagehood, and Socrates.* Cambridge: Cambridge University Press, 2014.

Brown, Raymond E. *The Semitic Background of the Term "Mystery" in the New Testament.* Facet Books Biblical Series 21. Philadelphia, PA: Fortress Press, 1968.

Brunt, P. A. "From Epictetus to Arrian." In his *Studies in Stoicism*, edited by Miriam Griffin and Alison Samuels, with the assistance of Michael Crawford. Oxford: Oxford University Press, 2013.

Bultmann, Rudolf. *History of the Synoptic Tradition.* Translated by John Marsh. Oxford: Basil Blackwell, 1972.

Burke, Kenneth. *Counter-Statement.* Berkeley: University of California Press, 1931.

Burridge, Richard A. *What Are the Gospels? A Comparison with Graeco-Roman Biography.* Society for New Testament Studies Monograph Series 70. 1992. Paperback edition, Cambridge: Cambridge University Press, 1995.

Casey, Maurice. *Jesus of Nazareth: An Independent Historian's Account of His Life and Teaching.* London: T&T Clark, 2010.

Charlesworth, James H, ed. *The Old Testament Pseudepigrapha*, 2 vols. Garden City, NY: Doubleday, 1985.

Chatman, Seymour. *Story and Discourse: Narrative Structure in Fiction and Film.* Ithaca, NY: Cornell University Press, 1978.

Chilton, Bruce D. "The Transfiguration: Dominical Assurance and Apostolic Vision." *New Testament Studies* 27, no. 1 (October 1980), 115–24.

Collins, Adela Yarbro. "Mark and His Readers: The Son of God among Jews." *Harvard Theological Review* 92, no. 4 (October 1999), 393–408.

Collins, Adela Yarbro. *Mark.* Hermeneia. Minneapolis, MN: Fortress Press, 2007.

Collins, John J. *Daniel: A Commentary on the Book of Daniel.* Hermeneia. Minneapolis, MN: Fortress Press, 1993.

Collins, John J. *Jewish Wisdom in the Hellenistic Age.* Old Testament Library. Louisville, KY: Westminster John Knox, 1997.

Cotter, Wendy. *Miracles in Greco-Roman Antiquity: A Sourcebook.* London: Routledge, 2009.

Crossley, James G. *The Date of Mark's Gospel: Insights from the Law in Earliest Christianity.* Journal for the Study of the New Testament Supplement Series 266. London: T&T Clark, 2004.

Delorme, Jean. *L'heureuse annonce selon Marc: Lecture intégrale du deuxième évangile*, 2 vols. Lectio Divina 219 and 223. Paris: Les Éditions du Cerf, 2007.

Dibelius, Martin. *From Tradition to Gospel.* Translated by Bertram Lee Woolf. New York: Charles Scribner's, 1965.

Dobbin, Robert F., trans. *Epictetus Discourses Book I*. Oxford: Oxford University Press, 1998.

Dodd, C. H. *The Parables of the Kingdom*. Glasgow: Collins, 1961.

Dorion, Louis-André. "Xenophon's Socrates." In *A Companion to Socrates*, edited by Sara Ahbel-Rappe and Rachana Kamtekar (Malden, MA: Blackwell, 2006), 93–109.

Dorion, Louis-André. *L'autre Socrates: Études sur les écrits socratiques de Xénophon*. Paris: Les Belles Lettres, 2013.

Dunn, James D. G. *Christology in the Making*, 2nd ed. Grand Rapids, MI: William B. Eerdmans, 96.

Eckey, Wilfried. *Das Markusevangelium: Orientierung am Weg Jesu: Ein Kommentar*. Neukirchen-Vluyn: Neukirchener, 1998.

Edwards, James R. *The Gospel According to Mark*. Pillar New Testament Commentaries. Grand Rapids, MI: William B. Eerdmans, 2002.

Ehrman, Bart D. "The Text of Mark in the Hands of the Orthodox." *Lutheran Quarterly* 5, no. 2 (Summer 1991), 143–56.

Epictetus. *Discourses, Fragments, Handbook*. Translated by Robin Hard. Oxford: Oxford University Press, 2014.

Evans, Craig A. *To See and Not Perceive: Isaiah 6.9-10 in Early Jewish and Christian Interpretation*. Journal for the Study of the Old Testament Supplement Series 64. Sheffield: Sheffield Academic Press, 1989.

Evans, Craig A. *Mark 8:27-16:20*. Word Biblical Commentary 34B. Nashville, TN: Thomas Nelson, 2001.

Flinterman, Jaap-Jan. *Power, Paideia, and Pythagoreanism: Greek Identity, Conceptions of the Relationship between Philosophers and Monarchs, and Political Ideas in Philostratus' Life of Apollonius*. Amsterdam: J. C. Gieben, 1995.

Fowler, Robert M. *Let the Reader Understand: Reader-Response Criticism and the Gospel of Mark*. Minneapolis, MN: Fortress Press, 1991.

Fredriksen, Paula. *Jesus of Nazareth, King of the Jews*. New York: Alfred A. Knopf, 1995.

Gnilka, Joachim. *Das Evangelium nach Markus*, 2 vols. Evangelisch-Katholischer Kommentar zum Neuen Testament. Züruck: Benziger, 1978.

Goddart, Timothy J. *Watchwords: Mark 13 in Markan Eschatology*. Journal for the Study of the New Testament Supplement Series 26. Sheffield: Sheffield Academic Press, 1989.

Gray, Timothy C. *The Temple in the Gospel of Mark*. Wissenschaftliche Untersuchungen zum Neuen Testament 2. Reihe 242. Tübingen: Mohr Siebeck, 2008.

Gray, Vivienne J. *The Framing of Socrates: The Literary Interpretation of Xenophon's Memorabilia*. Hermes Zeitschrift für Klassische Philologie 79. Stuttgart: Franz Steiner, 1998.

Guelich, Robert A. *Mark 1:8:26*. Word Biblical Commentary. Dallas, TX: Word Books, 1989.

Gundry, Robert H. *Mark: A Commentary on His Apology for the Cross*. Grand Rapids, MI: Eerdmans, 1993.

Guthrie, W. K. C. *Socrates*. London: Cambridge University Press, 1971.

Haenchen, Ernst. *Der Weg Jesus: Der Weg Jesu: Eine Erklärung des Markus Evangeliums und der kanonischen Pararallelen*, 2nd ed. Berlin: Walter de Gruyter, 1968.

Holladay, Carl R. *Theios Aner in Hellenistic Judaism: A Critique of the Use of this Category in New Testament Christology*. SBL Dissertation Series 40. Missoula, MT: Scholars Press, 1977.

Hooker, Morna D. *The Gospel According to Saint Mark*. Black's New Testament Commentaries. 1991. Reprint, Grand Rapids, MI: Baker Academic, 2011.

Horsley, Richard A. *Hearing the Whole Story: The Politics of Plot in Mark's Gospel*. Louisville, KY: Westminster John Knox, 2001.

Hultgren, Arland J. *Jesus and His Adversaries: The Form and Function of the Conflict Stories in the Synoptic Tradition*. Minneapolis, MN: Augsburg Press, 1979.

Iwe, John Chijioke. *Jesus in the Synagogue of Capernaum: The Pericope and Its Programmatic Character for the Gospel of Mark: An Exegetico-Theological Study of Mk 1:21-28*. Tesi Gregoriana Serie Teologia 57. Rome: Editrice Pontifica Università Gregoriana, 1999.

Jones, William H. S, ed. and trans. *Hippocrates*, Vol. 2. Loeb Classical Library 148. Cambridge, MA: Harvard University Press, 1923.

Hempel. Charlotte. "The *Treatise on the Two Spirits* and the Literary History of the *Rule of the Community*." In *Dualism in Qumran*, edited by Géza G. Xeravits, Library of Second Temple Studies. London: T&T Clark, 2010, 102–20.

Henderson, Suzanne Watts. *Christology and Discipleship in the Gospel of Mark*. Society for New Testament Studies Monograph Series 135. Cambridge: Cambridge University Press, 2006.

Hurtado, Larry. "The Gospel of Mark: Evolutionary or Revolutionary Document?" *Journal for the Study of the New Testament* 40 (1990), 15–32.

Iverson, Kelly R. "Jews, Gentiles, and the Kingdom: The Parable of the Wicked Tenants in Narrative Perspective (Mark 12:1-12)." *Biblical Interpretation* 20 (2012), 305–35.

Johnson, Brian E. *The Role Ethics of Epictetus: Stoicism in Ordinary Life*. Lanham, MA: Lexington, 2013.

Jones, Christopher P., ed. and trans. *The Life of Apollonius of Tyana Books I-IV*. Loeb Classical Library 16. Cambridge, MA: Harvard University Press, 2005.

Kaster, Robert A. *Guardians of Language: The Grammarian and Society in Late Antiquity*. Berkeley: University of California Press, 1988.

Kennedy, George A. *New Testament Interpretation through Rhetorical Criticism*. Chapel Hill: University of North Carolina Press, 1984.

Kingsbury, Jack Dean. *The Christology of Mark's Gospel*. Philadelphia, PA: Fortress Press, 1983.

Kirk, Daniel J. R. *A Man Attested by God: The Human Jesus of the Synoptics*. Grand Rapids, MI: William B. Eerdmans, 2016.

Klaiber, Walter. *Das Markusevangelium*. Die Botschaft des Neuen Testaments. Neukirchen-Vluyn: Neukirchener, 2010.

Kloppenborg, John S. *The Tenants in the Vineyard: Ideology, Economics, and Agrarian Conflict in Jewish Palestine*. Wissenschaftliche Untersuchungen zum Neuen Testament 195. Tübingen: Mohr Siebeck, 2006.

Kokenniemi, Erkki. *Apollonios von Tyana und neutestamentlichen Exegese*. Wissenschaftliche Untersuchungen zum Neuen Testament 2. Reihe 61. Tübingen: Mohr Siebeck, 1994.

Kokenniemi, Erkki. "The Philostratean Apollonius as a Teacher." In *Theios Sophistes: Essays on Flavius Philostratus' Vita Apollonii*, edited by Kristoffel Demoen and Danny Praet, 321–34. Leiden: Brill, 2009.

Loader, William R. G. *Jesus' Attitude toward the Law*. Wissenschaftliche Untersuchungen zum Neuen Testament 2. Reihe 97. Tübingen: Mohr Siebeck, 1997.

Long, A. A. *Epictetus: A Stoic and Socratic Guide to Life*. Oxford: Oxford University Press, 2002.

Lundbom, Jack R. *Jeremiah 1-20: A New Translation with Commentary*. Anchor Bible 21A. New York: Doubleday, 1999.

Mack, Burton L. "The Kingdom Sayings in Mark." *Foundations and Facets Forum* 3, no. 1 (1987), 3–47.

Mack, Burton L. *A Myth of Innocence: Mark and Christian Origins*. Philadelphia, PA: Fortress Press, 1988.

Mack, Burton L. "A Myth of Innocence at Sea." *Continuum* 1, no. 2 (Winter–Spring 1991), 140–57.

Mack, Burton L., and Vernon K. Robbins. *Patterns of Persuasion in the Gospels*. Sonoma, CA: Polebridge Press, 1989.

Marchant, E. C., and O. J. Todd, trans. *Xenophon*, Vol. 4. Revised by Jeffrey Henderson. Loeb Classical Library 168. Cambridge, MA: Harvard University Press, 2013.

Marcus, Joel. *The Mystery of the Kingdom of God*. SBL Dissertation Series 90. Atlanta, GA: Scholars Press, 1986.

Marcus, Joel. *The Way of the Lord: Christological Exegesis of the Old Testament in the Gospel of Mark*. Louisville, KY: Westminster John Knox, 1992.

Marcus, Joel. *Mark 1-8: A New Translation with Commentary*. Yale Anchor Bible 27. 2000. Paperback edition, New Haven, CT: Yale University Press, 2005.

Marcus, Joel. *Mark 8-16: A New Translation with Commentary*. Yale Anchor Bible 27A. New Haven, CT: Yale University Press, 2009.

Marrou, H. I. *A History of Education in Antiquity*. Translated by George Lamb. 1948. Reprint, Madison: University of Wisconsin Press, 1982.

Meier, John P. *A Marginal Jew: Rethinking the Historical Jesus*, Vol. 5, *Probing the Authenticity of the Parables*. New Haven, CT: Yale University Press, 2016.

Miller, Merrill P. "The Social Logic of the Gospel of Mark: Cultural Persistence and Social Escape in a Postwar Time." In *Redescribing the Gospel of Mark*, edited by Barry S. Crawford and Merrill P. Miller, 207–399. Atlanta, GA: SBL Press, 2017.

Moloney, Francis J. *The Gospel of Mark: A Commentary*. Grand Rapids, MI: Baker Academic, 2009.

Neirynck, Frans. "Le discours anti-apocalyptique de Mc. XIII." *Ephemerides theologicae Lovanienses* 45 (1969), 154–64.

Nickelsburg, George W. E. *Jewish Literature between the Bible and the Mishnah*, 2nd ed. Minneapolis, MN: Fortress Press, 2005.

Perrin, Norman. *Rediscovering the Teaching of Jesus*. New York: Harper and Row, 1967.

Resseguie, James L. *Narrative Criticism of the New Testament: An Introduction*. Grand Rapids, MI: Baker Academic, 2005.

Robbins, Vernon K. *Jesus the Teacher: A Socio-Rhetorical Interpretation of Mark*. 1984. Reprint, Minneapolis, MN: Fortress Press, 2009.

Royal, Mark, Iain McDougall, and J. C. Yardley. *Greek and Roman Education: A Sourcebook*. Routledge Sourcebooks for the Ancient World. New York: Routledge, 2009.

Saldarini, Anthony J. *Pharisees, Scribes, and Sadducees in Palestinian Society: A Sociological Approach*. 1988. Reprint, Grand Rapids, MI: William B. Eerdmans, 2001.

Sánchez, David A., ed. "Review Roundtable of *A Myth of Innocence: Mark and Christian Origins* by Burton L. Mack." *Journal of the American Academy of Religion* 83, no. 3 (2015), 826–57.

Sanders, E. P. *Paul and Palestinian Judaism*. Philadelphia, PA: Fortress Press, 1977.

Sanders, E. P. *Jesus and Judaism*. Philadelphia, PA: Fortress Press, 1984.

Sanders, E. P. *Judaism: Practice and Belief, 63 BCE-66 CE*. London: SCM Press, 1992.

Scott, Bernard Brandon. *Hear Then the Parable: A Commentary on the Parables of Jesus*. Minneapolis, MN: Fortress Press, 1988.

Snodgrass, Klyne. "Between Text and Sermon: Mark 4:1-20." *Interpretation* 67, no. 3 (2013), 284–6.

Stein, Robert H. *Mark*. Baker Exegetical Commentary on the New Testament. Grand Rapids, MI: Baker Academic, 2008.

Stephens, William O. *Stoic Ethics: Epictetus and Happiness as Freedom*. London: Continuum, 2007.

Stowers, Stanley K. *A Rereading of Romans: Justice, Jews, and Gentiles*. New Haven, CT: Yale University Press, 1994.

Telford, William R. *The Barren Temple and the Withered Tree: A Redaction-Critical Analysis of the Fig-Tree Pericope in Mark's Gospel and Its Relation to the Cleansing of the Temple Tradition*. Sheffield: JSOT Press, 1980.

Tolbert, Mary Ann. *Sowing the Gospel: Mark's World in Literary-Historical Perspective*. Minneapolis, MN: Fortress Press, 1989.

Trocmé, Etienne. *La formation de l'évangile selon Marc*. Études d'histoire et de philosophie religieuses 57. Paris: Presses Universitaires de France. 1963.

Vermes, Geza. *The Dead Sea Scrolls in English*. Revised and extended 4th ed. London: Penguin, 1995.

Vlastos, Gregory. *Socrates: Ironist and Moral Philosopher*. Ithaca, NY: Cornell University Press, 1991.

Vlastos, Gregory. "The Socratic Elenchus: Method Is All." In his *Socratic Studies*, edited by Myles Burnyeat, 1–29. Cambridge: Cambridge University Press, 1994.

Wallace, Daniel B. *Greek Grammar beyond the Basics: An Exegetical Syntax of the New Testament*. Grand Rapids, MI: Zondervan, 1996.

Weeden, Theodore J. *Mark: Traditions in Conflict*. Philadelphia, PA: Fortress Press, 1979.

Weeden, Theodore J. "The Heresy That Necessitated Mark's Gospel." Reprinted in *The Interpretation of Mark*, edited by William R. Telford, 2nd ed., Studies in New Testament Interpretation, 89–104. Edinburgh: T&T Clark, 1995.

Weitzman, Steven. *Surviving Sacrilege: Cultural Persistence in Jewish Antiquity*. Cambridge, MA: Harvard University Press, 2005.

Weren, W. J. C. "The Use of Isaiah 5,1-7 in the Parable of the Tenants (Mark 12,1-12; Matthew 21,33-46)." *Biblica* 79 (1998), 1–26.

Westerholm, Stephen. *Jesus and Scribal Authority*. Coniectanea Biblica New Testament Series 10. Lund: Gleerup, 1978.

Williams, Joel F. "Is Mark's Gospel an Apology for the Cross?" *Bulletin for Biblical Research* 12, no. 1 (2002), 97–122.

Wrede, William. *The Messianic Secret*. Translated by J. C. G. Greig. Greenwood, SC: Attic Press, 1971.

Wright, N. T. *Jesus and the Victory of God*. Minneapolis, MN: Fortress Press, 1994.

Index of Ancient Sources

Septuagint (LXX)

Genesis
2:3   101

Exodus
32:5   108
36:6   108

Deuteronomy
4:1   20
4:10   20
4:14   20
5:31   20
6:1   20
11:19   20
31:19   20

Joshua
18:1   151

1 Samuel (1 Kingdoms)
21:1-6   100

2 Kings (4 Kingdoms)
10:20   108
20:13   78

2 Chronicles (4 Kingdoms)
20:3   108
36:22   108

1 Esdras
8:23   21
9:48   21

2 Esdras (Ezra-Nehemiah)
7:6   90
7:10   21
18:8   21

Esther
6:1   20

1 Maccabees
1:13-15   79

2 Maccabees
1:10   20
2:5-7   171–2
4:9   79
6:18   91

4 Maccabees
6:33   78n. 7

Psalms
2:7   88
25:4   21
34:11   21
51:13   21
71:17   21
78:60   151
94:10   21
113:2   78
119:68   21
135:8   78

Ecclesiastes
8:8   78

Wisdom of Ben Sirach
24:11   79
30:11   79
38:24-39:11   91
39:1-4   91

Psalms of Solomon
17   83
17:32   83

Jonah	
1:2	108
3:2	108

Isaiah	
5:1-7	153
6:9-10	123
42:1	88
44:28	82
45:1-6	82
45:13	82, 83
56:7	148
61:1	108

Jeremiah	
7:11-15	151
26	151–2

Daniel	
3:2	79
4:17	80
5:7	80
7	80–3
7:15-27	126
8:15-26	126
9:20-27	126

Philo
On the Embassy to Gaius
94	108
100	108

On the Life of Joseph
16.86-87	21

On the Life of Moses
1.9	108
2.22	108

Josephus
Jewish Antiquities
1.168	21
3.93-94	21
9.208	108

The Jewish War
6.285	108

Qumran Documents
Community Rule (1QS)
3.13	115

New Testament
Matthew
4:6	121
7:28-29	86
10:32-33	140
26:54	134

Mark
1-7	138, 143
1:1	65, 90, 134
1:11	65, 152
1:9-11	65
1:14	107
1:14-45	69
1:15	69
1:21	86
1:21-28	3, 4, 67, 85–96, 100, 102, 103, 110, 138
1:22	3, 84, 87, 89, 92, 94
1:23	86
1:27	3, 84, 87, 94
1:27-28	86–7
1:34	104
2:1-12	96–100, 102
2:1-3:6	105
2:5	98
2:6-7	97
2:6-8	15
2:7	98
2:8	99
2:9	98
2:10	84
2:10-11	97
2:12	99
2:13-17	103
2:16	92
2:18-22	103
2:19-20	137
2:20	103
2:23-28	100–2, 103
2:25	101
2:27-28	101
3:6	105, 137
3:7-12	105

Index of Ancient Sources

3:11	89, 104	10:17-31	61
3:13-19	105–7,	10:23	69
3:15	84, 105	10:28-31	139–40
3:22	92	10:30	167
3:23	121	10:34	139
3:32	122	10:38-39	139
4	11, 138, 142	10:42-45	139
4:1-34	111–27	10:46-52	141
4:1-32	107	11:12-14	149
4:2	107, 112	11:15	146, 148
4:3	117	11:15-19	144–8
4:8	112	11:17	70, 148, 151, 154
4:9	117	11:18	92, 148, 151, 155
4:10	111, 117	11:20-24	149
4:11-12	111, 115, 117, 121, 122, 126	11:22-24	149
		11:27	92
4:11-13	112	11:27-33	156
4:12	125	11:28	84
4:13-15	113	11:29	84
4:14	118	11:33	84
4:19-20	118	12:7	153
4:21-32	124	12:9-10	152
4:23-24	117	12:12	156, 157
4:24	124	12:13-44	157–8
4:33-34	107, 111, 112	12:18-27	61
5:7	89	12:28	92
6:2	107	12:28-34	61
6:6b-13	105–7	12:34	69
6:7	84, 105	12:40	146
6:12	107	12:41-44	61
6:16	64	13	16, 62, 67, 68, 80, 107, 133, 141, 150, 159–62, 167
6:30	106, 110		
7:1	92		
7:1-23	61, 70, 87, 127–9	13:4	133
7:18-23	63	13:4-13	67
7:19	129	13:7	133
8:1-2	15	13:10	133
8:23-24	64	13:14	67, 133
8:27-30	132	13:26-27	133
8:31	70, 131, 139	13:34	84
8:31-32	132, 135–9	14:9	107
8:34	139	14:27	121
8:38	40	14:53-65	155
9:7	152	14:61	89
9:31	131, 139	14:64	98
9:35	139	15:6-15	153
9:47	63	15:39	65, 89, 173
10:2-12	63, 70	15:40-41	124
10:17-22	119	16:5-8	173
10:17-27	140		

Luke	
1:1-4	52
2:23	121
4:6	84
7:8	84
12:8-10	140
12:11	84
20:20	84
22:36-38	134
23:7	84
24:44-47	134

John	
8:17	121
12:34	134

Acts	
1:16	134
2:29	135
4:13	135
17:2-3	134

Romans	
9-11	124
9:6	124
11	116

1 Corinthians	
15	134

2 Corinthians	
3:12	135

1 John	
2:15-17	116
2:29	116

Revelation	
1:1	133
22:6	133

Other Ancient Literature

Aeschylus, *Eumenides*	
566	108

Aristotle, *Nichomachean Ethics*	
1161a	75
1332a	75

Aristotle, *Politics*	
1255b	76

Aristotle, *Rhetoric*	
1.3.5	64

Demosthenes, *Second Philippic*	
6.31	135

Epictetus, *Discourses*	
0.5	61
1.1	41, 43
1.2.1	48
1.2.5-6	48
1.2.8-9	48
1.11	42
1.11.4	43
1.11.27	43
1.12.15	45
1.16.12	108
1.18.1-4	44
1.22.10	43, 44
1.25.1-2	77
1.28	44
1.28.7	45
1.28.9	45
1.28.28-33	45
1.29.9	77
1.29.64	108–9
1.5	41
2.1.18	46
2.1.21-22	45
2.1.38-40	45
2.4	41
2.8	47
2.10	47
2.10.10	47
2.11.13	45
2.14	41
2.14.11-13	47
2.15	41
2.16.34-35	46
2.20	41
2.24	41
2.26	50
2.26.1-3	44
3.1	42
3.2	46
3.2.6	46

3.3.1	44	1.15.23	53
3.7	41	1.16.3	54, 56
3.9.11	47	1.16.4	56
3.10	41	1.17	56
3.12.15	50	1.18.-3.58	53
3.13.12	109	2.29.2-2.30	55
3.22	109	3.18	57
3.22.69	109, 110	3.19	55
3.22.70	109	3.30.3	56
3.23.4-5	47	3.32.2	56
4.6.23	109	3.41	57
4.13	41	3.50	55
		4.1	54
Enchiridion		4.2	56
14.2	77	4.19-20	54
53	57	4:20	95
		4.21	54
Euripides, *Medea*		4.24	54
1078-79	45	4.27	55
		4.31	55
Euripides, Fragments		4.32	55
362	75	4.36	58
738	75	4.36.2	58
775	75	4.37	58
		4.37.2	58
Hippocrates, *Law*		4.40	54
3	114	4.44	58
		5.21.1	57
Homer, *Iliad*		5.21.2-4	57
2.443	107	5.43-6.23	53
		6.3	56
Homer, *Odyssey*		6.11-12	55
2.7	107–8	7.1	55
		7.3.3-4.1	59
Philostratus, *Life of Apollonius of Tyana*		7.11.3	59
1.1	63	7.12.2	59
1.1-3	52	7.12.5	59
1.2	52, 63	7.13.2	59
1.2.3	59	7.14.1	60
1.3.1	52	7.14.2	60
1.3.2	52	7.14.10-11	60
1.4	52	7.15.1	60
1.5	53	7.22-26	60
1.7	53	8.5.4	60
1.7.2	53	8.6-7	60
1.8	53	8.10-13	60
1.11.2	53	8.29-30	60
1.12	53	8.29-31	53
1.13	53		

Plato, *Protagoras*
358d	33

Plato, *Republic*
359c	74
359d	74
606e	24

Plutarch, *Lives*
2.185a	108

Sophocles, *Electra*
1105	108

Sophocles, *The Women of Trachis*
97	108

Xenophon, *Anabasis*
3.4.36	108

Xenophon, *Memorabilia*
1.1-2	27, 30, 32, 39
1.1.2-4	30, 64
1.1.2-5	27
1.1.6-9	27
1.1.11-15	27
1.1.19	31
1.2	27, 33
1.2.1	27, 34
1.2.2-8	34
1.2.3	27
1.2.8	27
1.2.9	28
1.2.9-11	31
1.2.12	28
1.2.14-15	28
1.2.17	7
1.2.17-18	28
1.2.19	37
1.2.24	28
1.3	28, 29, 32, 36
1.3.1	28, 30, 35
1.3.1-4	32
1.3.5-8	34
1.3.5-15	32
1.3.8-13	39
1.4	27, 29
1.4.1	40
1.4.2	30
1.4.16	30
1.4.18	30, 63
1.5.1	34
1.5.4	33, 39
1.5.6	34
1.6.1-10	35
1.6.1-14	35
1.6.7-14	36
1.6.13	36
2.1.15	109
2.1.25	76
2.2	30, 39
2.3	30
2.4-6	30
2.6	39
2.6.24	76
2.7	36
2.7.5	36
2.7-8	31
3.1-7	31
3.6	35, 38, 39
3.6.3	35
3.6.11	76
3.6.18	38
3.8	31
3.8.1	32
3.9	31, 38
3.9.1	38
3.9.3	38
3.9.5	33
3.9.10	38
4.1	32
4.1.4	38
4.1.5	39
4.2	31, 32, 39
4.4	31
4.5.1-12	34
4.5.6	37
4.5.11	34

Augustine, *Confessions*
1.18	24–5

Index of Modern Authors

Ahbel-Rappe, Sara 26n. 12
Austin, J. L. 104n. 59

Bäbler, Balbina 51n. 53
Beck, Frederick A. G. 24n. 3
Best, Ernest 93n. 33
Betz, Hans Dieter 147n. 33
Black, C. Clifton 18n. 53
Bock, Darrell 3, 137n. 10, 147
Boesche, Roger 58n. 60
Booth, Wayne C. 14n. 38
Boring, M. Eugene 4, 67n. 75, 69n. 77, 106n. 60, 114, 116n. 74, 117, 124, 128n. 103, 129, 135n. 7, 144n. 26, 149n. 38, 150, 160n. 62
Bovon, François 52n. 56
Boyarin, Daniel 128
Brennan, Tad 48n. 43, 45–6
Brouwer, René 48n. 43
Brown, Raymond E. 125
Bruell, Christopher 29n. 17
Brunt, P. A. 40n. 29
Bultmann, Rudolf 86n. 16, 97, 140n. 17
Burke, Kenneth 5n. 16, 6n. 19
Burridge, Richard A. 5n. 14

Casey, Maurice 144n. 25
Chatman, Seymour 14n. 39, 15.45, 18
Chilton, Bruce D. 141n. 18
Collins, Adela Yarbro 2, 87n. 17, 88n. 22, 94n. 35, 111n. 64, 114, 120, 128n. 103, 141n. 20, 147n. 32, 149n. 39, 150n. 40
Collins, John J. 81n. 12, 91.30
Cotter, Wendy 95n. 37
Crawford, Barry S. 168n. 2
Crossley, James G. 159nn. 58–9

Delorme, Jean 112n. 66
Dibelius, Martin 13
Dobbin, Robert F. 47n. 41

Dodd, C. H. 141n. 19
Dorion, Louis-André 33–4, 37, 39n. 28
Dunn, James D. G. 79n. 10, 89n. 24

Eckey, Wilfried 93n. 34, 121n. 93
Edwards, James R. 114n. 68, 150n. 40, 157n. 56
Ehrman, Bart D. 90n. 26
Evans, Craig A. 123, 156nn. 51, 53

Flinterman, Jaap-Jan 55n. 57
Fowler, Robert M. 10, 13–17, 18, 99, 104, 142–3, 162, 174
Fredriksen, Paula 145n. 28

Gill, Christopher 40n. 31, 45n. 39
Gnilka, Joachim 112n. 65, 115n. 72, 133n. 4, 136n. 8, 147n. 35
Goddart, Timothy J. 157n. 54
Gray, Timothy C. 146
Gray, Vivienne J. 28–9, 32, 35, 39n. 27
Guelich, Robert A. 86n. 16, 121n. 92
Gundry, Robert H. 63n. 62, 65–8, 99, 133, 138
Guthrie, W. K. C. 26n. 12

Haenchen, Ernst 18
Hempel, Charlotte 115–16n. 63
Henderson, Jeffrey 26n. 11
Henderson, Suzanne Watts 138n. 12
Holladay, Carl R. 51n. 55
Hooker, Morna D. 101n. 50, 112n. 67, 117, 118, 120, 128n. 103, 140nn. 15–16, 147n. 35, 150n. 40, 157n. 55
Horsley, Richard A. 145
Hultgren, Arland J. 97n. 40, 104n. 58
Hurtado, Larry 11n. 33

Iverson, Kelly R. 153n. 47
Iwe, John Chijioke 92n. 32

Johnson, Brian E. 47-8, 49nn. 47-8
Jones, Christopher P. 51n. 53

Kamtekar, Rachana 26n. 12
Kaster, Robert A. 25nn. 9-10
Kennedy, George A. 173
Kingsbury, Jack Dean 89n. 25, 137n. 11
Kirk, J. R. Daniel 82n. 14
Klaiber, Walter 88n. 19, 120n. 88
Kloppenborg, John S. 152nn. 44, 46, 154n. 50
Koskenniemi, Erkki 51n. 54-5, 55n. 58

Loader, William R. G. 98n. 44
Long, A. A. 41n. 30, 42n. 34, 43n. 35, 44n. 38, 48n. 44, 49n. 49, 50
Lundbom, Jack R. 151n. 43

McDougall, Iain 24n. 3
Mack, Burton L. 10-13, 16, 17, 25n. 6, 64n. 63, 65n. 65, 101n. 54, 104, 114, 120, 127, 142, 145, 153n. 47
Marcus, Joel 2, 80n. 11, 86n. 16, 87n. 17, 88n. 20, 106n. 60, 117n. 81, 118 121n. 91, 123, 125n. 99, 128n. 103, 133n. 4, 156n. 52
Marrou, H. I. 23n. 1, 24nn. 3-5, 159n. 60, 160n. 61
Meier, John P. 152n. 45
Miller, Merrill P. 168-74
Moloney, Francis J. 67n. 75, 92.32, 94n. 36, 100n. 49, 117, 120n. 88, 148, 149n. 38 152n. 46, 158n. 57, 160n. 63

Neirynck, Frans 159n. 58
Nesselrath, Heinz-Günther 51n. 53
Nickelsburg, George W. E. 82n. 13

Perrin, Norman 119

Resseguie, James L. 18n. 51
Robbins, Vernon K. 5-10, 19, 25n. 6, 64n. 63, 95-6, 101-2, 125, 139, 142 143, 173
Royal, Mark 24n. 3

Saldarini, Anthony J. 90, 91n. 29
Sanders, E. P. 100n. 48, 146n. 29, 148n. 36, 151n. 42
Scott, Bernard Brandon 152n. 45
Snodgrass, Klyne 117
Stein, Robert H. 67n. 75, 93n. 33, 97n. 42, 106n. 60, 121n. 93, 138n. 12
Stephens, William O. 43n. 36, 44n. 37
Stowers, Stanley K. 42n. 34

Tannehill, Robert 104
Telford, William R. 137n. 11, 150n. 40
Tolbert, Mary Ann 101n. 51, 117n. 80, 118, 119, 122, 152n. 46
Trocmé, Etienne 132

Vermes, Geza 115n. 73
Vlastos, Gregory 33n. 22, 49n. 50

Weitzman, Stephen 168-74
Weren, W. J. C. 153n. 48
Wallace, Daniel B. 101n. 52
Weeden, Theodore J. 66, 131-2, 137n. 11
Westerholm, Stephen 91n. 31
Williams, Joel F. 67, 68n. 76
Wrede, William 89n. 25
Wright, N. T. 152n. 45, 153n. 49, 159n. 58

Xeravits, Géza 115-16n. 73

Yardley, J. C. 24n. 3

www.ingramcontent.com/pod-product-compliance
Lightning Source LLC
Chambersburg PA
CBHW070639300426
44111CB00013B/2170